Crisis, Issues and Reputation Management

CIPR

Crisis, Issues and Reputation Management

PR in Practice

Andrew Griffin

KoganPage

First published in Great Britain and the United States in 2014 by Kogan Page Limited

2nd Floor, 45 Gee Street
London EC1V 3RS
United Kingdom
www.koganpage.com

1518 Walnut Street, Suite 1100
Philadelphia PA 19102
USA

4737/23 Ansari Road
Daryaganj
New Delhi 110002
India

© Andrew Griffin, 2014

The right of Andrew Griffin to be identified as the author of this work has been asserted by him in accordance with the Copyright, Designs and Patents Act 1988.

ISBN   978 0 7494 6992 4
E-ISBN   978 0 7494 6993 1

British Library Cataloguing-in-Publication Data

A CIP record for this book is available from the British Library.

Library of Congress Cataloging-in-Publication Data

Griffin, Andrew, 1972-
   Crisis, issues and reputation management / Andrew Griffin.
      pages cm
   Includes index.
      ISBN 978-0-7494-6992-4 – ISBN 978-0-7494-6993-1 (ebk)   1. Corporate image–Management.
2. Crisis management.   3. Reputation.   4. Corporations–Public relations.   I. Title.
   HD59.2.G747 2014
   659.2–dc23

                                                                                            2014002589

Typeset by Graphicraft Limited, Hong Kong
Print production managed by Jellyfish
Printed and bound by CPI Group (UK) Ltd, Croydon, CR0 4YY

To all RL-ers, past, present and future.

CONTENTS

PR in Practice Series

Published in association with the Chartered Institute of Public Relations
Series Editor: Anne Gregory

Kogan Page has joined forces with the Chartered Institute of Public Relations to publish this unique series, which is designed specifically to meet the needs of the increasing numbers of people seeking to enter the public relations profession and the large band of existing PR professionals. Taking a practical, action-oriented approach, the books in the series concentrate on the day-to-day issues of public relations practice and management rather than academic history. They provide ideal primers for all those on CIPR, CAM and CIM courses or those taking NVQs in PR. For PR practitioners, they provide useful refreshers and ensure that their knowledge and skills are kept up to date.

Professor Anne Gregory PhD is Director of the Centre for Public Relations Studies at Leeds Metropolitan University, UK. She has authored over 70 publications; as well as being editor of the Kogan Page/CIPR series of books which she initiated, she is Editor-in-Chief of the *Journal of Communication Management*. Anne also leads specialist commercial research and consultancy projects from the Centre working with prestigious public and private sector clients. She is a non-executive director of Airedale NHS Foundation Trust. Originally a broadcast journalist, Anne spent 12 years as a senior practitioner before moving on to academia. She was President of the Chartered Institute of Public Relations (CIPR) in 2004, leading it to Chartered status and was awarded the CIPR's Sir Stephen Tallents Medal for her outstanding contribution to public relations in 2010. In June 2012 she became Chair of the Global Alliance of Public Relations and Communications Management, the umbrella organization of over 60 public relations institutes from around the world.

Other titles in the series:

Creativity in Public Relations by Andy Green
Effective Internal Communication by Lyn Smith and Pamela Mounter
Effective Media Relations by Michael Bland, Alison Theaker and David Wragg
Ethics in Public Relations by Patricia J Parsons
Evaluating Public Relations by Tom Watson and Paul Noble
Internal Communications by Liam FitzPatrick, Pamela Mounter and Klavs Valskov
Online Public Relations by David Phillips and Philip Young
Planning and Managing Public Relations Campaigns by Anne Gregory
PR and Communication in Local Government and Public Services by John Brown, Pat Gaudin and Wendy Moran
Public Relations in Practice edited by Anne Gregory
Risk Issues and Crisis Management in Public Relations by Michael Regester and Judy Larkin
Running a Public Relations Department by Mike Beard
The PR Professional's Handbook by Caroline Black
Writing Skills for Public Relations by John Foster

The above titles are available from all good bookshops. To obtain further information, please go to the CIPR website (**www.cipr.co.uk/books**) or contact the publishers at the address below:

Kogan Page Ltd
2nd Floor, 45 Gee Street
London EC1V 3RS
United Kingdom
Tel: 020 7278 0433
www.koganpage.com

FOREWORD
BY ANNE GREGORY

Many would say that the financial crisis that has recently engulfed the world is the first one in a truly globalized world. Things that happen in one country cannot be hermetically sealed in an era when we are all dependent on others and connected in ways that never seemed imaginable only a decade ago. The ripples cannot be contained and people and places that have nothing to do with finance and markets are feeling the effects. One of the astounding things that comes from an analysis of what happened is that it appears all the warning signs were there, but there was a refusal by leaders in governments and in organizations to accept them and to act upon them.

What happens on a global scale is also mirrored at a local level. Many of the crises and related reputational damage that have engulfed individuals, governments and companies were predictable – in hindsight.

In this updated edition of this best-selling book, Andrew Griffin again provides a comprehensive approach to managing situations that are fraught with risk and which may turn into crises. Unfortunately, not all crises can be envisaged and not all issues can be prevented from becoming crises, so he also covers in detail how to manage when that happens. His basic proposition is this: reputations cannot be managed, but behaviours can. To quote him, a good reputation comes from 'living your values, delivering for customers, making good decisions, meeting and exceeding performance standards and demonstrating good behaviours... across the organization. It is showing not telling'.

So reputation management begins from the inside, not in the corporate communication department. However it is usually that department that is responsible for building relationships with stakeholders and being in regular dialogue with them. They are the bearers of the corporate narrative, but more importantly they are the organizational antennae, ever in dialogue and listening and ever alert to danger signs. And it is in building relationships of trust that the organization builds a level of protection for itself when things go wrong. They are more likely to be believed, they will have others speaking in their defence and they will have a history of integrity behind them.

The corporate communication department is also the 'go to' department when things go wrong. They need to be prepared and ready. So when is it that an issue is likely to develop into a crisis? What is its life cycle? Who should be responsible for issues management? All these questions are answered in this book. How about crises? Well, it depends on the crisis and there are several types... all described here with their implications carefully explored in a variety of examples. Griffin carefully explains what planning needs to be done in preparation and goes through in detail the practicalities, including the legal implications, dealing with relatives and emergency services and of course the 24/7 on- and off-line media. Unfortunately, crises don't always finish when the press go home though. So how do you deal with the aftermath and how do you rebuild that most precious asset, reputation, if that has been damaged?

This is a careful and meticulous book based on many years of dealing with some of the largest and most complex crises. It is full of mini case studies and illustrations which explain the complexities that are involved, and, most importantly, it is full of insight and wisdom. Every practitioner who awaits the next issue, crisis or threat to reputation should have this book on their shelf and take it down regularly. Furthermore, every academic who wishes to teach and learn about the twists, turns, highs and lows of the subject should have *Crisis, Issues and Reputation Management* on their reading list, not only for its practicality, but because of its rigour and theoretically-informed thinking.

Professor Anne Gregory
Consultant Editor

FOREWORD
BY MIKE REGESTER

How can an international oil company, with so much previous experience of crisis management, still get the communications and stakeholder relations aspects of responding to a major physical incident so wrong? How can the world's most respected broadcaster, which surely understands that its reputation is by far its greatest asset, conspire to turn an issue about journalistic standards into a damaging corporate crisis? How can a media company, respected and feared for decades as a titan in its industry, fail to devise a competent crisis communications strategy when its values, products and reputation are on the line?

The crises faced by BP, the British Broadcasting Corporation (BBC) and News International suggest that even the world's biggest and most respected organizations have yet to crack crisis, issues and reputation management. All suffered major reputation damage and its knock-on effects: all saw their chief executives resign; all were restructured in some way; all saw real financial, commercial and/or strategic damage.

It seems nothing has changed since Judy Larkin and I wrote our first book on issues and crisis management 15 years ago.

Crises still happen. Every year, more and more crises play out in the public eye. Reputations are still destroyed, commercial and financial interests hit, and careers of senior leaders lost. Companies still make errors when faced with risks to reputation whether from a sudden incident or a developing issue. These errors usually have their origins in poor preparedness: those companies that are prepared for the worst are better at dealing with it.

But in other ways, an awful lot has changed. Most importantly, technology and the media have changed. Incidents now play out on 24/7 news channels, with opinion and visuals tweeted from the scene and social media conversations starting before the organization at the centre of the crisis has had a chance to convene a response.

Issues can now quickly snowball without the coordinating help of NGOs. This means the stakeholder mix has changed. Everyone is an NGO; everyone is a commentator; everyone is a journalist.

Scrutiny and expectation have changed. Organizations that are managing reputations are doing so in a climate of mistrust and high demand. As the world gets smaller through travel and technology, the boundaries of nation states seem more blurred and large companies are expected to make major societal contributions. If they fail, there are highly sceptical audiences waiting to expose and criticize them.

Risks to reputation have changed. Protecting reputation does not mean just managing the major shocks of incidents. Twenty-first-century reputation management is about spotting issues on the horizon, contributing to global societal debates, preventing performance-related issues, engaging in local issues and even defending the very premise of a company's existence.

Partly because of this, capability in reputation management has improved. Many big organizations are now reasonably well versed in strategic crisis management as well as the more tactical operational and functional responses. Having seen how reputations (their own, their peers or their competitors) can so easily be destroyed, companies have invested in the basic structures and processes to protect themselves should the worst happen. Some organizations have recognized that soft skills, like crisis leadership, are as important as the process; others have yet to start this journey.

Issues management has become more strategic. Because many companies down the years have lost reputation thanks to unresolved issues, companies have started to take issues management as seriously as incident management.

So why are issues and incidents still harming reputations? Organizations are battling to stay ahead of the curve in reputation, issues and crisis management. They are devising better structures and processes and they are developing better competence but, as they are doing so in a constantly changing world, crises and issues are still being mismanaged and reputations damaged.

Against this background, Andrew Griffin's new book, *Crisis, Issues and Reputation Management*, takes the thinking in this specialist discipline to a whole new level. It offers a new way of thinking about risks to reputation and a new life cycle for managing these risks. It builds on Andrew's many years of experience in advising clients of all shapes and sizes on reputation management. This includes a decade of leading the company Judy Larkin and I founded.

The book will, I hope, become the reputation 'bible' for communications professionals and other members of senior management for years to come. It focuses on reputation protection, but extols the need for a wider reputation strategy that appreciates the true financial value of a good reputation. It also provides an invaluable compendium of the lessons to be learned, both good and bad, from previous crises in corporate history. Times change but history has a habit of repeating itself.

What will be the 'next big case study' in reputation management? It could come at any time in any sector, whether from an unresolved issue or an incident. Organizations that learn the lessons of the past, and act on the advice in this book, will be in a much better place to protect their reputations whatever fate throws at them.

Mike Regester

PREFACE

Reputation is an outcome. It is the view, as held by others, of what you are like, based on their experience of you over time.

Organizations have thousands – or even millions – of people judging them every day. They are judged on their performance, products, services, decisions, announcements etc. These judgements come together over time as a collective view of what the organization is like: its reputation. Reputation may seem so all-encompassing – the collective view of everyone about everything – that an organization cannot hope to manage it. But whilst the outcome may seem unmanageable, all the actions, decisions, announcements, innovations and everything else an organization does can be controlled and managed. If they are managed in line with the good reputation that the organization has, or wants to have, then they are contributing to a positive reputation outcome.

So why is reputation management part of a book that also covers crisis and issues management?

For individuals and organizations alike, a reputation is far easier to destroy than it is to build. If an organization gets its response wrong to an issue that has emerged or an incident that has hit, its reputation is on the line. If reputation is on the line, then so are commercial and strategic interests. When customers change their minds about what you are like, they might change their buying habits; when employees see you differently, they might move on. A damaged reputation is an outcome; and this outcome can, in turn, damage the bottom line.

Managing risks to reputation places a particular strain on the communications function because such risks have the potential to play out very publicly. Everything the organization is doing and saying in response to the challenge facing them is being watched and judged by those who determine reputation and then make choices based on it. As a primary link between the organization, its stakeholders and the general public, communicators must respond well. Communications professionals are not only there to advise on delivery, but also on strategy. They need to bring the outside world into decision-making, help scenario plan and identify risks in the short and long term, advise on how different courses of action will be perceived and participate in making decisions that will have reputational impact.

The communications function is usually part of a wider corporate affairs department, which is only one of many parts of an organization involved when reputation is being built or protected. This book is therefore relevant to all those senior executives and board directors who are responsible for managing the interests of the organization and its shareholders/stakeholders.

The first half of this book examines reputation as a strategic asset that needs active care and attention (Chapter 1) and looks at the increasingly challenging external environment in which corporate reputations are managed (Chapter 2). It then looks at where reputation risks come from, and offers a new categorization system to help organizations understand the various risks they face (Chapter 3). The four categories of reputation risk are then discussed in further detail in Chapters 4 to 7, with Chapter 8 showing how some issues and crises cut across this model.

The second half of this book looks at a six-phase reputation risk life cycle, first introduced in Chapter 9. Chapters 10 and 11 look at how organizations can *predict* and *prevent* reputation risk. I then move on to examine how to *prepare* for acute reputation risk (crisis preparedness) in Chapter 12. Chapter 13 is the issues management chapter, which focuses on how organizations can *resolve* identified risks (issues) before they develop into crises. But despite all the prevention and resolution strategies organizations devise and execute, crises do happen and organizations need to *respond*. Chapter 14 is the extensive crisis management chapter. The book ends with a chapter on *recovery* (Chapter 15), which looks at how organizations can learn and improve after a crisis, rebuild reputation and make fundamental change.

Reputation is an outcome; but it is also a valuable, strategic asset. Crises and issues put it in jeopardy. This book provides guidance on how to think about and manage all three.

I will leave the last word of this preface not to one of the many philosophers and social commentators who have provided memorable quotes on reputation, but to a businessman who, I think, sums up well what reputation is and why crisis and issues management is so closely connected with it. Steve Marshall, who became Chief Executive of UK rail operator Railtrack soon after a train crash that killed four people in Hatfield, said: 'The fundamental truth, which you discover only when you have gone through the fires of hell, is that your reputation will always mirror the absolute reality of what you are.'[1]

Note

1 Randall, Jeff [accessed 21 June 2013] 'If banks and food companies want a good reputation, they should just be honest', *The Telegraph* [online] www.telegraph.co.uk/foodanddrink/foodanddrinknews/9865287/If-banks-and-food-companies-want-a-good-reputation-they-should-just-be-honest.html

ACKNOWLEDGEMENTS

I would like to thank Nasima Begum-Ali for her excellent research work and Lauren Welford for her project management.

Thanks also to those who agreed to be interviewed as part of my research, including: Simon Baugh, Julian Bishop, Robert Blood, Barnaby Briggs, Admiral Sir James Burnell-Nugent, Matthew Cain, Patrice de Vivies and colleagues, Niel Golightly, Truus Huisman, Christine Jude, Duncan Murray, Barney O'Kelly, Ben Peachey, Kate Slater, Andrew Vickers and Simon Walls.

Thank you to colleagues at Regester Larkin for contributing research and ideas: Komel Bajwe, Thomas Bolsin, Kate Brader, Alex Durnford, Jessica Evans, Jessica Frost, Ferelith Gaze, Kara Kovalsky, Toomas Kull, Alaina MacDonald, Chris Malpass, Afra Morris, Sarah O'Reilly, Ben Overlander, Roberta Ramsden-Knowles, Jacqueline Ratcliffe, Alex Rowbottom, Jennifer Smith, Claire Snowdon, Tim Wells, John Williams and Abigail Worsfold.

Thanks to Janine Elliot for her support, ideas and review and to Lew Watts, Eddie Bensilum, Tim Johnson and Kirsty Hall for reading and commenting on the manuscript. Thanks to Lorraine Warren for the usual reliable support. And finally thanks to Mike Regester for his kind foreword and for his enthusiastic support both on this project and throughout my career!

Andrew Griffin

01
Reputation: what it is and why it matters

Reputation, as a concept, is becoming part of normal corporate discourse, at least in large global companies. Once associated primarily with the corporate affairs department, reputation is now discussed in executive committees and boardrooms. Many companies have reputation (or reputation risk) committees of the board and some structure and process that bring reputation matters up to this senior level. Companies increasingly realize – and publicly declare – that their reputation is their most important asset; they claim that they make decisions with reputation in mind.

Not only is reputation in the boardroom, it is also beyond the boardroom. Shareholders are aware of the fragile and changing reputations of the companies in which they invest. They have seen, on many occasions, what losing reputation does to a company's commercial interests, people, morale, customer base and share price.

The transition of reputation from a 'nice to have' to a valued asset is well under way.

And reputation thinking is not confined to the world of business. Government departments, state schools and hospitals know that their funding, their ability to attract and retain talent and their survival can depend on their reputation. Charities and the not-for-profit sector understand that continued financial support and mission achievement will not come to those with bad reputations.

Many organizations have come to reputation negatively: either through having experienced a reputation-damaging crisis themselves or having seen a competitor or peer manage one. This is why reputation is often seen, first and foremost, as something to be protected. Indeed it is – and this book is primarily focused on reputation protection – but it is something that should also be seen positively. Reputation is a long-term, valuable strategic asset that organizations should think about proactively.

Although reputation has undoubtedly risen up the corporate agenda, it is one thing to 'talk' reputation and quite another to 'do' it. There is plenty of evidence to show that reputation is not as actively managed an asset as it should be. Some of the biggest and most respected companies have little or no crisis management structure, process and competence in place. Few have mature reputation risk and issues management frameworks. And there are many decisions and actions reported in the media that suggest the organization in question has failed to consider them through the lens of reputation. Partly this is because reputation is often discussed without being fully understood. It is sometimes confused with image, brand and values. Worse, it can be seen as something synonymous with ethics, sustainability and the corporate responsibility agenda. Leaders know it is not something that should be compartmentalized and managed by the corporate affairs department, but they are not quite sure where else to put it. They know it is valuable, but are not sure how to value it.

The good thing is that reputation now has an interested audience. This chapter seeks to define and explain the strategic value of this sometimes mysterious and often misunderstood asset.

Defining reputation

The Penguin English Dictionary defines reputation as: '1: overall quality or character as seen or judged by others; 2: fame, celebrity; 3: recognition by other people of some characteristic or ability'.

The key phrases here are 'as seen or judged by others' and 'recognition by other people'. Whether you are an individual or a multinational company, your reputation is not something that you own; it is something that is assigned to you by others. Furthermore, whilst there may be many different views about you and your various qualities and abilities, those others are acting as a group. You hear people saying, for instance, 'I know they've got a reputation for poor customer service, but I was extremely pleased with how they treated me.' This is a dissenting opinion to a group verdict. You can have different reputations amongst different groups, however. For example, a company might have a reputation for good customer service in one market but not in another.

It is also important to understand the distinction between reputation and brand. The two are often confused. Brand is a differentiator: a company actively projects its brands as promises and aspirations for its customer base to buy into. Reputation is not actively projected; it is earned. It is about acceptability and legitimacy to a much wider audience. Companies can have strong brands but weak reputations; and vice versa.

Brand, purpose, values and other things that an organization controls can have an impact on its reputation, as Figure 1.1 suggests. But this is marginal. Reputation derives from delivery – real or perceived – rather than promise.

FIGURE 1.1 A reputation framework

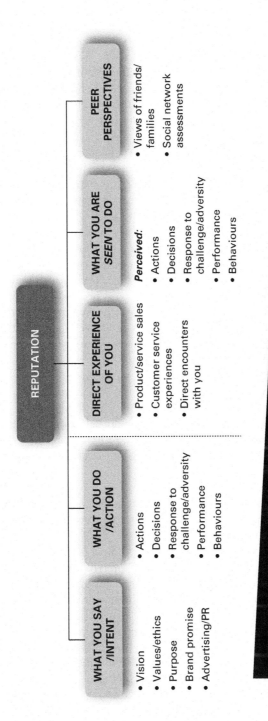

For example, your friend who is always there for you has this reputation not because she says it, but because she is. In fact, if she were to tell you repeatedly that she is always there for you, when the collective experience of you and your mutual friends is that she is not, it would make a bad reputation worse. Similarly in corporate life, if a company hails itself as 'best for customer service' across its markets, but does not live up to it in one, it will have a very different reputation in that market that no amount of PR will shift. As C G Jung reputedly put it: 'You are what you do, not what you say you do.'

So, if a good reputation comes from a promise delivered, this means the best reputation management happens in 'the business', not the corporate affairs department. The function can be the champion of reputation, but it should neither 'own' it nor feel prime responsibility for managing it. A good reputation comes from living your values, delivering for customers, making good decisions, meeting and exceeding performance standards, and demonstrating good behaviours... across the organization. It is showing, not telling.

To illustrate this, think about two airlines: one a global flag carrier, the other a low-cost regional or domestic airline. The two companies pursue very different strategies and have different brand promises: one based on quality and service, the other on convenience and price. One's advertising slogan is 'home comfort in the sky'; the other's is 'low-cost family flying'. You are already starting to form an image of these airlines and you may have *expectations* of what the customer experience with these airlines might be like, but this is not yet reputation.

If you fly with these airlines, you will experience what they do rather than hear what they say. You will have first-hand knowledge of their people, performance and customer service and you will judge for yourself whether they deliver on their promise. When you share your experience, you and many others like you will be forming the companies' reputations. Some people might not fly at all with these airlines, but it is likely that they will know others who have done so. Or they might read about, see or hear these airlines in the news, making announcements or contributing to a policy debate. All of this is, over time, forming two collectively held reputations of two different companies.

Let's say that, based on performance and perceptions, one of these airlines enjoys a good reputation and the other a terrible one. These different reputations will be very important if either, or both, of them faces a serious issue or crisis. Imagine they both experience crashes, killing all passengers and crew. Because of their reputations, you are likely to have very different assumptions of why this tragedy happened and how the companies will respond. And based on how they do respond to such an incident, their reputations could be enhanced or damaged. This, in turn, may impact your future flying decisions... and their bottom lines.

Importantly, it would be wrong to assume in the above example that the low-cost airline has the bad reputation. A low-cost airline could have a great reputation based on a 'cheap and cheerful' brand promise – if it delivers.

A flag carrier could have a terrible reputation based on a customer service excellence promise – if the reality as experienced and perceived by others does not match.

Valuing reputation

Reputation is undoubtedly valuable, but putting a financial value on reputation is difficult. One way of doing this might be to look at the share price or other financial indicators of a company that has, for whatever reason, lost reputation. But it is not easy to decouple the 'cost' of reputation damage from other costs associated with a crisis or issue, such as fines, clean-up costs and legal costs.

Take BP, for example. The oil giant is still counting the financial cost of the Deepwater Horizon oil spill in the Gulf of Mexico in 2010, and will be for many years to come (see Chapter 12 for a case study). The company has paid clean-up costs and fines, and set aside tens of billions of dollars to pay more fines and settle claims, and to do so it has had to sell assets across the world. The company's share price has suffered: the stock lost over half of its value on the US market in the three months after the disaster[1] and is still some way lower than its pre-crisis levels.

BP's reputation took a huge hit too. The human and environmental tragedy, and how the company responded to it, will sit in the public and stakeholder consciousness for a long time. Commentators and analysts can be heard saying that the long-term reputation hit will be far worse than the short-term financial hit. But can this reputation damage be measured? Is it feasible to separate actual balance sheet costs from the costs of reputation damage: the contract that will now not be awarded; the strategy in another part of the business that will have to be put on hold; the partner that drives a harder bargain in a joint venture (JV) arrangement; the senator who does not name check the company positively in speeches; the talented graduate who decides to go elsewhere; the consumer who chooses to fill up his car on a competitor's forecourt? It might be possible to put figures on some of these and their impacts – and it would be a powerful number to chase – but ultimately we have to accept that reputation is an intangible asset.

Suffice to say, in the wake of the Deepwater Horizon disaster, many companies in the energy and other sectors looked at what happened to BP and its senior management and thought 'There but for the grace of God go we.' Under regulatory, board and investor pressure, they initiated workstreams to check their crisis and reputation management structures, processes and capabilities. Even companies in other sectors with less risk of catastrophic infrastructure disaster (eg financial services companies) looked at the crisis and came to the same conclusion: if you do not understand the value of your reputation when it is riding high, you will certainly understand its value when you have lost it.

This may seem anecdotal rather than scientific, but that is the way reputation works. As it is about perceptions and experiences, it is often discussed within an organization – even at senior levels – in a conversational rather than a scientific way. Most organizations have tales of reputation good times and bad; employees are increasingly aware of how reputation was won or lost, and see how it impacts on their jobs and lives.

Although it is hard to value, there are of course ways of tracking reputation over time. There are many organizations that seek to measure reputation for companies. This is primarily done through surveys of stakeholder groups (as reputation is determined by others, the most obvious way seems to be to ask people) and/or analysis of media and other output. *Fortune* magazine's 'World's Most Admired Companies' index is perhaps the best known. PR agency Edelman's 'Trust Barometer' is another. Companies care about their positioning in trust or reputation surveys; whether they are up or down, and how they score against competitors. Everyone likes to be liked. A good result boosts morale and customer/stakeholder confidence, and it can even help create direct value by allowing a high-scoring company to charge a premium for its products and services.

All of this measurement is there in response to what now seems unarguable: reputation is a valuable asset. Having a good reputation brings benefits that are far from woolly. A good reputation can bring hard commercial benefits: it helps to build strong brands, launch new products, secure licensing deals, recruit the best staff and avoid intrusive regulation. Issues or incidents that damage reputation can undermine these benefits.

Consider the following fictional example, which shows how a badly managed issue can lead directly to reputation damage and knock-on commercial and financial consequences.

A British supermarket chain, FoodStores, discovers that there is horsemeat in some of its own-brand beef products. The contamination affects the supermarket's low-cost 'Quality Basics' range.

FoodStores immediately instigates the withdrawal of the products from its stores across the country, but in a statement buried on its corporate website – and only issued reactively to media – merely says that this is a 'precautionary measure pending further tests' and states that the fault, if there indeed was one, sits 'squarely with our supplier'.

As media interest grows, the company directs journalists to this supplier, which struggles to cope with the escalating issue. By the end of the first day, the supplier has started briefing the media that the supermarket has squeezed it so hard on price and pushed it so hard on quantity and delivery times that it has been forced to source its beef from farmers in other countries, which it now accepts have poor standards. The media report gleefully on the conflict between the supermarket and its supplier and demand that senior people from the supermarket are made available for interview. They are understandably interested in FoodStores (a household name), not the unknown supplier.

On the second day, the supermarket issues a proactive statement, apologizing to its customers. However, the statement asks shoppers to bring the 'unused product' back with 'proof of purchase'. Many customers call to complain that this is unfairly limiting, especially for a product that has the supermarket's own brand on it. FoodStores later reverses that decision, saying that products – even empty packaging – can be brought back for a full refund with no receipt necessary. But the damage has been done – many thousands of customers have been turned away.

Meanwhile, pressure groups such as Action on Animal Cruelty take an interest, seeing an opportunity to highlight the poor conditions animals are subjected to in the supply chain. Activists turn up in horse costumes at FoodStores across the country, causing disruption and attracting the attention of the media. British farmers also get involved, briefing the media and pressuring government to encourage better 'source from Britain' policies and singling out the supermarket as the 'worst in class' for sourcing cheap meat from untrustworthy sources.

A junior agriculture minister promises 'strong action' and 'tight regulation', saying the days of 'bully-boy tactics by the penny-pinching supermarkets' are over. An opposition spokesperson says that he believes consumers should be 'very wary' of the Quality Basics range. He later withdraws this statement, but the issue has been further escalated. Three respected news programmes run in-depth investigations, highlighting food quality issues and supply chain uncertainties.

By the second day, FoodStores' share price has fallen 8 per cent and stores are reporting customer footfall down by between 4 and 9 per cent. Senior management finally takes to the airwaves. As the Chief Executive is on a 'pre-arranged business trip to India', the head of quality is left to do the interviews. This is a disaster, with commentators saying that the spokesperson is out of his depth, incoherent and unsympathetic. 'Somewhere in an Indian hotel room', says one business analyst, 'a CEO is watching his company and his career implode.'

The supermarket's celebrity endorsers pull out after pressure from activists, and advertising campaigns are cancelled. After just one week, the decision is taken to terminate the 'Quality Basics' range entirely.

The consequences of the crisis are more than just financial. After the issue dominates the FoodStores annual general meeting some three weeks later, the Chief Executive decides to 'bring his retirement date forward' and leaves the company. The new Chief Executive makes a full public apology and vows to clean up the supply chain and re-emphasize the values of the company. He has much work to do: surveys show that trust in the supermarket has fallen from 67 per cent just before the crisis to 32 per cent. In six weeks, FoodStores has lost its leadership position and is trailing at number three behind its biggest rivals.

This may be a fictional example, but the issue was very real. There was a UK and European food industry crisis in 2013 involving horsemeat found in processed beef products. The supermarket involved from the start was Tesco. But, unlike the fictional FoodStores, Tesco handled the problem very well – it reacted swiftly, making a full public apology, terminating its contract with the supplier, offering full unconditional refunds and promising action to affect real, lasting change. Its action was decisive, showing care and control, commitment and contrition. The company suffered some reputational and commercial damage, of course, but their response spared them the sort of calamitous story told above (see full case study in Chapter 5).

The point of the fictional example is, I hope, that it is so believable. Companies can and do make errors such as those above when managing issues and crises, and these errors can have very real, negative impacts on their reputations. All of the errors in the fictional case study are either communication errors or errors in decision-making that corporate affairs professionals should be advising on.

From reputation management to reputation strategy

Reputation is valuable; if you manage a risk to your reputation poorly, you will see the value of what you have lost. But stating that you value something does not necessarily mean fully appreciating its strategic and financial value. Managing something does not necessarily imply that a comprehensive strategy has been put in place to maintain, enhance, protect and utilize it for the achievement of business goals and to create genuine long-term shareholder value.

This change – from reputation management to reputation strategy – is the final step that organizations need to take in order to show themselves, their stakeholders and shareholders that they not only value reputation but are actively addressing it with positive strategies.

What is a reputation strategy? Can you have a strategy for something that is not in your control? You can indeed. Essentially, a reputation strategy looks at four pillars: maintain, enhance, protect and utilize.

Being good at the day job – delivering on your corporate and brand promises – helps to *maintain* and *enhance* your reputation. It also serves to *protect* by building reputational capital in the bank – an important shield for when a crisis or issue comes along. This aspect of reputation strategy derives from everyday performance, behaviours, delivery, quality and service.

Reputation can, to an extent, be *enhanced* by specific initiatives, decisions, changes and announcements as well as excellent performance in the delivery of the organization's objectives. This could be a significant change such as dropping a product or launching a global citizenship programme.

Protecting reputation is about making sure that your organization is as resilient as possible. Elements of this can be compartmentalized and given to departments to manage/oversee, but again these are matters that require buy-in and action from across the organization. Protecting your reputation covers all the strategic crisis, issues and reputation risk management activities that this book is primarily about. It is everything from actively making sure (through reputation risk architecture, process and culture) that reputation is in the room when key decisions are taken, to crisis management manuals, training and testing.

Finally, a good reputation should be *utilized* – or 'leveraged' – for the achievement of strategic goals. Enlightened organizations can deploy the value of their reputations to create the climates in which they can better perform their core business or purpose. This is done, for example, through policy, positioning and public affairs programmes: making contributions to debates and leveraging relationships and goodwill to influence policy. The company at the top of *Fortune's* 'Most Admired Companies' index is Apple.[2] It has a reputation that gives it access, influence and power.

These four aspects of reputation strategy do not fit neatly into any one function. Whilst some of the above activities can be compartmentalized for management (citizenship and crisis management, for example), reputation as a whole has no natural home. Whilst some organizations have given reputation to a named senior executive (usually in corporate affairs), on balance it is not advisable to house reputation as a concept or function anywhere in an organization. It encourages a sense of compartmentalization, which is the exact opposite of how reputation should be considered.

Many leaders say that reputation is owned by everyone in their organization. This is a powerful, empowering and inclusive sentiment and, if all employees went about their daily work with reputation top of mind, there would undoubtedly be fewer issues and crises to manage. But it needs to be led from the top. If anyone should be the Chief Reputation Officer, it is the Chief Executive. Were leaders to take on this mantle, it would truly be a demonstration of reputation being treated as a valuable and strategically important asset.

Notes

1 Smith, Hannah [accessed 8 March 2013] 'BP one year on: How events unfolded' [online] www.ifaonline.co.uk/ifaonline/news/2044806/bp-events-unfolded

2 Fortune [accessed 27 February 2013] 'World's Most Admired Companies', *CNN Money* [online] http://money.cnn.com/magazines/fortune/most-admired/

02
The challenging climate in which reputations are managed

If, as argued in the previous chapter, reputations are determined by others, these 'others' are increasingly sceptical, critical, demanding, informed, empowered and interconnected. The reputational playing field is both full and chaotic. Organizations in all sectors, but perhaps most obviously global, privately held companies, are seeking to devise reputation strategies in a hostile and seemingly uncontrollable environment.

It is not easy to compartmentalize this challenging climate, as there is so much connectivity between its various aspects, but this chapter discusses each of the following:

- declining trust;
- low risk tolerance;
- international regulation;
- local and global expectations;
- the information 'anarchy' of traditional and new media; and
- empowerment and activism.

Declining trust

At times of economic hardship and austerity, one would hardly expect positive or increasing trust – especially when failures by privately-held banks and regulating governments are seen as the causes of the crisis – but trust levels were in fact barely better over the economic boom years. Whilst levels of trust in some organizations, sectors or professions periodically increase or decrease, underlying trust is weak.

The PR agency Edelman publishes an annual 'Trust Barometer', which looks at trends in trust across industries, sectors, countries etc. Its 2013 publication started with the finding that 'less than one fifth of the general public believes business leaders and government officials will tell the truth when confronted with a difficult issue'.[1] The report focused on the 'crisis of leadership', in which leaders are significantly less trusted than the organizations they represent (whilst 50 per cent claim to trust in business, only 18 per cent trust business leaders). Whilst the report suggested that trust is 'on the rise', the overwhelming picture presented by this and other similar reports and surveys – as well as anecdotal evidence – is that trust is a valuable asset that is increasingly difficult to earn from a public made sceptical by scandals, crises and controversies.

The biggest change has happened over the past few decades rather than the past few years. A good example of how attitudes have changed in this time period is the perception of, and trust in, banks. The 'bank manager' was once the personification of sense and stability in a local community, characterized in television sitcoms as the portly gentleman in a three-piece suit and spectacles. How times have changed. 'Bankers' are now perceived (and portrayed) as the unacceptable face of capitalism, gambling the hard-earned cash of ordinary people on risky foreign ventures that line their own pockets.

This is part of a general rejection of traditional authority figures. In recent years, the reputation spotlight has fallen not only on the usual suspects (politicians, journalists), but also on the church, public broadcasters, the police and doctors. Indeed it is hard to think of any organization that has maintained any sort of 'untouchable' status as far as trust is concerned. The Edelman 'Trust Barometer' refers to this as a 'democratising trend'[2] – a redistribution of influence away from chief executives and other authority figures towards peers, employees, and those with credentials such as academics or technical experts. Companies have been on to this for some time, which is why advertising campaigns feature 'ordinary workers' just getting on with their jobs to bring us the food, energy, products etc that we want.

In addition, what now seems to be happening is that the rejection of traditional figures of authority has been enhanced by a rejection of traditional *structures* of authority. Just in the last few years, there have been revolutions in the traditional sense in the Middle East and North Africa, in part fuelled by revolutions in how politics and the traditional structures of a market economy are seen and experienced. Social and political movements and everyday activism are aided by new information networks that are horizontal (peer to peer) rather than vertical (top down).

There seems to be an underlying assumption in much of current social and political discourse that business is a force for bad rather than a force for good. In many ways, business has only itself to blame, both because of the high-profile issues and crises it has faced (and, as we shall see later, often mismanaged) and because it has failed to put its worth and its contribution across more positively. Business has allowed others to characterize its behaviours and motives, which has led to distrust, in turn causing further retreat: a vicious circle. There is an argument to say that a global economic crisis is not the time for business to proclaim more loudly what it stands for, especially as its leaders are so mistrusted and as business is perceived as a villain of the piece, fuelling the boom that led to the bust. But there is a counterargument to say that this is exactly the right time to extol the virtues of private enterprise – after all, the wealth needs to be created somewhere so that governments can start spending it again.

Either way, the underlying trust gap means that organizations are on the back foot when designing strategies to maintain, enhance, protect and utilize their reputations. At the same time, it puts an even greater premium on reputation: if the climate of trust is low, then the value of a good reputation and good relationships is extremely high when issues or crises arise.

Low risk tolerance

Society's diminishing risk tolerance is related to declining trust in that people are even less prepared to tolerate risk (whether real or perceived) when they do not trust those who are seeking to impose it. The result is that in developed countries, whereas once we accepted a certain amount of risk associated with our lives and jobs, we now want a near zero-risk environment. We crave certainty, but technological and scientific innovation presents uncertainties even if it also presents societal benefits.

The low-risk climate has been causing reputation (and commercial and financial) risks for many years, and the fear of the unknown is a key dynamic in the challenging climate in which organizations manage reputation. There are plenty of examples of issues that have developed from real risk or perceptions of risk. Some of the most famous include:

- **Genetically modified (GM) foods:** efforts led by Monsanto in the 1990s to bring GM food technology to Europe failed when European interest groups, politicians and the general public reacted with fear and opposition. Instead of being perceived as delivering technology that could help the developing world beat famine, GM companies were seen as the profiteering creators of 'Frankenstein foods'. Retailers responded to consumer pressure by withdrawing GM foods from the supermarket shelves, and politicians and regulators kicked the technology into the long grass, where it still languishes.

- **Deep vein thrombosis:** 'Economy class syndrome' was a medical scare that reached its peak in the early 2000s and which led to airlines encouraging passengers to take small amounts of exercises on long-haul flights.

- **Mobile phone masts:** for many years, campaigners attempted to prevent the telecoms industry from erecting new mobile phone masts, believing that the frequencies emitted were causing cancer clusters in local communities. This is largely an issue that has been resolved, thanks to proactive communications strategies by the companies involved (see case study in Chapter 13).

A case study that is 'one to watch' in this regard is the shale gas debate. This is following the classic risk issue path. It is a new application of technology in a controversial industry. It involves a process which, whilst not new (energy companies have been fracturing rock for decades), is perceived to be new and 'dangerous'. The perception of risk, fuelled by the media and campaigners (including a Hollywood movie), is high. The risk involves very typical 'fear' components: water contamination, earth tremors, property blight.

So what is driving this low tolerance of risk? Whereas scientists and engineers think about hazards (the risk outcome and likelihood of it happening), the general public adds a layer on top of that which experts in this field tend to call 'outrage'. This outrage factor covers all the emotional responses, values and biases that drive attitudes and opinions. One of the biggest drivers of outrage is fear: the fact is that we fear before we think, which puts organizations (and their communicators) on the back foot where risk is concerned.

There are various factors that risk communication experts have identified that help organizations to understand how people are likely to respond to a real or perceived risk. These include:

- **Fear:** the pure 'dread' of the potential outcome of the hazard. This is usually a health outcome, and often cancer.
- **Noise:** what are the media, politicians, NGOs, scientists, community leaders, academics etc saying about the risk?
- **Nature:** is the risk natural or man-made? People fear the man-made risks (nuclear technology, pesticides, GM foods) more than the natural (such as weather events).
- **Detectability:** can people see, quantify and contain the risk? In the case of mobile phone masts, viruses such as SARs, radiation etc the fear is amplified because people cannot detect and therefore seek to avoid it.
- **Benefit:** people are more likely to tolerate a risk from which they derive a benefit. This benefit can be something direct (such as using a mobile phone because it is so convenient, despite concerns about the safety of base stations, masts and handsets) or indirect, such as jobs and wealth coming to a local community.
- **Choice:** did I choose to take this risk or has it been imposed upon me? Risk communication experts all tell anecdotes which show the distinction here. For example, a public meeting is held where local community members are up in arms about a theoretical contamination risk from a chemical plant which increases the chances of contracting cancer (already a significant chance for any human being) by

one-in-a-million. After the heated meeting, half the participants go outside to smoke a cigarette. The point is that people are more afraid of (or certainly more outraged by) a small risk that is imposed on them by others than a major one that they choose to take themselves.

Another factor to be wary of is that campaign groups who understand these emotional dynamics will use risk as a 'Trojan' to fulfil a different campaign goal. Some of those opposing mobile phone masts were in fact more worried about the visual impacts of a new mast than they were about risk, but health risk was the angle more likely to generate support and action. Similarly, some environmental NGOs are primarily opposed to shale gas development because they want to take fossil fuels out of the energy mix, but the hooks they use to achieve their aim are classic risk perceptions: earthquakes, aquifer pollution and 'destruction' of the countryside. It is worth stressing, of course, that campaign groups are not bound by the same rules as government bodies or companies. They can flood the media (including, of course, social media) with inaccuracies designed to scare.

The public's changing attitude to risk is a key factor in understanding the challenging climate in which reputations are managed; companies and their communicators would do well to understand it in greater depth.

International regulation

Companies also need to deal with changing, hardening and more rigorously enforced regulations on their international operations. Anti-bribery regulation is a case in point. Over the past 15 to 20 years, not only has there been an increase in the amount of anti-bribery regulation, but also its enforcement has become far tougher. This presents financial and reputational risks to global companies because, whilst few would argue that bribery is an acceptable way of doing business, becoming bribe-free is no mean feat.

One of the earliest pieces of 'global' anti-bribery legislation was the United States' Foreign Corrupt Practices Act (FCPA) 1977, which outlawed the bribery of foreign officials by US-listed organizations.[3] This Act was not strictly enforced until 1997, when the Organisation for Economic Co-operation and Development (OECD) introduced its Anti-Bribery Convention.[4] In 1998, in response to the Convention, the United States amended the FCPA so it would also apply to foreign firms that committed bribery in the United States.[5] The OECD Convention was a driving force in the creation of the UK Bribery Act,[6] which was introduced in June 2011.

The UK Bribery Act applies to any organization with operations in the United Kingdom, and covers its operations in any part of the world. It requires companies to be able to prove they have done everything they can through 'adequate procedures'[7] to prevent bribery from occurring in any part of the world at any time. If accused of bribery, a company's only defence will be that it had adequate procedures in place to prevent it. Put simply, 'we had no idea this was happening' is not acceptable, but 'we can prove that we did everything we could to prevent it' is.

Over the past five years, prosecutions have increased globally, in terms of number and the size of resulting penalties. Since 2008, the FCPA has handed out its 10 largest penalties to multinational companies.[8] This pattern is expected to continue as authorities increasingly work together and share data. For example, in April 2012 Siemens was investigated by German authorities for potentially corrupt payments to a Russian company. The company is now facing probes from 14 jurisdictions, all rooted in the initial German investigation.[9] The likelihood of companies being targeted by whistle-blowers has increased significantly, as legislation has been introduced that encourages employees to step forward. In the United States, the Dodd–Frank Act gives financial rewards to employees who provide information that results in prosecution.[10]

The only way companies can truly protect themselves from the financial and reputational risk of being found to be guilty of bribery is to become bribe-free. As this is ultimately impossible to guarantee, then at least they need to be able to show proactively that they had taken all reasonable measures to become bribe-free. To achieve this, companies are introducing anti-bribery policies and procedures: the 'hard' changes. Changes will include updating disciplinary procedures, establishing investigation procedures for when an individual is suspected of committing bribery, and introducing whistleblowing policies.

However, these policy and procedural changes must be supported by attitudinal and cultural change too. This 'soft' change is just as important in minimizing exposure to prosecution. When any organization looks to effect change of this nature, it is looking ultimately to change behaviours. Figure 2.1 shows 'behaviour' in the corporate context.

FIGURE 2.1 Behaviour in the corporate context

	FEEL	DO
INDIVIDUAL	ATTITUDE	BEHAVIOUR
ORGANIZATION	CULTURE	SYSTEM

Figure 2.1 shows that:

- what an individual thinks is his/her attitude;
- what an individual does is his/her behaviour;
- what an organization thinks is its culture; and
- what an organization does is its system.

Organizations usually seek to change behaviour through introducing systems (or policies, procedures etc – the 'hard' changes described above) and demanding compliance. But this needs to be accompanied by attitudinal and cultural change, the other key drivers of behaviour. Anti-bribery regulation is just one example of the hardening nature of international regulation. International efforts on banking regulation and corporation tax are others. This is not necessarily a bad development. Indeed, many companies lobby for clearer, tougher regulation in order to create level international playing fields. But it is another component of the high scrutiny and expectation in modern international commerce.

Local and global expectations

Global regulation is a direct answer to some of the questions raised by 'globalization'. This term – once a controversial topic of debate as if it was something that could be turned up or down, on or off – is simply the name given to the unstoppable international integration that has happened as a result of developments in information technology and the accessibility and affordability of international travel.

It means the world is getting smaller, and that people are far more aware of how the world economy is interlinked. We never used to think about where our toys and clothes were made; now we have seen pictures of them being made in Asian factories. For global organizations, this means that there really is no such thing as a 'little local difficulty' in some distant outpost which will never make it to the news agenda. One-asset mining companies, for example, are becoming acutely aware that, even if their asset is tucked away in an African nation that few could place on a map, there is the potential for stakeholder interest at the local and international level that could swiftly translate into reputation and financial damage. Similarly, the luxury of time has well and truly disappeared. Something that happens at this asset today is not only potentially front-page news tomorrow, it is also potentially the headline of a blogger's latest offering today.

This small world is also a free world. According to Freedom House's *Freedom in the World 2013 Report*, 65 per cent of the world's population now live in free or partly free countries.[11] Of the 35 per cent of those not classified as living in a free country, more than half are in China.[12] In many countries where questioning authority and demanding change were once extremely rare, individuals, communities and consumers are becoming more aware of their rights, their powers and their ability to effect change in both the public and private sectors.

In this globalized world, companies need to deal with international expectations in a local context and local expectations in an international context.

When operating in a local context, as well as increasingly onerous international regulation, companies also face the challenge of international 'soft law'. Soft law means different things to different people, but it essentially refers to the codification of non-binding norms or codes of conduct agreed to by various parties. It is essentially self-regulation: the corporate adoption of principles and codes that no government has imposed. It allows companies to take the lead on issues that might otherwise result in reputation damage and/or hard regulation. But companies need to be careful about what they are committing to.

The UN Guiding Principles on Business and Human Rights[13] is a good example of soft law. These principles – drawn up by the former UN Secretary General's Special Representative for Business and Human Rights, John Ruggie – establish amongst other things a global code of practice that is expected of all states and corporations with regard to business and human rights. The principles explain that companies have a 'responsibility to respect' human rights whilst states have a 'duty to protect' them.

When managing an incident or an issue – and especially when in some sort of conflict situation – companies are acutely aware of their 'hard law' legal obligations. But responding based solely on hard law is no longer enough. This soft law matters, and there is a lot of it.

Campaigners, of course, seek to turn soft law into hard law. They are increasingly looking to governments and the courts to ensure commitments and expectations that companies sign up to or are encouraged to abide by – which do not have the status of law – are upheld. A recent Supreme Court ruling in the United States provided a hard law answer to a soft law question. The US Alien Tort Statute of 1789 allows non-US nationals to bring civil lawsuits in US federal courts for violating the 'law of nations or a treaty of the United States'.[14] The Statute was barely used until the 1980s, when it started to be used (primarily by campaign organizations) to bring companies to court in the United States for alleged violations abroad. A recent US Supreme Court ruling has put a brake on this: in *Kiobel vs Royal Dutch Petroleum (Shell)*, the court held that the Statute does not apply to actions committed by foreign companies. It also cautioned against efforts to apply US law outside the United States. The consequence of this ruling is that, essentially, foreign nationals cannot use US courts to sue foreign companies for acts committed on foreign soil.

Whilst this case can be seen as a victory for multinationals, it was just one attempt at firming soft law into hard law. But soft law is hardening every day. If there is a genuine gap between the two, law usually catches up with societal expectation. Until it does, compliance with the hard law rather than the soft law of expectation may not be enough to avoid reputation damage.

But at the same time as being expected to abide by 'soft' international codes and guidelines, companies are also expected to respect local cultures and resist the cultural homogenization that some see as the unwanted consequence of globalization. Can companies really think and act locally, whilst working to uphold international business codes? It is not difficult to see how companies might see themselves as stuck between a rock and a hard place.

Take the following fictional dilemma. A company once manufactured industrial chemicals at a site in a developing country. The site has long been redundant, but the company wants to help turn the land back from industrial to residential or other use. On investigating the land, it discovers that some chemical residues remain in the soil. Initial tests and an assessment of the risk reveal that there is no threat to human health or the environment. The local regulatory regime is immature. But the company recognizes that if it were to apply standards it has previously used in developed countries, it would probably address some pockets of contamination before changing the land use.

Acting responsibly in accordance with what it sees as its global standards, the company decides that it should indeed take some remedial action on the land. But the relatively immature regulatory regime is confused. Seeking a permit to clean up the land is complex, and will involve regulator engagement and education.

Regulatory engagement leads to political, and then community, interest. Local NGOs start to question what is happening and politicians become interested in why the company seems so keen to clean up land it does not legally need to worry about. After some to-ing and fro-ing, the local mayor declares that the permits are all eminently grantable, but suggests that before any signatures are in place, the company might consider creating a leisure centre in an adjacent area for the local community to enjoy.

So here is the dilemma: is the creation of the leisure centre a locally and culturally acceptable way for a global company to ensure that its own international standards are adhered to in a developing country, or is it a facilitation payment to smooth the resolution of a difficult contamination issue that some might say shows the company has put health and the environment at risk?

There is no right answer to this or many similar dilemmas that companies face when balancing the local with the global and hard law with soft law. But, ultimately, operating in this changing and globalized world is about delivering on promises. Reputation, as described in Chapter 1, comes from a promise delivered, not from a promise made. Soft law may be a soft promise, but it is still a promise. Companies need to get used to the fact that, in this small world, they will increasingly be held to account for these promises on both an international and a local stage.

The information 'anarchy' of traditional and social media

The world is small partly because we travel more, and our horizons are broader. But even those who have not enjoyed the luxury of foreign travel are interconnected through both traditional and new media.

The past 20 years have seen rapid change in the media and news industry, largely driven by advances in technology. Across the world, households can access many more television channels, including 24-hour news channels, and can now do this via laptops, tablets and smartphones.

The most critical change in traditional media relates to time. The old cycle of deadlines and first editions has been gradually dismantled by 24-hour news and, more recently, online editions and social media. A story breaking in the print edition of a newspaper still does happen, but it is rare.

These developments have radically affected the concept of deadlines. Journalists now need to turn their stories around fast and need to fill space 24 hours a day, 365 days of the year. So the predictable pattern of news no longer exists, whilst the sheer volume and amount of news needed to fill all this space have rapidly expanded.

Just 20 years ago, journalists dealing with a crisis or escalating issue would likely face one deadline, probably late in the afternoon. If the story was big enough to feature on broadcast news, coverage would consist of a three- or four-minute package within a half-hour evening bulletin on a terrestrial channel. If the organization at the centre of an issue or crisis decided to field a spokesperson, the demands on them would be limited. The infancy of the internet meant there were no bloggers, no online newspapers and no Twitter. Most members of the public didn't own a mobile phone, and they certainly didn't have smartphones that could shoot video footage.

Fast forward two decades and it is a very different picture. Today, a story can escalate extremely quickly and the first pictures of a physical incident may well be taken by a member of the public. Anyone with a smartphone is now a 'citizen journalist'.

The life of a journalist has changed too. Cuts in advertising budgets saw the media badly hit by the financial crisis; there are fewer journalists, expected to do more. Not only do they have to turn their hand to any medium, they are also expected to cover an ever more diverse range of subject matter. This, for some publications, has meant the end of specialist correspondents and subject experts in the newsroom.

The most extraordinary change, of course, is the growth of social media. It has dramatically changed the media and societal context in which reputations are managed. We have moved from an environment in which reputation management was based on 'one-to-many' structured communications to one of 'many-to-many', non-hierarchical conversations.

Two case studies demonstrate this changing context. On 11 July 2012, mobile phone company O2 experienced a major service outage in the United

Kingdom. The organization lost all 2G and 3G network services, resulting in the crash of mobile, landline and broadband connectivity for customers. Thousands immediately took to Twitter. New followers on the microblogging site increased from an average of 155 to 13,500 per day.[15] However, O2 turned a potential reputation disaster into a triumph, and it did so almost exclusively by virtue of how it engaged with customers on social media. Indeed, the organization's nimble, personalized and humorous response to the crisis almost eclipsed the outage (and resulting outrage) itself. *The Telegraph* called it a 'social media master class'.[16]

By contrast, the social media aspect of BP's response to the Deepwater Horizon oil spill was heavily criticized. BP did not begin communicating via social media in earnest until one month[17] after the spill happened. When it did engage, it bought search terms on the three major search engines to secure visibility for a sponsored link highlighting its clean-up efforts. The photographs of these efforts, however, appeared to look nothing like the reality. And when BP tried to deploy the technique of crowdsourcing solutions to problems, this backfired: asking a lay audience for ideas about how to plug a leaking oil well did not give the impression of a company in control of a crisis. It is perhaps not surprising that the parody @BPGlobalPR Twitter account had more than 10 times the following of BP's official account less than two months after the incident occurred.

Social media are now just part of reality for organizations and communications functions. It is almost unthinkable that the management of a major incident or issue – whether or not a crisis is called – would not involve a social media dimension. But it is worth looking at the specific ways in which the advent of social media, with their unique characteristics, has affected reputation risk management.

First, social media can *trigger* reputation risks. For example, in June 2013, a photo appeared on the internet showing a Taco Bell employee licking a stack of tacos. The photo quickly went viral on Facebook and Twitter, where it attracted angry comments from customers. Taco Bell's hygiene and quality standards were widely brought into question. Indeed, the company's YouGov BrandIndex Buzz (a brand perception measurement) score dropped into the negatives from +9 to −1 following the appearance of the photo.[18]

Second, social media can *escalate* issues. In January 2013, disgruntled HMV employees hijacked the company's official Twitter account to express their dissatisfaction with the retailer's redundancy programme. Whilst only seven tweets were posted, the incident showed that the company had failed to take precautions in how it managed its online assets (one tweet read, 'Just overheard our Marketing Director... ask 'How do I shut down Twitter?'[19]). It also confirmed the view that the company was in free fall after filing for bankruptcy.

Third, an organization's use of social media can *be* the issue. In April 2013, not long after the Boston bombings, food website Epicurious tweeted that everyone could do with 'a bowl of breakfast energy to start today'. It proceeded to tweet, 'In honour of Boston and New England, may we suggest whole grain cranberry scones!'[20] Needless to say, its attempt to leverage the tragedy for commercial ends was poorly viewed by stakeholders and customers alike.

Fourth, and more positively, social media can help *resolve* the issue. The O2 case study, as described above, is a good example of this. Another can be found in FedEx's response to a YouTube video posted in January 2012 by a disgruntled customer. The video depicted a FedEx employee delivering a computer monitor by throwing it over a gate and into the garden of the buyer. The video went viral, and was viewed 5 million times in the first five days.[21] FedEx responded quickly, posting an apology on YouTube from Senior Vice-President, Matthew Thornton III. They also reimbursed the customer and announced publicly that the video would be used for training purposes. The company also used Twitter to amplify its apology, winning praise from professionals.

Social media have therefore introduced new dimensions to specific reputation risks. Moving from the specific to the general, the growth of social media has also changed the *context* in which reputations are managed in the following ways:

- More people now make a direct contribution to the formation of an organization's reputation.
- Reputations can change faster than ever before.
- Traditional approaches to communication are no longer enough.

Social media are all-pervasive. More than 70 per cent of the internet population uses social networks of one form or another.[22] In 2011, social networking accounted for one in every six minutes spent online.[23] Social media are no longer the realm of teenagers either. Facebook's biggest demographic is now between 35 and 54 years old and the average profile age on Twitter is 37 years[24] – a demographic with greater political sway and purchase power. The online world is fast resembling the offline one, with all of its variety and complexity.

As explained in Chapter 1, an organization's reputation is heavily informed by individual, family and peer group experiences of it, which are much more compelling than anything an organization says about itself through marketing or PR. One of social media's most important contributions has been its creation of hundreds of thousands of forums for users to share opinions about products, services and brands. According to recent polling, 43 per cent of consumers who use social media do so to complain about a product; 43 per cent use it to ask for peer recommendations and 47 per cent use it to share their experience of a product or a service with others.[25] All this sharing can impact an organization's reputation and, more importantly, its bottom line.

But what has perhaps contributed most to social media's influence on reputation management is the high level of visibility this user activity has. This visibility has encouraged increasing numbers of 'establishment' figures to use the medium. Journalists, for example, can exploit Twitter for the access it gives them to new stories, case studies, personal testimonies, and rapid eyewitness accounts. For example, when an Asiana aircraft crashed on arrival in San Francisco in July 2013, journalists from Sky News and Bloomberg instantly contacted Krista Seiden, a bystander who had tweeted a photo of the crash from the airport lounge via her Twitter account.

In this and other ways, 'ordinary' people can more easily contribute to the way we think about an organization. At the same time, the historical influencers of opinion – the media, politicians etc – are able to access and amplify these peer-to-peer exchanges using traditional channels of communication.

Additionally, social media operate on a different timescale to other communications channels: its impact is immediate. When a helicopter crashed in Vauxhall, London in January 2013, Twitter beat the traditional media to the story with instant pictures, witness accounts and videos. Within 20 minutes of the Asiana crash in July 2013, personal testimonies from passengers were running on Facebook, Twitter and Weibo. When O2 experienced its service outage in 2012, roughly 1.7 million people had seen negative coverage of customers' experiences by the end of day one.[26]

This speed has been accentuated by the increasing sophistication of mobile technologies and the ubiquity of smartphones. The availability of social media on handsets turns everyone into an amateur journalist, social commentator, news photographer or professional critic. Negative (or positive) opinion about a product, a service or a company can be instantly communicated and then amplified by any number of friends, contacts or followers. Given that social media do not respect geographical borders either, anything posted can rapidly gain traction in markets across the world, often before an organization's in-house communications team has had the opportunity to understand what has happened. Reputations are more volatile assets than ever before.

The purpose of social media is the formation of communities. These communities might be small and temporary. They might be large and involve multiple interactions between members every day. But they have dialogue as a central organizing principle. This contrasts with the historical approach to corporate communications, where companies were in control of what they said, when they said it, to whom they said it, and on what platform it was communicated. Organizations could expect some responses from stakeholders and consumers, but had limited incentive to engage in conversation with their critics. Social media have changed this. Users expect organizations to engage with them on the terms they set. They expect companies to speak plainly and honestly, to answer their questions and address their concerns. They expect them to respond quickly and to continue talking.

Social media have changed the *tactics* of communication and the *context* in which reputations are managed, but the *principles* have not changed. Organizations still need to seize the communications initiative in a crisis, for example, to prevent a vacuum forming around them. They still need to communicate directly with their key stakeholders and speak to them plainly and honestly. And they still need to deploy their messages through whatever media or communications channels their audiences use. Social media websites, whether Twitter or Facebook, Google+ or YouTube, are additional platforms for organizations to communicate through, albeit in a different and less structured way. They are faster and resource-intensive, but they offer one of the most direct forms of stakeholder engagement available. Social media may have sparked a paradigm shift in how companies should think about communication, but the real change is tactical rather than strategic. And, most importantly, those organizations that can harness the power of social media can find new opportunity in both peacetime and adversity.

Empowerment and activism

The final part in the jigsaw of this climate in which reputations are managed is the increase in 'activism'. Activism is not necessarily the direct action taken by vociferous issue-driven groups. It is the everyday activism that has been created by the information anarchy, the low tolerance of risk, the rejection of traditional power structures and all the other aspects of the challenging climate as described in this chapter. Developments in communication technologies coupled with a changing media landscape mean that now any individual – member of staff, customer, neighbour, or even just an individual with an opinion – can spot a problem or escalate an issue. But the NGO remains the key organizing and campaigning vehicle for activism... for now at least.

The term 'NGOs' sits proudly as a category in just about any corporate stakeholder list, whether it is a list compiled for a particular issue/risk or one that is used for general proactive engagement on a range of matters. Since the inception of the modern NGO in the 1970s, these groups have wielded significant power; they have driven the 'external issues' discussed in Chapter 4, bringing attention, interest and organization to key topics of debate. Even those who are not fans of NGOs will admit that, on some issues, they have helped improve corporate performance and made a positive difference to the world.

The term 'international NGO' was first used during the establishment of the UN. It was defined in 1950 as 'any international organization that is not founded by an international treaty'.[27] It was an attempt to describe organizations such as the International Red Cross/Crescent, which do good work and are worthy of special recognition. There are now more than 2 million NGOs in the United States alone, and 40,000 NGOs which can legitimately be called international.[28] Not all of them are as worthy of special recognition as the Red Cross.

The power of NGOs has come partly from their 'independent' status and the perception that they are staffed with people who are 'more ordinary' than those in governments, businesses and the media. The truth is that most

NGOs are very partial, unelected and unaccountable, except to their members. They are like businesses: they have priorities, incomings and outgoings, forward strategies and customers. The global lobby groups and charities are huge professional businesses in their own right, with massive advertising budgets.

The NGO community, and its outlook and tactics, has changed significantly over the years. The evolution of NGOs, and their relationship with business in particular, has happened in three distinct phases: the adversarial era, the era of cautious engagement and the current era of polarization.

Early NGOs focused on the civil rights and anti-war movements, choosing to target governments directly with the aim of impacting policy and legislation. However, the rise of global corporations saw many NGOs shift their focus to the social and environmental ills perceived to have resulted from the operations of 'big business'. There was an explosion of NGOs that realized they had access via the mass media to the customers and other key audiences of corporations, and saw that some of those companies perceived to be all-powerful and untouchable were in fact thin-skinned when it came to bad publicity.

Particularly in the 1980s, campaign groups identified key social and environmental issues, bringing them to public attention and forcing governments and the private sector into action. Most NGOs considered themselves to be a vital 'social' check on the power of corporations, and relations between the two groups were primarily antagonistic. At this time – the adversarial era – the idea of engaging with NGOs was rarely accepted in the business world.

The 1990s saw the advent of a period of 'cautious engagement', with global companies recognizing that 'engaging' with their stakeholders (including NGOs) was a more constructive way of managing the issues the groups were raising. By this time, the success of some NGO campaigns had created a generation which cared more about global social and environmental issues. NGOs grew in size and stature, and some came to look like those they criticized: professional, slick, articulate and well-resourced. Companies cautiously reached out to NGOs, seeking to understand their motivations and explain their own policies and needs. Some went further, recognizing the need to change on issues identified by NGOs, and inviting some groups to be part of the solution. Some NGOs accepted this invitation; others declined, preferring to remain confrontational. But even the positive relationships between corporations and NGOs remained for the most part strained: they were relationships born of the need to manage each other, rather than driving towards a common goal.

Since the turn of the century, and especially during the last few years, there has been a 'polarization' amongst NGOs. The attitudes and concerns that NGOs had helped instil in younger generations became mainstream. Companies hired bright young professionals straight from further education, or from NGOs themselves, to lead environmental and social issues from within the organization. This was the private sector seeking to shape the agenda and affect the direction of externally driven issues that were in danger of damaging their reputations. Some of the most talented people likely to make a difference in big global societal issues were now sitting in the corporate headquarters of the world's biggest and wealthiest companies. With the machinery of capitalism now behind the key issues of the day, and collaboration with NGOs seen as a natural next step beyond cautious engagement, NGOs were in a position where they could either embrace collaboration or retain a combative stance. In fact they have done both. On one end of the scale are 'thinkers': NGOs who want to contribute constructively to realistic and intelligent policy debate and who measure their success in genuine outcomes. On the other side are 'shouters': groups whose *raison d'etre* is to agitate, campaign, disrupt and embarrass, and who have agendas that are, to many people, unreasonable, unrealistic and almost always anti-corporate. As with any scale, there are some groups at either extreme and many in between.

'Thinkers' are less worried about being seen as corporate sell-outs and are more willing to engage and compromise. Their approach is more scientific and rational, building solutions through dialogue and policy work. Some have forged strong and lasting relationships with corporations aimed at tackling some of the world's most pressing issues. 'Shouters' are those campaign groups too ideologically inflexible to make cooperation feasible. They retain what NGO analyst Robert Blood refers to as a 'quasi-religious' belief that they are right and that they must expose the wrongs of big companies. Engagement is not an option with these groups. Whilst companies happily sit down with the 'thinkers' with a view to creating better policy and practice, there is no prospect of meaningful dialogue with 'shouters'.

The more confrontational NGOs need publicity to keep their members happy. They therefore seek innovative ways of drawing attention to themselves and key issues, but their aggressive tactics appeal to a dwindling number of people. With the rise of social media, people do not need NGOs to organize discontent; it can be done via a Facebook campaign. For example, Greenpeace's campaign against Shell on the oil major's plans to drill for oil in the Arctic shows creativity in tactics but ultimately not much strategic success. The 'Save the Arctic' campaign, launched in 2012, called for the region to be established as a sanctuary. The campaign initially consisted of the collection of over 3 million signatures (including those of a number of high-profile celebrity backers), the occupation of Shell petrol stations in Edinburgh and London, and the boarding of Shell's drillship in Port Taranaki by activists. These are all familiar tactics that cause headaches but get little mainstream media coverage and low public attention. Greenpeace switched tactics and launched a 'brand-jacking' campaign. Using a fake Twitter handle and website to ridicule Shell's own 'Let's Go' advertising campaign, Greenpeace got attention. However, this attention came primarily from its existing supporters. Furthermore, some social media commentators felt that this was a move too far; with so much uncertainty on the internet, adopting the identity of another is considered a faux pas. In July 2013, trying to escalate the issue with a further stunt, six Greenpeace campaigners scaled London's tallest building, The Shard, and placed a 'Save the Artic' flag at its pinnacle. This got some media coverage but more for the action rather than the issue. The activists were criticized for putting their own safety and that of rescue crews at risk. The campaign may have raised some income for Greenpeace (much needed, as NGOs have been hit by the recession too) but it has not moved the debate.

Some argue that the 'thinkers' and 'shouters' feed off each other nicely (and purposefully). The 'shouters', ineffective in the policy space, create enough noise and corporate discomfort to encourage more concessions from companies in their discussions with the 'thinkers'. One creates this problem; the other solves it. This is possibly true in some cases, but the gulf between the solution-oriented 'thinkers' and the confrontational 'shouters' is widening, and respect between the two diminishing.

The next challenge for NGOs is the arrival on the scene of big Russian, Chinese and other non-Western companies, particularly in the extractives industry, where environmental activism has its home. When competing for contracts in some developing countries, Western companies rightly agonize over social and environmental impacts and proceed in a way that reflects hard and soft law obligations. Some other companies do not, and can win contracts on simpler grounds. At some point NGOs will surely need to switch their attention from the converted to the unconverted, and collaborate more closely with those companies that espouse positive environmental and social values. In the meantime, many corporations have found the best way to deal with NGOs: take the issues that NGOs have raised over the years, set the agenda in a more positive and constructive way, hire the best people, engage meaningfully and beat NGOs at their own game. Those NGOs motivated by real change have joined companies on this journey, and can see that the change in global companies represents a victory for their hard work. But some just cannot contemplate sleeping with the enemy, and will continue to play to the (dwindling) crowd.

Shareholder activism

Activism is not limited to organized campaign groups on social issues. Companies can face activism from individuals or loosely formed groups, or indeed from the business and financial communities. Shareholder activism has hit the headlines in recent years; its development has further complicated the environment in which corporate reputations are managed.

Chief executives and their boards work on behalf of their shareholders to create value (ie to grow the share price and/or increase dividend return). The activist shareholder thinks they know how to do this better. To prove this they acquire a relatively small shareholding in a company to give them the voting platform (and voice) they need to attend annual general meetings, table shareholder resolutions and ultimately convince the existing board, its management, shareholders and stakeholders that their alternative strategic or financial approach is the right one.

Shareholder activists range from private individuals to global funds but typically take the form of private investment vehicles (ie hedge funds such as David Einhorn's Greenlight Capital Inc which successfully persuaded Apple to reduce its cash pile and pay special dividends in 2013), or institutional investors (ie pension funds, mutuals, religious organizations and labour unions).

Europe and the United States have seen a rising tide of shareholder activism, typified by the 'shareholder spring' of 2012, during which activists targeted the remuneration policies of companies including Aviva, Barclays, Novartis, Tesco and WPP. These activist campaigns frequently 'won' for the shareholders the significant and very public curtailment of senior executive pay. Shareholder activism is not, however, a new trend. Benjamin Graham, author of *The Intelligent Investor* and often credited with being Warren Buffet's investor mentor,[29] gained notoriety in 1928 for his activist stance against John D Rockefeller's Northern Pipeline Co, when he united a coalition of support against the board.

During the 1980s, shareholder activism was more often carried out via publicly traded companies and even in the 1990s, when private investment companies (ie hedge fund activists) began to be active, it was largely restricted to the banking sector. However, there is little doubt that, following the 2008 financial crisis and the ensuing focus on corporate governance supported by regulation (eg 2010 Dodd–Frank Act), shareholder activism has infected the mainstream. Shareholder activism has, over the past few years, forced out chairmen and board members (Chesapeake Energy 2012), reduced executive pay (Aviva 2012), increased dividend payments (Apple 2013) and influenced deals (Glencore Xstrata 2013).

Boards, Executive Committees and their communications advisers navigating the already complex stakeholder environment must be prepared to listen and proactively engage with the increasingly active and vocal shareholder activist. Although in some cases the shareholder activist can launch a 'surprise attack', the campaign for change generally begins in private, with a direct approach by the activist to the board or chief executive. In some cases, organizations may seize the opportunity to access 'free' management consultancy and take on board enough of the recommendations to appease the activist and generate further value. However, this conversation may stall and become public, forcing the target company's management team into issue or even crisis management mode.

Regardless of the identity of the shareholder activist, their approach, or indeed the validity of their proposal, the speed of the target company's response and its willingness to engage are critical to protecting its reputation and that of its management team. As with any risk, companies and their management teams must be able to predict, prepare for and respond to an activist approach as they would any other issue or crisis.

Chapter summary

The climate in which any organization manages its reputation is more challenging now than it was even a decade or two ago. Underlying levels of trust in business, government, public services and the media are weak. Tolerance of the risks associated with progress is, in developed countries at least, low. Expectation of success is high, as is scrutiny fuelled by intrusive and demanding media; acceptance of failure is low. Problems and issues play out very publicly, whilst corporate success is rarely lauded by a suspicious public. There are potentially billions of citizen journalists and activists empowered by social networks that allow them to access, share, analyse and broadcast information and opinion. And the world, whilst made smaller by information technology and travel, remains characterized by cultural and societal differences that global organizations need to navigate carefully.

Many of the aspects of the climate as described in this chapter are beyond the control of organizations. They are just facts of life in a changing world. The one thing that organizations can seek to change proactively, however, is trust. Those that deliver for their customers and stakeholders, live their values, meet performance standards, behave responsibly and make good decisions can earn trust.

Notes

1 Edelman [accessed 27 February 2013] *Edelman Trust Barometer Executive Summary*, New York: Edelman [online] www.edelman.com/trust-downloads/executive-summary/

2 Edelman [accessed 27 February 2013] *Edelman Trust Barometer Executive Summary*, New York: Edelman [online] www.edelman.com/trust-downloads/executive-summary/

3 Baker Hughes [accessed 16 May 2013] *Foreign Corrupt Practices Act (FCPA) Compliance Guide*, Texas: Baker Hughes [pdf] www.bakerhughes.com/assets/media/assets/4dc40248fa7e1c6400000001/file/07_code-of-conduct-guide-and-fcpa-guide-5_2011.pdf

4 AIG Chartis [accessed 15 May 2013] *Global/Anti-bribery regulation: Laws against bribery and other forms of corruption have become stricter and more global*, New York: Chartis Inc [pdf] www.aig.co.uk/chartis/internet/uk/eni/Global-Anti-Bribery-Regulation_2590_446637_tcm2538-446809.pdf

5 Cook, Christopher and Connor, Stephanie [accessed 15 May 2013] *The Foreign Corrupt Practices Act: An Overview*, US: Jones Day [pdf] www.jonesday.com/files/Publication/3325b9a8-b3b6-40ff-8bc8-0c10c119c649/Presentation/PublicationAttachment/d375c9ee-6a11-4d25-9c30-0d797661b5ff/FCPA%20Overview.pdf

6 Cannon , Lista and Pegram, Ian [accessed 25 July 2013] 'The Bribery Act: one year on', *Risk.net* [online] www.risk.net/operational-risk-and-regulation/opinion/2186552/the-bribery-act-one-year-on

7 Gillespie, Roy and McEvoy, Megan [accessed 25 July 2013] ANTI-BRIBERY COMPLIANCE. Protect yourself against unscrupulous third parties, *The Times*.

8 AIG Chartis [accessed 15 May 2013] *Global/Anti-bribery regulation: Laws against bribery and other forms of corruption have become stricter and more global*, New York: Chartis Inc [pdf] www.aig.co.uk/chartis/internet/uk/eni/Global-Anti-Bribery-Regulation_2590_446637_tcm2538-446809.pdf

9 AIG Chartis [accessed 15 May 2013] *Global/Anti-bribery regulation: Laws against bribery and other forms of corruption have become stricter and more global*, New York: Chartis Inc [pdf] www.aig.co.uk/chartis/internet/uk/eni/Global-Anti-Bribery-Regulation_2590_446637_tcm2538-446809.pdf

10 AIG Chartis [accessed 15 May 2013] *Global/Anti-bribery regulation: Laws against bribery and other forms of corruption have become stricter and more global*, New York: Chartis Inc [pdf] www.aig.co.uk/chartis/internet/uk/eni/Global-Anti-Bribery-Regulation_2590_446637_tcm2538-446809.pdf

11 Freedom House [accessed 4 April 2013] *Freedom in the World 2013: Democratic Breakthroughs in the Balance* [pdf] www.freedomhouse.org/sites/default/files/FIW%202013%20Charts%20and%20Graphs%20for%20Web_0.pdf

12 Freedom House [accessed 4 April 2013] *Freedom in the World 2012: The Arab Uprisings and Their Global Repercussion* [online] www.freedomhouse.org/article/freedom-world-2012-arab-uprisings-and-their-global-repercussions

13 Office of the High Commissioner for Human Rights [accessed 4 April 2013] *Guiding Principles on Business and Human Rights: Implementing the United Nations "Protect, Respect and Remedy" Framework* [pdf] www.ohchr.org/Documents/Publications/GuidingPrinciplesBusinessHR_EN.pdf

14 USA Engage [accessed 4 April 2013] 'Alien Tort Statute' [online] http://usaengage.org/Issues/Litigation/Alien-Tort-Statute-/

15 Wired [accessed 22 July 2013] 'Calming a twitstorm: O2's masterclass in dealing with "outage outrage"' [online] www.wired.co.uk/news/archive/2012-07/17/o2-outage-social-media-masterclass

16 Warman, Matt [accessed 22 July 2013] 'O2's social media masterclass', *The Telegraph* [online] www.telegraph.co.uk/technology/social-media/9398450/O2s-social-media-masterclass.html

17 Wired [accessed 22 July 2013] www.wired.com/business/2010/06/bps-social-media-campaign-going-about-as-well-as-capping-that-well/

18 BrandIndex [accessed 22 July 2013] 'Taco Bell Handling Of 'Taco Licker' Seems To Reassure Consumers', *Forbes* [online] www.forbes.com/sites/brandindex/2013/06/13/taco-bell-handling-of-taco-licker-seems-to-reassure-consumers/

19 Jones, Sam [accessed 22 July 2013] 'HMV workers take over official Twitter feed to vent fury over sacking', *The Guardian* [online] www.theguardian.com/business/2013/jan/31/hmv-workers-twitter-feed-sacking

20 Olenski, Steve [accessed 22 July 2013] 'Epicurious Uses The Boston Marathon Tragedy To Cross That Line', *Forbes* [online] www.forbes.com/sites/marketshare/2013/04/18/epicurious-uses-the-boston-marathon-tragedy-to-cross-that-line/

21 Ko, Vanessa [accessed 22 July 2013] 'FedEx Apologizes After Video of Driver Throwing Fragile Package Goes Viral', *Time* [online] http://newsfeed.time.com/2011/12/23/fedex-apologizes-after-video-of-driver-throwing-fragile-package-goes-viral/

22 Brenner, Joanna [accessed 22 July 2013] 'Pew Internet: Social Networking', *Pew Internet* [online] http://pewinternet.org/Commentary/2012/March/Pew-Internet-Social-Networking-full-detail.aspx

23 Parr, Ben [accessed 22 July 2013] 'Social Networking Accounts for 1 of Every 6 Minutes Spent Online', *Mashable* [online] http://mashable.com/2011/06/15/social-networking-accounts-for-1-of-every-6-minutes-spent-online-stats/

24 Dugan, Lauren [accessed 27 July 2013] 'The Typical Twitter User is a 37 Year Old Woman', All Twitter [online] www.mediabistro.com/alltwitter/twitter-age-gender-2012_b27885

25 Qualma, Erik [accessed 22 July 2013] 'Statistics Show Social Media Is Bigger Than You Think', *Socialnomics.net* [online] www.socialnomics.net/2009/08/11/statistics-show-social-media-is-bigger-than-you-think/

26 Wired [accessed 22 July 2013] 'Calming a twitstorm: O2's masterclass in dealing with "outage outrage"' [online] www.wired.co.uk/news/archive/2012-07/17/o2-outage-social-media-masterclass

27 United Nations Economic and Social Council (ECOSOC) (27 February 1950) 'Resolution 288 B (X)'

28 LSE Centre for Civil Society and Centre for the Study of Global Governance (2001) *Global Civil Society 2001*, US: Oxford University Press

29 Carlen, Joe [accessed 2 July 2013] 'How Benjamin Graham Revolutionized Shareholder Activism', *Bloomberg Echoes* [online] www.bloomberg.com/news/2013-05-17/how-benjamin-graham-revolutionized-shareholder-activism.html

03
What are the risks to reputation?

This chapter looks at the different reputation risks that organizations face and suggests a new categorization system to help better understand and, ultimately, manage them. In doing this, it moves away from the simplistic terminology of issues management and crisis management.

Most people – including me in the title of this book and in other publications – refer to issues management and crisis management as if they are quite different disciplines. In some ways, they are, but the absolute distinction is not helpful and can be counterproductive.

Crisis management is still most often associated with incidents that happen suddenly, presenting an organization with an immediate and fast-moving operational and communications challenge that unfolds in the public arena. These incidents might be explosions, fires, oil spills or train crashes, for instance. They cause intense pressure and scrutiny in a short time frame, with the organization(s) involved coming under the spotlight for all the wrong reasons. To address such acute and serious challenges, crisis management requires the invocation of a 'non-business as usual' modus operandi: the crisis procedures or plan.

Issues management is less clear in current terminology. In some organizations, issues management is seen as 'just what we have to deal with every day'. In others, an issue describes a problem or challenge that requires strategic intervention over time. It is sometimes also used to describe an opportunity that an organization has identified that has an element of controversy or risk attached to it. Or it can be a political or social issue that has emerged as a risk necessitating an organizational, wider industry or sector response.

In these commonly used definitions, what distinguishes issues management from crisis management is the assumption that the organization has more space and time to resolve an issue. It is, perhaps, the space and time that mean issues management is less advanced a discipline and is seen as the less immediate, or important, part of managing reputation risks.

In short, most literature and most practitioners broadly see crisis management as an immediate response to an incident (an acute risk) and issues management as a longer-term response to a slower-burning risk.

There are many case studies that fit neatly into these two categories. The 2010 rig explosion and oil spill in the Gulf of Mexico, for example, is a classic crisis case study – a physical incident that happened suddenly and unexpectedly, which required emergency and incident response, put BP, Transocean and others under intense public and stakeholder scrutiny and led to serious reputational, financial and commercial impacts. Staying in the energy industry, shale gas extraction ('fracking') is a classic issue: a developing debate where there are clear stakeholder and public expectations and concerns which energy companies interested in shale gas need to factor into their strategies, and mitigate and manage.

But in other ways, these definitions are unhelpful in understanding risks to reputation and how companies manage them. Some of the biggest corporate crises and reputation meltdowns of recent years have come not from incidents but from issues: for example, News International and the phone hacking scandal; the British Broadcasting Corporation (BBC) and the posthumous uncovering of one of its star entertainers as a prolific sex offender; Barclays (and the wider banking industry) and the LIBOR-fixing scandal. These were clearly crises – and were labelled as such by the media and other stakeholders – despite the fact that they did not involve burning platforms, train wrecks or air accidents.

These definitions of crisis management and issues management have persisted perhaps because of how they emerged and developed within many organizations. Crisis management as a discipline developed from incident management, emergency response and business continuity and therefore traditionally sat in the more operational part of an organization. Issues management was born more in the corporate affairs and communications departments. Whilst crisis management has in many organizations moved into corporate affairs, sometimes the terminology has not kept up. Some of those organizations that evolved their crisis management capabilities from their incident management capabilities have failed along the way to demerge the two and bring slow-burn or rising-tide crises into their planning.

This book moves away from this classic dichotomy of issues and crisis management – at least partially. Instead it looks at all risks to reputation as potential crises that are either incident-led or issue-led.

With this in mind, let's look at the definition of a crisis. *Crisis management: guidance and good practice* is a consultative document drafted by the Cabinet Office in the United Kingdom and the British Standards Agency. The document is a 'publicly available specification' (*PAS 200*), a precursor to a 'standard'. It is designed to provide guidance to companies as they develop their own policies and processes in crisis management. *PAS 200* defines a crisis as an 'abnormal, unstable and complex situation that represents a threat to the strategic objectives, reputation or existence of an organization'.[1]

This is a good definition. There are two key points to mention here. First, a crisis in this definition is a 'situation'. A situation could stem from an incident, but equally it might not. The authors distinguish between sudden crises (incidents) and smouldering crises (issues) and suggest that most crises are of the smouldering type. Second, a crisis is big news. A crisis threatens the very core and existence of an organization. By implication, crisis management procedures should not be invoked lightly. Organizations have incidents all the time – but few would qualify as crises by this definition.

Because crises are not synonymous with incidents, the document explains that crisis management is very different from incident management: '[crises] develop in unpredictable ways, and the response usually requires genuinely creative, as opposed to pre-prepared solutions. Indeed, it is argued that pre-prepared solutions (of the sort designed to deal with more predictable and structured incidents) are unlikely to work in complex and ill-structured crises. They may, in fact, be counterproductive.' This is absolutely correct.

My definition of crisis management is: 'making, implementing and communicating strategic decisions under exceptional circumstances of intense scrutiny, acute pressure and high organizational risk'. It is not the same as incident management, emergency response or business continuity. All of these operational response capabilities are vital but crisis management sits above them at the highest strategic level.

What identifies a crisis is not the nature of what has happened but what is at stake – reputation, the bottom line, the licence to operate and the future of the organization – and the immediacy of the threat.

So where does that leave issues management? I define it as: 'the management over time of non-acute risks to an organization's strategic, commercial and reputational interests which, if left unresolved or if ignited by a "trigger" event, could escalate into a crisis'.

So reputation risks either come from incidents or issues; and either can be or become a crisis. This is the first of two elements of the categorization used in this book.

The second part of the categorization looks at whether these risks to reputation and potential crises derive from internal or external incidents or issues. This is an important distinction. Incidents or issues that are internally driven imply a failure of performance, whether acute or chronic. They are self-inflicted. Incidents and issues that are externally driven are either inflicted or led/developed by an external party or force.

These two variables provide a four-category model which is captured in Figure 3.1. The four categories are:

- **External issues.** These risks are often policy or political issues, or could emanate from controversies or societal 'outrage'. They are usually not specific to one organization; rather they affect a wider sector or sectors. They require careful positioning, policy development, communication and often – and most importantly – change in order to manage them. The risk of bad management is to become the 'poster child' of an escalating societal or political issue; the opportunity in managing these externally driven issues is to steal a march on competitors and improve trust and reputation. Examples include: societal/political issues such as obesity and climate change; and risk (real or perceived) issues such as concern about hydraulic fracturing/shale gas or genetically modified (GM) crops.

- **Internal issues.** This is a huge category as it essentially covers all issues relating to the performance of the company. This could include: inappropriate behaviour, product failure, supply chain issues, job losses, poor financial performance etc. As this category implies some sort of chronic organizational failure, it can be the hardest to manage. No organization wants to accept it suffers from poor performance and/or poor behaviour. Examples include: malpractice, such as the LIBOR-fixing scandal and the Enron/Arthur Andersen scandal; product issues or recalls, such as the horsemeat issue in Europe in 2013; and perceived corporate or governance failure, such as was uncovered by the Olympus 'CEO whistle-blower' in 2012. This category also includes potential issues with positive developments. The misjudged product launches, marketing initiatives or other supposedly good news stories that go wrong: Coca-Cola's launch of Dasani water in the United Kingdom and the opening of Heathrow Terminal 5 are two examples.

- **External incidents.** This category covers the sudden and often very acute/extreme incidents which are not the fault of, or not in the control of, the organization or organizations impacted. They do, however, require an immediate response to protect people, the environment and the organization's reputation. These incidents include terrorist attacks, piracy and sabotage. One of the most famous good crisis management case studies was Johnson & Johnson's handling of a product sabotage and attempted extortion. The category also covers: sudden health scares, such as the swine flu pandemic; political revolution and unrest, such as was seen in North Africa during the Arab Spring; and natural/weather events, such as Hurricane Sandy, the Asian tsunami and the volcanic ash cloud that grounded flights and left passengers/tourists stranded in 2010. Whilst this category implies that the organization handling the crisis is not the 'villain' of the piece – something has been done *to* you rather than *by* you – the need to respond well is no different.

- **Internal incidents.** These risks are the incidents that are, or are perceived to be, in an organization's direct control. They are the classic 'crises' from the commonly used definitions referred to earlier in this chapter, often involving loss of life and/or environmental impact. Examples include: transport disasters, such as plane crashes, train derailments or shipping incidents (eg the Costa Concordia sinking off the coast of Italy in 2012); and infrastructure failures, such as mining disasters or oil rig explosions. The incidents in this category present immediate, potentially catastrophic risk to an organization which is thrown – often alone – under the stakeholder, media and public spotlight.

The examples used in this categorization below are all case studies covered in this book.

FIGURE 3.1 Categorization of reputation risks and potential crises

	INCIDENT-LED	ISSUE-LED
INTERNAL	*Typically:* Industrial accidents Transport accidents System failures *Examples:* RBS system failure BP Deepwater Horizon oil spill Costa Concordia cruise ship disaster Elgin gas leak BP Texas Refinery explosion	*Typically:* Fraud/malpractice Corporate governance failure Poor practice/behaviour (perceived or real) Corporate/strategic failure *Examples:* HMV job losses Dasani launch Persil Power launch Cadbury sports campaign Hoover flights promotion Heathrow Terminal 5 opening Olympus scandal Enron scandal Tesco horsemeat contamination LIBOR-fixing scandal Shell reserves News International phone hacking BBC Jimmy Savile scandal Toyota recalls
EXTERNAL	*Typically:* Cyber attacks Health scares Terrorism Piracy Natural disasters Political revolution/unrest *Examples:* Pan Am flight 103 (Lockerbie) Madrid train bombing Hurricane Sandy Fukushima disaster Piracy in the Gulf of Aden Lonmin Marikana incident Tylenol sabotage Heathrow snow disruption	*Typically:* Policy issues Investigations/allegations Religious/cultural/political controversies Societal outrage *Examples:* McDonald's and healthy food General Electric and climate change UK corporation tax avoidance: Amazon, Google and Starbucks Nestlé baby milk issue Mobile phone health risk perceptions Obesity GM crops Sweatshops Fracking

Chapters 4 to 7 look in more detail at these four categories of reputation risk, highlighting the different challenges they present to organizations and providing case studies.

Note

1 British Standards Institution (2011) *PAS 200:2011 Crisis Management – Guidance and Good Practice*, London: BSI. This document has now been superseded by a draft standard which is out for consultation at the time of writing. The definition used in the draft standard, BS11200, has changed slightly since PAS200. It reads: 'abnormal and unstable situation that threatens an organisation's strategic objectives, reputation or viability'.

04
Externally driven issues

Externally driven issues present opportunities as well as risks. As they are rarely specific to one organization, those that address and manage them most successfully have the opportunity to derive a reputational, commercial and strategic benefit. But getting to that place is not easy. Externally driven issues, by definition, are identified, escalated and led by others – often NGOs, campaign groups, interest groups or politicians. They therefore require careful positioning, policy development, communication and often – and most importantly – change in order to manage or resolve them.

This chapter looks at the challenges presented by this category and examines some of the ways in which they can be managed. The later chapters of the book look in more detail at strategies and tactics for dealing with these, and other, risks to reputation.

An external issue tends to have the following characteristics:

- As it emerges, the main 'narrative' of the issue is not held or controlled by the organizations that are expected to change and/or contribute to its management. Ownership of the agenda is held elsewhere, and is being shaped by a multitude of different stakeholders and interest groups.

- The issue affects a whole sector, a number of sectors or sometimes (as with the case of climate change, for example) practically all organizations in all sectors. This may seem like safety in numbers but, more often than not, those campaigning for change will focus their attention on specific organizations that they see as the main offenders and/or who have the highest profile and most to lose from reputation damage. The risk of becoming a poster child for the issue is significant.

- The issue plays out over time and there may never be full 'resolution': it just becomes a permanent risk in the background for organizations involved. Again, climate change seems unlikely to disappear as an issue, with the merits of certain courses of action and changes to be debated for decades to come.

- The issue is fundamental, deep-seated and difficult to tackle. There are few 'quick wins' to be had from external issues, and they will not be resolved through PR and gimmicks.
- The issue is almost always political, with those driving it seeking certain public policy and regulatory outcomes, as well as demanding change from the organizations they perceive to be at the centre of the issue.
- The concept of 'outrage' is more often than not important in an external issue. As discussed in Chapter 2, 'outrage' is an important driver of how people perceive risks; it is also important in how moral, ethical and other societal issues are discussed.

Although usually sharing these characteristics, there are subtly different forms of the externally driven issue:

- Societal and political attention on a broad problem.
- Societal and political outrage at specific organizational behaviour/ performance.
- Societal and political outrage at a new risk (real or perceived) imposed by an organization/sector.

Societal and political attention on a broad problem

These are the big issues of the day that tend to feature in political and societal discourse over many years. With this sort of issue, the external world, often driven by NGOs and politicians, is saying: 'We have a problem; these organizations are contributing to it; they need to change.'

Examples of this type of issue are climate change and obesity. Although each of these issues has required action and communication by a number of organizations, each has had a poster child (or various 'poster children') over the years. ExxonMobil, Shell, McDonald's and Coca-Cola all spring to mind. These are deep-seated, fundamental issues: the energy we use and the food we eat. And they are all unlikely to be entirely solved any time soon.

The obesity 'crisis'

Obesity is an external issue currently being addressed by the food industry. If we are to believe those setting the agenda for this externally driven issue, it is a major threat to the health of the world's people and economies that has yet to be resolved despite a decade or more of high public attention, governmental action and industry change. A recent report published by leading medical journal *The Lancet* predicted that, if obesity rates were to increase at current levels, 26 million Britons and 163 million Americans could be obese by 2030.[1]

Like all external issues, obesity is highly politicized. US President Barack Obama announced the start of National Childhood Obesity Awareness Month in 2012 saying: 'Over the past several decades, childhood obesity has become a serious public health issue that puts millions of our sons and daughters at risk.'[2] Meanwhile, in the United Kingdom, Prime Minister David Cameron has backed calls for a 'war on sugar', stating that fatty and sugary foods pose 'one of the biggest public health challenges that we face in our country'.[3]

There is little doubt that the media, together with most politicians and others driving the agenda, see 'junk food' or 'fast food' as the cause of the obesity crisis. The following headlines give a flavour of the reporting: 'Junk food raises asthma risk in children "by 40 per cent"';[4] 'Junk food as bad for babies as smoking';[5] 'Junk food diet "could damage your child's IQ"';[6] 'Junk food diet takes 11 years off child's life';[7] 'Junk food linked to bad behaviour';[8] 'Junk-food ads lure kids to bad diets'.[9] Speaking to *Forbes*, Sam Kass, Senior White House Policy Advisor on healthy food initiatives, said: 'We will only solve the obesity epidemic if the food industry takes substantial action toward a healthier marketplace.'[10]

With the blame apportioned, various efforts to impose stricter regulation on the food industry have followed:

- A New York ban on large soft drinks (over 473 ml) was blocked by the judge a day before the law was to take effect. The judge's decision is currently being appealed.[11]

- In the United Kingdom, some MPs are attempting to introduce rules banning pre-watershed advertising of junk food. The initiative has support from the Food Standards Agency (FSA). The current ban in place prevents junk food advertising during children's programming.[12,13]

- Some local councils in the United Kingdom have introduced, or are in the process of introducing, rules restricting fast food outlets from opening within 400 metres of schools and other areas frequented by children, such as parks.[14]

- The US Agriculture Department has announced plans to ban junk food from schools as part of the 'Smart Snacks in Schools' programme. The new regulations, in place for the 2014–15 academic year, will extend to vending machines that sell high-calorie drinks. The ban conforms to the child nutrition law passed in 2010.[15]

Regulatory and political intervention has, as ever, been accompanied by legal interest. In the United States, McDonald's (in 2002) and Kraft (in 2003) have been sued unsuccessfully for selling unhealthy food, with particular reference in both cases to the vulnerability of children. The parents who brought the case against McDonald's argued that the chain was unforthcoming about the fat content in its foods, but the case was thrown out for lacking evidence to show customers were unaware that eating too much McDonald's food would be unhealthy.[16] The Kraft lawsuit was filed in regards to fatty biscuits. The lawsuit was dropped after Kraft launched a trans-fatfree reformulation of Oreo biscuits.[17] These unsuccessful cases kept obesity on the agenda and kept pressure on industry high, and are unlikely to be the last obesity-related cases brought against food companies.

So where is the food industry in this flurry of blame, regulatory reform and legal action? The industry is, as you would expect, taking this issue extremely seriously. Food companies are worried that obesity in their customers today could come back to bite them financially tomorrow, just as smoking-related illness has hit tobacco companies.

External issues can be met with two basic responses: win the argument and/or change. The food industry has chosen the latter. It has done an enormous amount in recent years to change in response to this debate:

- Food companies have changed their products, by reformulating them to contain less salt, less sugar and less fat, to increase choice and to cut larger portions. McDonald's has famously removed 'Supersize' options from its UK and US menus, has switched to healthier ingredients and reduced the levels of sodium in its food. The UK Food and Drinks Federation's *Recipe for change* (2009) illustrates how prominent UK brands, such as Walkers, j2o, Dairylea, McVities and Kingsmill, have reformulated recipes to make them healthier.[18]

- Food companies have changed their labels to show consumers what is contained in the product in terms of fat, salt, sugar and so on. Both the traffic light system and the Guideline Daily Amount system have been adopted by food companies in the United Kingdom. Prominent British companies have also voluntarily signed up to the Government's 'Responsibility Deal', pledging to label and reformulate products in a bid to be healthier. In the United States, Walmart introduced the 'Great for You' icon to help consumers instantly identify healthy products. In 2013, the UK government announced a new consistent labelling system to make nutritional information easier for consumers to understand. A number of major food manufacturers and retailers have already signed up to use the new system including Mars UK, Nestlé UK, PepsiCo UK, Tesco, ASDA, Morrisons, Co-operative, Waitrose and McCain Foods.[19]

- Food companies have changed their marketing drives, to include initiatives aimed at helping combat obesity. In 2009, Coca-Cola UK published its 'Responsible Marketing Charter' pledging not to target the marketing of any of Coca-Cola's drinks, in any media, to children under 12.[20] Mars introduced the 'Just Play' campaign to encourage children to play football, whilst McDonald's ran the 'Mascotathon' campaign to publicize sports and the Olympics.

- Food companies have changed their advertising, to stress to consumers that they should 'enjoy responsibly' or 'be treat wise'. The Children's Food and Beverage Advertising Initiative (CFBAI) was established in 2006 by the US food industry. So far 17 major food companies have signed up to the voluntary programme pledging to change advertising targeting children to encourage healthier choices.[21] Meanwhile, Kellogg's official UK website has undergone a transformation to remove stand-alone websites for certain brands and has removed games across its website.

But despite all of these changes, industry continues to get the blame. In the United States, the Associated Press–NORC Center for Public Affairs Research conducted a poll in 2013 which found that 53 per cent of people polled felt the food industry had a very large responsibility for solving the country's obesity problem. The same poll found that 75 per cent of people blamed inexpensive and easy to find fast food as the major reason for the country's obesity problem.[22]

So has the food industry got its strategy and tactics right in response to this externally driven issue? There is an argument that the food industry has not changed enough; there can always be more change. But it could also be argued that this is a problem the industry has created itself by failing to successfully change the debate at the same time as it has offered up change in its products and practices. The obesity debate remains focused on food (energy in), rather than exercise (energy out).

Although the obesity debate has been around for some years now, it is still in its infancy. As with most issues in this category, the identified problem is not easily resolved. Unless the food industry changes the direction of the debate, the changes it makes to products and practices will perhaps never be enough.

Societal and political outrage at specific organizational behaviour/performance

External issues in this subcategory are more specifically targeted at one or more organizations that have been identified as doing something that is not in society's interests. These issues are usually laden with moral outrage and public indignation, egged on by an NGO, media and/or political campaign. The external world is saying: 'have you seen what these organizations do or how they behave? They need to change.'

There is a crossover between these types of issues and the internally driven issues that I will turn to in the next chapter. But there is a difference. Take bankers' bonuses, for example.

This is the issue that surfaces regularly (at bonus time) and which has dramatically increased in salience and outrage since the global financial crisis. This could be described as an internally driven issue: something that has arisen because of the actions of companies. The issue wouldn't exist, after all, if banks were not paying their high-performing staff what seem to many to be eye-watering sums of money. But the issue was 'born' outside the banks. It did not surface after an internal realization that there was an issue that needed addressing; rather, it was imposed on banks by external actors. The banks needed to follow the agenda and react. This issue is still playing itself out. At the time of writing, the European Union finance ministers have agreed to cap bankers' bonuses despite strong opposition from the UK government, seeking to protect the City of London.[23]

Other examples of this type of issue include: child labour, which is partially resolved; methods of energy extraction, such as deepwater drilling and oil sands; and controversies about companies operating in certain markets such as South Africa in the 1980s and, more recently, Zimbabwe and Burma. In the latter case, campaigners single out companies to highlight human rights abuses in a particular country: if Burma will not listen, the Western companies who operate there and who are sensitive to reputation risk will.

An example of an externally driven issue that developed into a crisis for the companies involved is the corporation tax issue that was high on the political and media agenda in the United Kingdom during 2012 and 2013. This case study is notable for how rapidly the issue developed, catching those involved off guard, and for how societal outrage became keenly focused on companies that had done nothing legally wrong but had, according to some, acted unethically.

Taxing times in the United Kingdom

Tax avoidance had been simmering as an issue in the United Kingdom and elsewhere since 2009, but the issue gained sudden momentum when Reuters published a report revealing how US coffee chain Starbucks 'avoids' UK corporation tax.[24] Amazon and Google (also, notably, US multinationals) were targeted by the media and politicians for their tax affairs soon there-after. All three were accused of utilizing low-tax jurisdictions and complex internal tax arrangements to pay little or no corporation tax. Since this time, many other companies have come under the corporation tax spotlight: Apple has faced congressional questioning in the United States, whilst Thames Water and Vodafone have faced scrutiny in the United Kingdom.

Coming against the backdrop of the global economic downturn and austerity in public spending, the issue struck a chord with the public. Politicians, NGOs and journalists did not suggest that the companies had committed a crime, but the public's sense of right and wrong was awakened, and this externally driven issue became a crisis of ethics and responsibility for those most heavily targeted. UK Prime Minister David Cameron spoke about the issue at the World Economic Forum in January 2013, and led the debate again during the G8 summit in June 2013 where the Lough Erne declaration was agreed to 'fight the scourge of tax evasion'.[25]

Pressure group UK Uncut organized a boycott of Starbucks and sit-in protests in UK branches. This led to the extraordinary and unprecedented move by Starbucks to offer to pay more tax – £20 million more over two years – than it needed to. A public apology in paid-for newspaper advertisements accompanied the announcement: 'We know we are not perfect. But we have listened over the past few months and are committed to the UK for the long-term.'[26] Crises can push companies into making gestures beyond their legal obligations. A £20 million tax 'contribution' by Starbucks may have been enough to stop the spread of a boycott but it attracted criticism too, demonstrating for some the company's cavalier attitude towards the payment of tax. Starbucks paid its first instalment of £5 million in corporation tax on 23 June 2013, with a further £5 million to follow in 2013 and £10 million in 2014.

Neither Amazon nor Google offered such concessions. Starbucks' high street presence made it more susceptible to a boycott; boycotting online companies is less visible and there is no potential for disruptive sit-ins. Google's Chief Executive, Eric Schmidt, commented that he was 'perplexed' by the anger towards legal tax practices in the United Kingdom. He said that Google paid the amount of tax legally required in the United Kingdom and that it was up to governments if they wanted to change tax arrangements: 'If the British system changes the tax laws, then we will comply... That is a political decision for the democracy that is the United Kingdom.'[27] Amazon's defence was similar: after it was revealed that Amazon received more in government grants than it contributed in corporation tax, the company reiterated that: 'Amazon pays all applicable taxes in every jurisdiction that it operates within. Like many companies, Amazon has received assistance in relation to major investments in the UK.'[28]

The UK parliamentary spending watchdog, the Public Accounts Committee (PAC), requested the appearance of Google, Starbucks and Amazon at a public hearing. All three gave evidence on 12 November 2012. Matt Brittin, Vice-President of Google's Central European Sales and Operations, firmly upheld that the tax minimization practices Google engaged in were not illegal. Andrew Cecil, Director of Public Policy at Amazon, seemed less prepared and was criticized by Margaret Hodge, chair of the PAC, who vowed to haul in a more senior representative for questioning. Troy Alstead, Starbucks' Chief Financial Officer, appeared apologetic but said that the public furore had caught the company off guard. The PAC published its report on tax avoidance on 13 June 2013 and appeared to single out Google for criticism. Margaret Hodge said that Google's 'highly contrived tax arrangement has no purpose other than to enable the company to avoid UK corporation tax'.[29] Following the publishing of the PAC report, a Google spokesman said: 'It's clear from this report that the Public Accounts Committee wants to see international companies paying more tax where their customers are located, but that's not how the rules operate today... We welcome the call to make the current system simpler and more transparent.'[30]

Externally driven issues are often moral outrage issues. In this case, being legally right was seemingly not enough. PAC chair Margaret Hodge said: 'We're not accusing you of being illegal; we are accusing you of being immoral.'[31] The law is a lagging indicator of societal outrage and this outrage can be whipped up at an alarming speed.

When the issue has a moral or ethical dimension (perceived greed, in this case), there is a demand for punishment and retribution. The appetite for early political humiliation on such issues is growing. UK select committees, like congressional hearings in the United States, can convene on such an issue quickly, and big companies are good political targets in times of austerity.

Margaret Hodge's carefully executed sound bite during the PAC's second grilling of Google – 'you do evil'[32] – a take on Google's motto 'Don't be evil', encapsulates the danger of the externally driven issue perfectly. The corporation tax issue is an excellent example of political expediency, stoking public outrage at companies' legal but, as was suddenly collectively decided, ethically questionable tax practices. The spectacle of politicians castigating companies for practices they concede are legal, when only the politicians themselves have the prospect of legislating for change, seems ironic. But such is the nature of the often irrational and almost always highly emotive externally driven issue.

Societal and political outrage at a 'new' risk imposed by an organization/sector

Chapter 2 contained a brief overview of the increasingly risk-averse society in which we live. Many external issues centre on an actual or perceived risk. The external drivers of these issues are asking: 'Do you know the risks associated with these developments/innovations? These organizations are imposing these risks on you. They need to change.' This may seem like a minor variation on the theme, but this sort of external issue has different dynamics and requires a different sort of strategic management. Rather than being outraged at corporate behaviour or performance, interest groups, communities, politicians and others are 'outraged' by a perceived new risk that they believe is being imposed upon them and wider society.

Chapter 2 used mobile phone infrastructure/handsets, genetically modified (GM) crops and hydraulic fracturing (fracking) to illustrate the dynamics of risk issues. Others include nuclear power (especially decommissioning of nuclear waste) and nanotechnology. Chapter 13 includes some guidance and a case study on risk communication.

Challenges in managing externally driven issues

The first challenge associated with managing external issues is *predicting how, where and when they might develop*. Although these issues are externally driven, the assumption should not be that they are unpredictable. Should, for example, the fast food industry have predicted the emergence of the obesity issue? What should the alcoholic drinks industry be looking out for next in the development of the binge drinking and alcohol misuse issue? What should both industries have learned from the tobacco industry about 'outrage' issues directed at specific sectors? One role of the communications professional is to understand how these sorts of issues emerge and develop, and to be the organization's eyes and ears as they start to unfold. This involves stakeholder knowledge and engagement as well as a finely tuned 'radar'.

Another related challenge for the communications professional is to help the organization *understand the issue and how it is perceived* by those who are driving it, supporting it or engaging with it. Organizations can sometimes develop a 'bunker mentality' when they, or the sector they belong to, are suddenly at the centre of a new or fast-developing issue, driven by a determined and vociferous set of what seem like opponents. 'Bringing the outside in' is central to a successful strategic response; eyes, ears and minds need to be open if these issues are to be addressed.

Another challenge is the *development of policy, positioning or a 'narrative'* on the issue. This is easier said than done. In many large organizations, it is difficult to find and articulate a common position on an issue that has developed externally and is seen as a threat or potential threat to the organization's interests or ways of working. It often falls to the corporate affairs function to help broker a position, trial it internally with policy testing and refinement sessions, and advise on whether, how and when it should be communicated externally.

Organizations must also decide their *positioning amongst their peers and competitors*. Do we want to put our heads above the parapet on this issue? Do we want to see a joined-up industry response, or should we go it alone? Is this an opportunity for us? Many companies are reluctant to be seen to be a leader on any issue that is externally driven and therefore difficult to control. This is quite understandable, especially for companies that have been bitten in the past and know what it is like to become a poster child for a controversial issue.

Some organizations are naturally more courageous, and want to be seen to lead, either because it suits their positioning within the industry, their wider corporate strategy or their style (and that of their leaders). Some have leadership thrust upon them by virtue of being the biggest, best known and most successful organization in the sector, or because they have a disproportionate interest in the issue. Shell, for example, has little choice but to take a leading position within the energy industry on Arctic drilling as it is the company that has the most advanced plans to pursue it. Similarly, Monsanto became the poster child for the GM foods issue in the United Kingdom by virtue of being at the forefront of the technology. Others in the industry – some of whom had interests equal to Monsanto in seeing the issue managed well – did not intervene to challenge the company's lightning rod status. But there is no room for complacency: an organization that sees its partner/competitor facing an issue would be wise to make sure it is in a position to deal with the issue, just in case.

Some industries have formed strong membership organizations empowered to manage – at least partially – controversial externally driven issues. One such industry is the mining industry, which came together to form the International Council on Mining and Metals (ICMM).

Recapturing the sustainability agenda in the mining industry?

By the late 1990s, executives in the mining industry had recognized that the industry had a poor reputation for sustainability. The reputation challenge was a fairly obvious one: many people on whom the industry depended perceived it to be routinely harming employees, communities and the environment in developing world countries and believed that these communities and countries saw little of the financial benefits. This was an externally driven moral outrage issue which had all the signs of escalation. It needed to be addressed.

The Global Mining Initiative (GMI) was set up in 1999. Its Chair, Sir Robert Wilson, stated that: 'there is a gap, which sometimes seems like gulf, between the mining industry's self-perception and how others see it. Society's standards and priorities have shifted. Industry's behaviour must not only shift in line but must where possible try to anticipate future shifts.'[33]

The industry understood that this poor reputation, if not addressed, was going to affect its key points of access. The mining industry needs access to land, for which it requires good relationships with governments and communities; it needs access to capital, for which it requires good relationships with investors; and it needs access to markets, for which it requires good relationships with customers.

As part of the Global Mining Initiative, the Mining, Minerals and Sustainable Development initiative (MMSD) was set up. It was a two-year programme to gather evidence and knowledge and engage stakeholders, providing a foundation for shared understanding amongst all stakeholders – from the executives of the mining companies to the communities in which these companies operated. Friends of the Earth Founder, Richard Sandbrook, agreed to head the MMSD, provided it was given independence from industry. This persuaded some of the industry's 'antagonists', such as Oxfam (an organization that had refused to talk to the industry), to engage with the MMSD process. A new dynamic between the industry and NGO community began.

A 2002 GMI Conference in Toronto marked the closing of the MMSD process and the GMI, and established the International Council of Mining and Metals (ICMM) as a flagship Chief Executive-led organization that would take forward the industry's responsibilities in sustainable development. The ICMM now counts 22 mining and metals companies as its members, together with national and regional mining associations and global commodity associations. It serves as an 'agent for change and continual improvement'[34] on issues relating to mining and sustainable development. Three key characteristics of its approach stand out:

- **It is based on member commitments.** The ICMM promotes principles such as 'implement and maintain ethical business practices and sound systems of corporate governance' and 'uphold fundamental human rights and respect cultures, customs and values in dealings with employees and others who are affected by our activities'.[35] It requires member companies to make a public commitment to improve sustainability performance and report against progress on an annual basis.

- **It has a multi-stakeholder approach.** The ICMM engages with a broad range of stakeholders – governments, international organizations, communities, civil society and academia – to build partnerships. This was envisaged by the industry back in the late 1990s. According to a report by the International Institute for Environment and Development (IIED), 'MMSD+10: Reflecting on a decade of mining and sustainable development' (2012), the industry was at the time seeking 'an alternative to the adversarial, advocacy based approach that characterized interactions at the time, and was ready for a move towards a shared agenda involving all the main stakeholders'.[36]

- **It is Chief Executive-led.** The ICMM is supervised by a council composed of the Chief Executives of all ICMM member companies, together with representatives from the member associations. This ensures that, unlike other bodies in other industries that operate through technical cooperation, the ICMM is strategic. As with almost any corporate initiative, senior involvement and endorsement helps drive good practice.

All of the above has helped the ICMM to improve the reputation of the mining industry amongst its key stakeholders. It, perhaps more than any other organization, now drives the agenda of mining sector sustainability. It has changed an 'externally driven issue' into one that is driven by the industry with a constructive multi-stakeholder approach. Importantly, investors now look to the ICMM as an arbiter of what good practice should look like in the sector and they are keen that mining companies should belong to the ICMM because adherence to the principles helps manage investor risk.

This is not to say that the issue of sustainability in mining is resolved. Indeed, challenges remain for the ICMM. The agenda may now be set in a positive way, and the principles are those that most stakeholders can agree on, but the real challenge remains implementation. K H Haddow, writing in the *Journal of Energy and Natural Resources Law*, argues that 'the way forward is not one of finding the right laws or policies or creating new ones. Mining companies operating anywhere in the world now probably have all the tools (as well as rules) they need available to them. What needs to improve, certainly in consistency of performance, is the industry's implementation of consultation.'[37] This is a view echoed by the IIED, which states that the sector needs 'an agenda focused on operationalizing good practice'.[38]

The ICMM's role will perhaps need to adapt to these new challenges – moving from a driver of policy to a driver of compliance. Whilst members of organizations much prefer to feel they are being 'steered' rather than 'policed', an agenda focused on delivery will test the credibility of an organization that has never expelled a member for breaking its principles. As a good reputation comes from a promise delivered not a promise made, perhaps the biggest challenges to the reputation of the mining industry still lie ahead.

Another challenge associated with the external issue is *shaping the agenda*. Organizations should not resign themselves to being followers of the agenda that has been set externally. Communications professionals need to help the organization step back and assess whether the agenda that is being set by others is the agenda they want to engage with; if not, they need to challenge it. As a simple example, the aforementioned issue of 'bankers' bonuses' is pretty much an unwinnable one for banks, especially during an economic downturn. But the issue of 'the role of banks in society' is more positive territory. It does not mean that the issue of bonuses can be avoided, just that it can be framed as part of a more positive agenda.

Challenging the agenda: Nestlé and infant formula[39]

The issue of child nutrition is an emotive one. Few would contest that breastfeeding is the best, cheapest and safest way for mothers to feed their babies. But not all mothers are able to breastfeed. Whether from a medical condition or necessity to work, some mothers have either chosen to, or had no other option, but to seek alternatives to breastfeeding, even for very young babies. Unfortunately, the foods that mothers have substituted for breast milk (unpasteurized cow's milk, rice water, fruit juices etc) have been prone to contamination and have led to infant death. Henri Nestlé developed infant formula products in the 19th century. Even then, the inventor recognized that breastfeeding is best for babies, and that his product was only suitable for mothers who had to find a substitute.

About 100 years later, Henri Nestlé's products started to attract controversy. The issue started in the mid-1960s, when a child nutritionist, Dr Derrick B Jelliffe, developed the idea that the infant formula industry was responsible for infant mortality in the developing world. This provoked little reaction, with most established bodies (including the UN Protein Advisory Group) promoting the use of infant formulae amongst vulnerable groups. However, in the early 1970s, some other child nutritionists started to support the condemnation of infant formula companies. Nestlé invited stakeholders to come to their headquarters in Switzerland to learn more about infant formula. A representative of campaign group War on Want visited and subsequently wrote a publication called *The Baby Killer*. This then was picked up by another organization who wrote a campaigning pamphlet called 'Nestlé kills babies'. Not long thereafter, boycotts started in various markets and the issue took hold.[40]

The argument put forward by anti-Nestlé campaigners is flawed on so many different levels. But once moral outrage sets in, it is hard to shift. External issues are emotive, and those driving them have confidence in their convictions. As the issue grew, infant formula manufactures participated in the creation of the World Health Organization's (WHO) 'Code of Marketing of Breast-Milk Substitutes'. Whilst this Code ended some of the boycotts, it did not stop the issue completely. Indeed, the Code established a set of standards which no global company can ever guarantee it can meet 100 per cent of the time. For example, the Code bans incentives such as product promotions on infant formula, but how can a company like Nestlé ever totally eliminate the possibility that an independent shop owner in India will do a two-for-one offer on its infant formula? The Code therefore invites people to police it, and the anti-Nestlé campaigners happily do this because it keeps the issue firmly on their agenda.

In the late 1990s, Nestlé started to communicate better with its stakeholders, although at first the focus of the communication was the company's compliance with the Code. Literature was developed which set out allegations made against the company, and explained the truth as the company saw it. These were well-intentioned initiatives showing compliance with an international set of standards, but part of a defensive strategy. It was only from 1999, when Nestlé started to address student union meetings in the United Kingdom (some student unions had long boycotted Nestlé products), that the company started to regain the initiative. These meetings, although sometimes heated and fraught, were a success and allowed Nestlé to start communicating more on its territory. For the first time, some students and campaigners were hearing the real history and importance of infant formula products, and hearing it from Nestlé employees from the developing world, some of whom were themselves working mothers.

The Nestlé infant formula issue has not completely gone away. It is too institutionalized in some NGOs for it to do so. But the issue is now far less troublesome for the company. The main reason for this is that the company started to show its commitment to the product, articulate its belief in the product, engage with stakeholders and communicate on its own agenda.

A final challenge identified is the most fundamental: being willing to change. Nestlé changed the debate, but only after it had changed policy and practice to make absolutely sure that any allegations could be addressed.

The most difficult thing to effect in any organization is change. But externally driven issues arise out of a demand for change and sometimes change is the best – or indeed the only – answer. That may include changing products (as the food companies have done in response to the obesity debate), services, policies, supply chain or an entire business strategy. On some issues, organizations or sectors may find that if they do not volunteer change, change will be forced upon them through regulation.

Of all the categories of risk identified in this book, the externally driven issue presents the most opportunity. The opportunity comes through change – accepting that an issue needs to be addressed, working collaboratively with stakeholders to address it and in so doing improving competitive positioning, finding a more sustainable business model and leading to a positive reputation outcome.

Below are some examples of companies that have successfully changed in response to an externally driven issue, and derived some reputational capital from it.

Unilever and the Marine Stewardship Council

During the 1990s, Unilever, at the time one of the largest fish buyers in the world, was coming under increasing pressure to address sustainability issues in the fishing industry. Environmental NGO Greenpeace was stepping up its campaign against unsustainable fishing and Unilever was a perfect poster child for this externally driven issue.

Unilever's response was to effect a major corporate change and move the agenda on to different territory. Bypassing Greenpeace, Unilever established a partnership with World Wide Fund for Nature (WWF) to create a market-based mechanism for ensuring fishery sustainability. The result was the Marine Stewardship Council (MSC), jointly set up by the multinational company and the environmental NGO. The MSC was established to recognize and reward sustainable fisheries through a certification scheme, build a market for sustainable seafood and give buyers and consumers an easy way to source seafood from a sustainable fishery – the blue 'MSC-certified' label.

The result was that Unilever was applauded for its role in bringing sustainability to the industry and was seen as a leader of positive change in its sector: most of its competitors and most retailers in the United Kingdom soon announced that they would only source MSC-certified fish in the future. The reputation 'bounce' that Unilever received was accompanied by the obvious more strategic 'win' – Unilever's future fish business depended on there being a sustainable supply of fish, and the company's actions had helped ensure this.

General Electric and climate change

General Electric (GE) often faces criticism from environmental activists, but the rise of climate change as a political and social issue was perhaps its biggest challenge, as it potentially posed a threat to the organization's core businesses.

Jeffrey Immelt, Chief Executive of GE, believed that GE could position itself to benefit from the rise of the issue by helping customers improve their environmental performance. Immelt's vision led to the launch of 'Ecomagination', an environment-focused research and development programme, in 2005. Ecomagination aimed to provide innovative solutions to environmental challenges faced by businesses whilst also fuelling economic growth. Immelt stated that it was 'not just good for society, it's good for GE investors – we can solve tough global problems and make money doing it... This is good business.'[41]

GE's innovative approach to the issue of climate change has won it numerous accolades from the media, politicians and environmentalists alike. The *Financial Times*, *The Wall Street Journal* and *The Washington Post* have all hailed the company's environmental leadership, whilst US Senator John McCain has been a vocal supporter of the initiative. Eileen Claussen, President of the Pew Center on Global Climate Change, has also applauded Ecomagination, saying, 'GE is deploying the biggest and most ambitious climate strategy in corporate America, and taking an incredibly gutsy stand in favour of greenhouse gas regulations.'[42] Whilst an organization in the space GE occupies will never win over everyone, this is not a bad stakeholder outcome for a company once assumed to be on the wrong side of environmental sustainability.

McDonald's and healthy food

In the mid-1980s, Greenpeace UK accused McDonald's of selling addictive and unhealthy junk food; a reputation-sapping legal dispute ensued. The 2004 documentary, *Super Size Me*, did much to publicize the calorie and fat content of McDonald's menus. Recognizing that this externally driven issue was not going away, McDonald's took the initiative to transform its menu.

Amongst other things, McDonald's removed 'Supersize' options from its menus, began to sell Happy Meals that included fruit, switched to healthier ingredients, such as trans-fat-free frying oil, and reduced sodium levels in its food. McDonald's President and Chief Executive, Don Thompson, said: 'McDonald's has the unique ability to encourage kids to get into the routine of enjoying foods like fruits and vegetables in a way that's fun for them and convenient for the parents.'[43]

McDonald's has won praise for its efforts to improve the healthiness of its menu. By concentrating efforts on improving its offerings for children, McDonald's has protected one of its key customer groups – parents. Even celebrity chef Jamie Oliver, known for his crusade in the United Kingdom against unhealthy school dinners, has admitted that McDonald's is 'doing its bit'.[44]

Chapter summary

Change – in strategy, product, services and marketing – is not the preserve of the 'business'. The role of the communications function is not to sit back and wait for change to happen, but to help organizations change when change is the right answer.

The key lessons from this chapter are:

- Externally driven issues can affect a whole sector, a number of sectors or just one organization; there is always the risk of being selected as the poster child.

- These issues are emotive and deep-seated, with a sense of outrage directed at the organizations in question.

- The agenda of the issue is initially set and dictated by others but organizations can challenge this to regain the initiative.

- Sometimes change is the best, or even only, strategy for resolving externally driven issues.

The externally driven issue may seem like the worst risk to reputation: others are driving a debate with moral or ethical connotations, and you need to react. It questions what you do, how you do it and what effect it has on individuals, communities and society at large. It sees unwelcome attention – often at a global level, fuelled by the interconnected world – and demand for change.

But there are two ways of dealing with this: win the argument, or at least regain control of the agenda; and/or change. The right answer is usually a mix of both. And the most enlightened will always see the opportunity as well as the risk.

Notes

1 Wang, WC *et al* (2011) Health and economic burden of the projected obesity trends in the USA and the UK, *The Lancet*, 378(9793), pp 815–25

2 Obama, President Barack [accessed 12 July 2013] 'Presidential Proclamation – National Childhood Obesity Awareness Month 2012', *The White House* [online] www.whitehouse.gov/the-press-office/2012/08/31/presidential-proclamation-national-childhood-obesity-awareness-month-201

3 HC Deb 16 January 2013, vol 556, col 867

4 Taylor, Joel [accessed 12 July 2013] 'Junk food raises asthma risk in children "by 40 per cent"', *Metro* [online] http://metro.co.uk/2013/01/15/junk-food-raises-asthma-risk-in-children-by-40-per-cent-3352176/

5 Little, Emma [accessed 12 July 2013] 'Junk food as bad for babies as smoking', *The Sun* [online] www.thesun.co.uk/sol/homepage/woman/health/health/4604229/Junk-food-as-bad-for-babies-as-smoking.html

6 Staff reporter [accessed 12 July 2013] 'Junk food diet "could damage your child's IQ"', *Metro* [online] http://metro.co.uk/2011/02/07/junk-food-diet-could-damage-your-childs-iq-637523/

7 Fletcher, Victoria [accessed 12 July 2013] 'Junk food diet takes 11 years off child's life', *The Daily Express*

8 Staff reporter [accessed 12 July 2013] 'Food linked to bad behaviour', *The Sydney Morning Herald* [online] www.smh.com.au/lifestyle/diet-and-fitness/food-linked-to-bad-behaviour-20110413-1dduj.html

9 Staff reporter [accessed 12 July 2013] 'Report: Junk-food ads lure kids to bad diet', *The Richmond Times* retrieved from the Factiva database

10 Cardello, Hank [accessed 11 July 2013] 'How Free-Market Forces Are Fighting Obesity – and Can Be a Model for Industries Far Beyond Food', *Forbes* [online] www.forbes.com/sites/forbesleadershipforum/2013/04/15/how-free-market-forces-are-fighting-obesity-and-can-be-a-model-for-industries-far-beyond-fooid/

11 Staff reporter [accessed 12 July 2013] 'New York City large-soda ban blocked by judge', BBC News [online] www.bbc.co.uk/news/world-us-canada-21747568

12 Staff reporter [accessed 11 July 2013] 'Call for pre-watershed ban on junk food advertising', BBC News [online] www.bbc.co.uk/news/uk-scotland-17414707

13 Derbyshire, David [accessed 11 July 2013] 'Ban all junk food ads before 9pm, says watchdog', *The Telegraph* [online] www.telegraph.co.uk/news/uknews/1521313/Ban-all-junk-food-ads-before-9pm-says-watchdog.html

14 Bodden, Tom [accessed 12 July 2013] 'Sugary drinks, chocolate, sweets and fatty burgers all off the menu in Welsh schools', *The Daily Post* [online] www.dailypost.co.uk/news/health/sugary-drinks-chocolate-sweets-fatty-5759944

15 Staff reporter [accessed 12 July 2013] 'Junk foods banned by federal government in public schools', *The Christian Science Monitor* [online] www.csmonitor.com/The-Culture/Family/2013/0627/Junk-foods-banned-by-federal-government-in-public-schools

16 Staff reporter [accessed on 12 July 2013] 'McDonald's obesity suit thrown out', CNN [online] http://edition.cnn.com/2003/LAW/09/04/mcdonalds.suit/

17 Kraft Foods Company [accessed 12 July 2013] *Fact Sheet: OREO 100th Birthday: A Global Taste of the World's Favorite Cookie* [pdf] www.kraftfoodscompany.com/sitecollectiondocuments/pdf/Oreo_Global_Fact_Sheet_100th_Birthday_as_on_Jan_12_2012_FINAL.pdf

18 Food and Drink Federation [accessed 11 July 2013] *Recipe for change*, London: Food and Drink Federation [pdf] www.fdf.org.uk/publicgeneral/Recipe_for_change_Jul09.pdf

19 Department of Health [accessed 11 July 2013] 'Final design of consistent nutritional labelling system given green light', GOV.UK [press release] www.gov.uk/government/news/final-design-of-consistent-nutritional-labelling-system-given-green-light

20 Coca-Cola GB [accessed 11 July 2013] *Responsible Marketing Charter – A Refreshed Approach* [pdf] www.coca-cola.co.uk/downloads/Responsible_Marketing_Charter_full_version.pdf

21 Better Business Bureau [accessed 11 July 2013] 'Children's Food and Beverage Advertising Initiative: About the Initiative' [online] www.bbb.org/us/about-the-initiative/

22 Tompson, T *et al* [accessed 12 July 2013] 'Obesity in the United States: Public Perceptions', *The Associated Press-NORC Center for Public Affairs Research* [pdf] www.apnorc.org/PDFs/Obesity/AP-NORC-Obesity-Research-Highlights.pdf

23 Waterfield, Bruno [accessed 6 May 2013] 'George Osborne is defeated 26 to 1 on EU bonus caps', *The Telegraph* [online] www.telegraph.co.uk/finance/financialcrisis/9909798/George-Osborne-is-defeated-26-to-1-on-EU-bonus-caps.html

24 Staff reporter [accessed 30 July 2013] 'Special Report: How Starbucks avoids UK taxes', *Reuters* [online] http://uk.reuters.com/article/2012/10/15/us-britain-starbucks-tax-idUKBRE89E0EX20121015

25 Staff reporter [accessed 1 August 2013] 'Tax Evasion: G8 Leaders Vow Tougher Stance', Sky News [online] http://news.sky.com/story/1105333/tax-evasion-g8-leaders-vow-tougher-stance

26 Jones, David [accessed 30 July 2013] 'Starbucks: Well-intentioned voluntary tax is not the way forward', *The Telegraph* [online] www.telegraph.co.uk/finance/comment/9732219/Starbucks-Well-intentioned-voluntary-tax-is-not-the-way-forward.html

27 Staff reporter [accessed 1 August 2013] 'Google's Eric Schmidt 'perplexed' over UK tax debate', BBC News [online] www.bbc.co.uk/news/business-22676080

28 Rushton, Katherine [accessed 1 August 2013] 'Amazon received more money from UK grants than it paid in corporation tax', *The Telegraph* [online] www.telegraph.co.uk/finance/personalfinance/consumertips/tax/10060229/ Amazon-received-more-money-from-UK-grants-than-it-paid-in-corporation-tax.html

29 UK Parliament Commons Select Committee [accessed 30 August 2013] 'MPs publish report on Google's tax avoidance', GOV.UK [online] www.parliament.uk/business/committees/committees-a-z/commons-select/ public-accounts-committee/news/tax-avoidance-google/

30 Staff reporter [accessed 1 August 2013] 'HMRC must fully investigate Google over tax, say MPs', BBC News [online] www.bbc.co.uk/news/business-22878460

31 Staff reporter [accessed 31 July 2013] 'Starbucks, Google and Amazon grilled over tax avoidance', BBC News [online] www.bbc.co.uk/news/business-20288077

32 Bowers, Simon and Syal, Rajeev [accessed 30 July 2013] 'MP on Google tax avoidance scheme: "I think that you do evil"', *The Guardian* [online] www.theguardian.com/technology/2013/may/16/google-told-by-mp-you-do-do-evil

33 International Council on Mining and Metals [accessed 5 May 2013] *Meeting the Challenges to 21st Century Mining* [pdf] www.icmm.com/document/106

34 International Council on Mining and Metals [accessed 5 May 2013] 'About us' [online] www.icmm.com/about-us/about-us

35 International Council on Mining and Metals [accessed 5 May 2013] '10 Principles' [online] www.icmm.com/our-work/sustainable-development-framework/10-principles

36 Buxton, Abbi [accessed 5 May 2013] *MMSD+10: Reflecting on a decade of mining and sustainable development*, International Institute for Environment and Development [pdf] http://pubs.iied.org/pdfs/16041IIED.pdf?

37 Haddow, KH (2013) Consultation, the Way Forward, *Journal of Energy and Natural Resources Law*, 31(1), p 82

38 Buxton, Abbi [accessed 5 May 2013] *MMSD+10: Reflecting on a decade of mining and sustainable development*, International Institute for Environment and Development [pdf] http://pubs.iied.org/pdfs/16041IIED.pdf?

39 Edited extract from case study first published in Griffin, A (2008) *New Strategies for Reputation Management*, London: Kogan Page

40 Green, S, Jones, S and Sidgwick, C (July 2006) The Nestlé issue from an evidence based midwifery perspective, *British Journal of Midwifery*, 14 (7)

41 McClenahen, John [accessed 12 March 2013] 'GE's Immelt Sees Green In Being Green', *Industry Week* [online] www.industryweek.com/environment/ ges-immelt-sees-green-being-green

42 Griscom Little, Amanda [accessed 5 March 2013] 'G.E.'s Green Gamble', *Vanity Fair* [online] www.vanityfair.com/politics/features/2006/07/ generalelectric200607

43 McDonald's Newsroom [accessed 21 February 2013] 'McDonald's Takes Olympic Stage to Announce Advances in Children's Well-Being, Menu Innovation and Access to Nutrition Information' [press release] http://news.mcdonalds.com/press-releases/mcdonald-s-takes-olympic-stage-to-announce-advance-nyse-mcd-0913306

44 Reynolds, John [21 February 2013] 'Jamie Oliver praises McDonald's healthy eating agenda', *Marketing Magazine* [online] www.marketingmagazine.co.uk/article/1142906/jamie-oliver-praises-mcdonalds-healthy-eating-agenda

05
Internally driven issues

As the case studies in this book demonstrate, internally driven issues are responsible for the some of the highest-profile corporate crises in recent years. The LIBOR-fixing crisis, the crisis at the British Broadcasting Corporation (BBC) over its *Newsnight* programme, the News International 'phone hacking' crisis and the 2013 horsemeat scandal all belong in this category. Internally driven issues are perhaps the hardest of all risks to manage, because they usually arise from some sort of failure which calls into question the organization's behaviour, performance, governance, strategy, values and even purpose.

This category is an interesting one to study as it is the only one containing risks that could conceivably be resolved with minimal, or even no, public or stakeholder scrutiny. Unlike the incident-based risks (which are by definition almost always very visible/public) and the externally driven issues (which are instigated and driven by NGOs, communities, politicians or other external stakeholders), some internally driven issues may never be known about outside the organization managing them.

To illustrate this point, consider the following scenario, which is a fictionalization (and simplification) of a very real internal issue with which my company was recently involved. A pharmaceutical company – PharmaCo – has a facility in Estonia that manufactures a range of its products for distribution and sale across the world. The facility fails an inspection by the regulator after whistleblower allegations of non-adherence to good manufacturing practice are found to have merit. All production is halted and all product held in the facility is quarantined until further investigations take place although, after tests show no contamination of product had happened, the regulator allows existing stocks in the supply chain to be used. The facility is the single source for some lifesaving drugs which do not have competitors on the market for patients to switch to. The time until some markets see 'stock out' of these key drugs is less than 40 days. The company needs to act fast to move stocks around the world, relabel product and seek regulatory input and approvals. It also needs to prepare for the worst: draft communications to patients, doctors, stakeholders and the media, think through the worst-case scenarios and rehearse how it would manage them if necessary. After five weeks of running a virtual crisis operation involving dozens of full-time employees seconded on to the project, a second source for the key drugs is identified, production timetables are shifted and key drugs are able to be produced and taken through the supply chain just in time before serious stock outs. An issue that could have become a hugely damaging crisis, knocking confidence in the company and its products and leading to commercial, financial and reputational implications, ends before any significant scrutiny and attention are felt.

But with this seemingly positive concept of 'quiet resolution' comes a major warning: in these circumstances, out of public sight should not mean out of corporate mind. When there is no immediate external scrutiny, there can be a temptation to sweep issues under the carpet, fail to address them and hope they go away. In the long term, failure to have managed and identified problems can have serious reputational consequences; the perception is almost inevitably created that the organization is or was not being entirely open and honest about its own performance and failings.

And, of course, not all issues in the 'internal issue' category can be managed away before scrutiny and pressure are felt. Some play out immediately in the public domain and may be declared crises from the moment they are identified. Many require a proactive announcement of bad news, an admission of a problem that has already had external repercussions or a consultative approach with stakeholders.

In fact, so large and diverse is this category, it warrants a sub-classification. Whilst there is some overlap, these subcategories provide a guide to the different sorts of internal issues that organizations face. This, too, is a four-category model with two variables. The first variable is whether the organization is being *reactive* to something or is able to be *proactive*: it's the difference between 'this has just come to light and we have to manage it now' and 'this is coming on the horizon so we have to prepare for it'. The second variable is whether the matter is generally a *negative* or a *positive* development. The idea of a positive development may seem odd in a book about reputation risk, but there are plenty of risks attached to developments that organizations believe to be positive. This variable is the difference between 'we have a bad situation to resolve' and 'we have some risk associated with our new development'.

The four subcategories are therefore:

- A proactive stance on a negative development (eg we are going to make 1,000 people redundant and we need to develop the strategy for the announcement).

- A proactive stance on a positive development (eg we are about to launch a new marketing campaign but we recognize there will be some controversy attached to it which we need to assess and manage).

FIGURE 5.1 Internally driven issues subcategories

	NEGATIVE	POSITIVE
PROACTIVE	*Typically:* Job losses Changes to portfolios Bad results *Examples:* UBS job losses HMV job losses Crown Estate asset divestment Church Commissioners asset divestment Shell reserves	*Typically:* New market entry New product New joint venture *Examples:* Shale gas investment
REACTIVE	*Typically:* Product problems Performance issues Bad practice Scandal *Examples:* Enron scandal Arthur Andersen scandal LIBOR-fixing scandal News International phone hacking Olympus scandal Perrier contamination Toyota recalls Tesco horsemeat contamination	*Typically:* Product launch/change Marketing push *Examples:* Victoria Bitter reformulation New Coke launch Dasani launch Persil Power launch Hoover flights promotion Cadbury sports campaign Heathrow Terminal 5 opening

- A reactive stance on a positive development (eg we have just spent millions of dollars advertising our new product only to find the launch stocks are wrongly labelled, and we need to respond).

- A reactive stance on a negative development (eg we have just found out our Chief Executive has been charged with bribery and we need to respond).

Figure 5.1 shows the case studies mentioned in this chapter, subdivided into these four categories.

The rest of this chapter looks at these four subcategories, explaining their characteristics, providing examples and case studies and identifying some of the key challenges faced by communications professionals when managing them.

The 'proactive negative' internal issue

This subcategory covers issues in which some bad news or a difficult/controversial decision needs to be proactively communicated or resolved. The characteristics include:

- The issue is usually bad news happening to just one organization – it is your problem and yours alone. It is most often a decision that the organization would rather not have to take, but is being forced into it through strategic, commercial or financial realities.
- It is likely to be very high profile, at least amongst a certain set of stakeholders. These may be external stakeholders, internal stakeholders or both.
- It is often a classic 'victims, villains and heroes' issue. Bad news means some will lose or perceive themselves to be losing (the victims), some will come vocally to their support with outrage and suggested solutions (the heroes) whilst the organization at the centre of the issue is portrayed as the villain of the piece.
- It may involve formal and/or informal consultation processes.

The most obvious examples of this sort of issue would be job losses and corporate restructuring. All organizations at some stage go through difficult times or periods of significant change, potentially affecting many thousands of people and the local communities in which they live. There are, of course, formal processes for consultation around job losses and, depending on the market and sector, there may or may not be powerful and vocal trade unions. But despite the fact that so many companies have had to communicate bad news in this way, some still find the challenge difficult. In October 2012, Swiss bank UBS announced that it would be cutting up to 10,000 jobs. Some of those affected found out the bad news when they tried to enter their place of work, only to discover that their pass was no longer activated. Although UBS was perhaps rightly preventing a bigger reputation risk (the possibility that some people about to lose their jobs could get to their desks and start trading), finding out that you have lost your job because you cannot swipe in in the morning seems particularly brutal. Many took to Twitter to complain about their treatment and that given to their colleagues.

But this subcategory is not just about job losses; it can include other sorts of corporate change or controversial decisions. For example, organizations sometimes need to divest assets that are seen by others (both inside and outside the organization) as worthy of protection or in some way special or vulnerable. Both the Church Commissioners (which manages the assets of the Church of England) and the Crown Estate (which manages the historical assets of the British monarchy) faced fierce campaigns when they decided to sell their affordable housing assets in London. People who had believed they were tenants of the church or the monarch were to be transferred to a new (and, they believed, potentially less benevolent and certainly less prestigious) landlord. Both organizations managed the communication extremely carefully but the nature of this sort of risk is that, however good the communications and consultation process, you are always working with what, to many, will be bad news.

Communication of a health risk – such as an asbestos find or a chemical contamination – would also fall into this subcategory. My consultancy helped a chemical company for many years as it prepared to assess and remediate contamination at various sites around the world. This involved communicating (mainly around health and environmental risk) with local people, employees and former employees, local stakeholders (and in particular regulators and politicians) and the media. But, importantly, this was not just a communication challenge. Reputation management in this instance is about doing the right thing environmentally and for the health and welfare of people. So the strategy also involved commissioning independent reports and setting up health panels, for example.

Chapter 15 contains a case study about the Shell reserves crisis of 2004 from the perspective of how the company changed its business and recovered its reputation after the crisis was over. This, too, was a 'proactive negative' issue in theory – the company had bad news to impart (that it had fewer provable oil and gas reserves than it had previously claimed) and, theoretically, time to get the strategy and communications plan right. E-mail traffic showed that the company had been discussing the issue internally at the most senior levels for some time. The news was imparted in a short press release and conference call, in which neither the Chairman, Sir Philip Watts, nor the Chief Financial Officer, Judy Boynton, participated. The media picked up the story and were highly critical of the manner in which it was communicated. Just two months after the bad news was announced, the Chairman, Chief Financial Officer and Head of Exploration and Production (E&P) had resigned.

There are many challenges associated with the 'proactive negative'. One is the challenge of *making the tough decision* in the first place. Good reputation management means factoring reputational considerations into all key decisions. Those that understand how certain news or developments will be heard and how stakeholders will respond need to feed this into the decision-making process from an early stage. Making tough decisions means weighing up all aspects of the issue – financial, commercial, strategic, legal and reputational – before deciding on a course of action. Being reputation-led, or at least reputation-conscious, in decision-making would be expected in crisis management, as we shall see later, and so too should it be in managing issues.

Following on from this is the challenge of *communicating bad/difficult news*. No organization wants to have to communicate something bad. Some fall into the trap of trying to 'spin' a bad news story into a positive one. This rarely works. Whilst the narrative around job cuts can include commentary about the organization restructuring for better times ahead and to deliver for shareholders and stakeholders, any suggestion that this is the lead narrative will play badly when there are 'victims' already feeling aggrieved and the media are looking for conflict.

This subcategory requires excellent *stakeholder engagement and consultation*. It is during the bad times that companies show their true colours, and those that show themselves to be listening, engaging organizations who understand they have responsibilities beyond their shareholders will emerge better. Communications professionals in particular need to help organizations not only to think like those affected and communicate well with them, but also to make decisions with them in mind. Organizations now regularly enter into consultations on difficult decisions, even when there is no legal requirement to do so.

A very specific challenge is *getting the communications cascade right*. For some issues in this category, a very careful communications plan needs to be developed and followed so as to ensure all stakeholders hear the right message, in the right way and in the right order. I once helped a professional services firm after it had learned that one of its senior members of staff was to be charged with a serious crime. Communicating this to a number of different audiences required precision planning and timing to avoid leaks and rumour whilst ensuring people heard the news and were given support in a controlled way.

Finally, a challenge common to this sort of issue is *keeping a positive internal mindset* and managing internal communications. Bad news can understandably cause a sense of gloom in the organization that is experiencing it and about to communicate it. Making sure that internal stakeholders not directly affected understand what is happening and why, and trying to balance the need for seriousness and empathy with the need to stay upbeat and positive as an organization require much thought, skill and delicacy.

The 'proactive positive' internal issue

This subcategory covers reputation risks that have been identified with an otherwise positive development. Examples of this sort of issue are product launches, the creation of new joint ventures or other contracts with new partners/suppliers or entry into a new technology or sector that has some controversy associated with it. In the energy sector, for example, there are plenty of scenarios in which companies should – and do – consider all the reputational risks of acquiring assets in oil sands, shale gas etc. Despite all the opportunities these technologies might provide, there is a need to assess the downside risk of causing stakeholder anxiety and outrage (often called the 'non-technical' or 'above-ground' risk).

These issues require sensitive management to prevent a good news story turning bad. The characteristics of these issues include:

- There is often complex technical, scientific and legal information to consider as part of a conversation about the reputational risks attached to a certain course of action.

- This sort of issue usually allows some time and space for careful assessment and consideration, unless there is a launch timetable or contractual negotiation that is difficult to row back from.
- There is often a team representing different functions and businesses (marketing, product development, commercial, legal etc) that has come together to complete a deal or launch.

In any industry, the launch of a new product can present a risk. As a case study (fictionalized but again based on a real issue), consider the launch of a new cleaning product, 'MegaClean'. The consumer goods company behind MegaClean is convinced that it will be the most powerful domestic cleaning product in the market, thanks to a new ingredient that it has sourced from a chemical company and to which it has exclusive rights. The company is planning to replace its already market-leading brand with the new one, fully confident that it can further extend its market share by focusing on the new brand. It has booked a major advertising campaign as part of a multi-market launch.

Rather late in the day, the team managing the product launch has been alerted to the fact that the new active ingredient in the product has a particular risk label attached to it because of its chemical composition. In its undiluted form, it needs to be labelled in containers with: 'Warning: possible risk of impaired fertility'. When the undiluted ingredient arrives at the manufacturing facility, it will carry this label. After manufacturing, it is in such a diluted form that the finished product does not need such labelling. The technical experts in the team are content that the risk is 'theoretical' rather than real and that the standard safety procedures at manufacturing facilities are more than adequate to deal with any such risk. They are also reassured that the risk label will never feature on the final product.

But there are clearly risks associated with proceeding to launch, and the company commissions a full reputation risk assessment together with further health and environmental risk assessments. The reputation risk assessment looks at worst-case scenarios, the likely perceptions of those who will be working with the chemical with the new risk phrase, the likelihood of the risk phrase becoming knowledge outside the manufacturing facility gates, how the media and other stakeholders (including competitors) might perceive and report it, and how consumers might respond if the issue becomes public. It looks at worst-case scenarios, the triggers for these scenarios and the potential commercial, financial and reputational consequences of these scenarios happening. It also suggests a reputation strategy for mitigating the risks and a response plan for how any trigger could be dealt with.

In so doing, the reputation risk assessment gives the company the information it needs to make a judgement: is the identified and assessed reputation risk, with its potential impacts, worth taking given the potential commercial benefits of the product and the assessment of how manageable the risks are? In this case, the launch went ahead after an extremely careful internal communications plan was executed and a crisis exercise held to give comfort to senior management that even the worst case was manageable.

This was another example of issues management behind closed doors, where a team comes together to work on an issue, the only external result of which is an unproblematic product launch. This is in some respects the most satisfying of all reputation risk management projects: not only is a negative outcome avoided, but also the positive outcome that many have worked hard for over many months or years comes to fruition.

But there are, of course, many challenges associated with this subcategory. The first, and most self-evident, is *bringing risk and bad news into a positive project*. When at least one part of the organization (the part that developed the new product, negotiated the new deal, devised the new campaign) is likely to be raring to hit the 'go' button, it is difficult to be the bearer of bad tidings. It is not good to be seen as the 'reputation police', introducing or talking up problems at a late stage of a positive project. Reputation specialists need to help colleagues or clients understand the risks associated with the development they have been working so hard on.

Related to this is *scenario planning*: looking at all the potential scenarios, what could trigger them, what could escalate the triggers, what this would look and feel like and what impacts it could have on the development in question or indeed the wider organization. The concept of the 'perfect storm' is helpful here, to demonstrate how even the smallest of triggers can, given the right circumstances (a small but media-savvy campaign group, an inquisitive journalist, celebrity interest, a relevant link issue, for example), escalate into a worst-case scenario.

Another challenge is conducting a full *reputation risk assessment*. This is where reputation specialists must come together with others in the business to help assess whether the risk – if a risk has been identified and quantified – is worth taking. The key questions to explore and answer are: How serious is the risk? What strategies can we employ to mitigate it? How confident are we that these strategies will work? Could we stomach (and manage) the worst-case scenario that we have identified? Chapter 10 looks in detail at how to conduct a scenario planning exercise and construct a reputation risk assessment.

The final challenge is *helping to make the call*. Are the financial and commercial upsides of this course of action worth the reputation risk? This question is usually asked of senior management who can give the go/no go decision, but the information that is presented for that decision is usually drafted and coordinated by the cross-functional team that has been assessing the risk and opportunities from all angles.

The 'reactive positive' internal issue

The third subcategory covers similar ground to that above – a risk associated with a positive development – but in this case the risk is not identified and managed before it is too late, putting the organization involved on to a reactive footing. The characteristics of these risks include:

- The issue is usually very public and very embarrassing – having to beat a retreat or manage a problem associated with something it has been working on for some time is the ultimate 'banana skin moment' for an organization.
- It is also likely to test one of the most important relationships any organization has: the one with its customer.
- It might immediately be declared a crisis, and therefore managed outside 'business as usual' (if there is a clear and serious problem), or it may be managed as an issue (if there is gradually growing disquiet about a new development).
- It will almost certainly involve an operational response, such as a product recall, as well as communications response.

Dear Victoria Bitter drinkers, we've heard you... and we're fixing it. A few years ago, we made several changes to the recipe of your favourite beer. We altered the brewing process and we got it wrong. But we've listened to you – our loyal customers – and now we are determined to make it right. Today I'm pleased to announce that we are restoring Victoria Bitter back to the recipe that made it the best cold beer.[1]

So wrote the Chief Executive of Carlton and United Breweries in Australia in an open letter to customers in September 2012. It is a seemingly simple apology and change, but admitting mistakes and rectifying them are challenging for all organizations. This one took three years and the loss of the leading market position before the change was made and communicated.

It was not the first nor will it be the last such mistake to be made and rectified by consumer goods companies. A quarter of a century before the Victoria Bitter story came one of the most famous case studies in this sub-category. After successful taste tests of a new formula, New Coke was launched by Coca-Cola in 1985 to great fanfare. However, public reaction was overwhelmingly negative. Boycotts were organized, lawsuits filed and 1,500 complaints inundated Coca-Cola every day. Coca-Cola was caught off guard by the level of public hostility towards the new drink and eventually bowed to public pressure. Executives announced the return of the original formula on 10 July, less than three months after New Coke's introduction.

Coca-Cola had another such issue to contend with when its Dasani brand of water was launched in the United Kingdom on 10 February 2004, accompanied by a £7 million publicity campaign. The British public took issue with the source of Dasani – tap water – when the drink was being marketed as 'pure, still water'. Coca-Cola defended the product, claiming the source of the drink had been misunderstood. The company stated that the tap water underwent a 'highly sophisticated purification process',[2] but this was later contested, denting the product's credibility further. Finally, when the chemical bromate was found in Dasani, Coca-Cola admitted defeat and withdrew the product, leaving the company with a £25 million loss from cancelled contracts and advertising campaigns as well as a need to rebuild reputation.

These product launches may have been misjudged, but at least the products did no real harm. Persil Power, however, did. In the mid-1990s, Unilever's Persil brand was losing its dominance of the UK detergent market, especially with the launch of arch-rival P&G's Ariel Ultra. In response, Persil Power was launched. P&G soon claimed that the product's new manganese ingredient rotted clothes after frequent washing and released photos of damaged garments to the media. The clothes-damaging properties of Persil Power were confirmed in independent tests conducted by The Consumers' Association. After denials, reformulations and relaunches failed to solve the problem, Unilever eventually withdrew the brand with the Chairman admitting it was the 'greatest marketing set-back we've seen'.[3] Unilever had to write off stock to the value of £57 million and it was estimated the product failure cost the company £250 million in total.

It is not just product launches or relaunches that fit into this subcategory. Things can go wrong with marketing campaigns too. For example, in August 1992, Hoover launched a promotion in the United Kingdom offering two free return flights to Europe for customers who bought at least £100 worth of Hoover products. The promotion was received positively and the company launched a second promotion widening the destinations on offer to include the United States. The company soon found itself overwhelmed by the demand for its products. Some senior Hoover executives were dismissed following an exposé which uncovered staff encouraging telesales staff to dissuade redemption of the offer. Maytag Corporation, Hoover's US parent company, set aside $30 million to pay for free flights. The Hoover Holidays Pressure Group was established, and several lawsuits were brought against the company which led to a number of compensation payouts.

In 2003, Cadbury launched 'Get Active', a £9 million scheme to give away 'free' sports equipment to schools across the United Kingdom. The campaign encouraged the collection of tokens which could then be exchanged for sports equipment by schools. The promotion faced criticism due to the large amounts of chocolate that would need to be consumed in order to qualify for free sports equipment. Criticism was widespread with The Food Commission, the Chairman of the government's obesity taskforce and the National Union of Teachers (NUT) all condemning the scheme. Initially, Cadbury defended the promotion, claiming it encouraged brand switching rather than extra (or excessive) consumption. But the company ultimately decided to overhaul the scheme by removing the token-collection aspect, a move which was welcomed by hitherto critics.

One of the biggest launch crises of recent years was the launch of Heathrow's new Terminal 5, which opened to the general public in March 2008 to high expectations, not least because it had a price tag of £4.3 billion. Airport operator BAA lauded the 'world class' baggage system, intended to halve the number of bag delays and losses. However, a chain of events on launch day eventually resulted in a ban on checking in luggage and 33 cancelled flights. This number rose to 300 cancelled flights during the first five days of opening. The airport's biggest airline, British Airways (BA), released a statement on the opening day apologizing to customers, set up a helpline and said customers not yet checked-in would receive a refund or could rebook. On the opening day, BA shares fell 3 per cent, wiping £90 million off the carrier's value.[4]

Some of the challenges associated with these issues have already been covered in this chapter: scenario planning is very important in this subcategory, as is keeping a positive mindset (the 'crash' from positive launch or development to major crisis is potentially debilitating for any organization).

One additional challenge to mention here is *accepting fallibility*. 'We got it wrong' and 'we let you down' are hard messages because they involve people admitting that they have created, authorized, spent money on and signed off something that was supposed to win them plaudits but has instead caused a problem. It involves action, change, internal scrutiny and public embarrassment. But to minimize reputation, commercial and financial damage, organizations must be in a position both structurally and culturally to be able to do this.

Related to this is the *art of the apology*. Saying sorry does not need to mean an absolute admission of liability, which is the reason some legal advisers are keen to ensure they are consulted in advance of the 's' word being used. In circumstances where the organization has clearly made an error, an apology is entirely appropriate and reputationally necessary. There are some circumstances where an admission of liability would be wrong, but saying sorry is still right. There is a difference, and communications professionals need to help their organization to understand this; if they don't, the lack of a 'sorry' may become another part of what is already a reputation-damaging situation.

The 'reactive negative' internal issue

The final subcategory is the 'reactive negative'. This is where something bad comes to light (usually, but not always, quite suddenly) which the organization needs to react to and resolve. This sounds like the worst of all worlds – it is an inherently bad internal development of which those tasked with managing it had no prior knowledge. Examples would include product problems, performance issues and bad practice (social, environmental, ethical). These are often extremely serious reputation risks as they hit at the very heart of the organization: its values, its practices, its products, its services and its people.

Typically, these risks will be characterized by the following:

- There might be an opportunity for the issue to be successfully resolved with little or no scrutiny, but this is not always the case. The issue could require immediate disclosure (for legal, regulatory or reputational reasons), or the organization may even hear about the issue at the same time as other stakeholders (as could be the case with a whistleblower or dawn raid, for example).

- Crisis procedures might need to be invoked from the beginning, either to manage the immediate external scrutiny and pressure, or to use the structure and process of crisis management to resolve the issue as soon as possible.
- Without the deaths, injuries and/or physical damage (and therefore sympathy) associated with incidents, stakeholders are unlikely to grant a 'window of goodwill' to the organization facing the issue. Instead, the outrage, blame and recriminations start immediately.

Corruption scandals are extremely dangerous risks to reputation, hitting trust hard from the moment they are uncovered. The Enron and Arthur Andersen scandal spelt the end for both these organizations in the early 2000s. The LIBOR-fixing scandal in banks is still running (see case study in Chapter 15 on how Barclays bank is seeking to rebuild its reputation in light of the practices to which it and other banks have admitted). The damage to the UK newspaper industry following the phone hacking scandal – in terms of new regulation and lost reputation – has shown how the illegal and immoral actions of a few can have a lasting effect on an entire industry.

Another recent example was the scandal faced – eventually – by Olympus. In 2011, acting on claims made by a Japanese magazine, Michael Woodford, the new President and Chief Operating Officer of Olympus, raised concerns with the executive board about irregularities in the company's accounting practices. The irregularities included large fees paid to undisclosed financial advisers and overpriced acquisitions. Finding the board's response unsatisfactory, Woodford called in external auditors to investigate. The results of the audit corroborated Woodford's suspicions. His reward was to be dismissed, after which he turned whistleblower. Led by the Chairman, Tsuyoshi Kikukawa, the company initially denied Woodford's allegations but later admitted to hiding losses amounting to $1.7 billion. By January 2012 Olympus was suing 19 of its executive board members. The scandal resulted in the company's share price plunging 80 per cent. Although Olympus avoided being delisted from the Tokyo Stock Exchange (TSE), the company's stock was placed on its three-year 'on alert' list and the TSE imposed the maximum fine of 10 million yen. The Tokyo Metropolitan Police, the Financial Services Authority (FSA), Japan's financial watchdog, and the Securities and Exchange Surveillance Commission (SESC) all launched investigations into the concealment of losses, which led to the arrest and trial of senior executives.

'Scandals' come from bad behaviour, but can also come from poor performance. Whilst the above case studies look at corruption, fraud and unethical practice, this subcategory also covers more straightforward performance failure. As argued in Chapter 1, the first thing any organization has to do to protect and enhance its reputation is to fulfil its fundamental purpose. This is the aspect of reputation over which it has most control. If reputation is won by delivery rather than promise, then failure to deliver (or delivering, or being perceived to deliver, badly) is as fundamental a reputation risk as any other.

Product problems, often accompanied by recalls, are examples of this. Some are managed better than others. Perrier's belated global recall of its contaminated bottled water in February 1990 ultimately led to the company being taken over; Toyota's recall of millions of cars in 2010 led to it losing its market-leading position. What both have in common is that not only was the product faulty or contaminated, the brand positioning had been called into question at the most fundamental level. Perrier's brand promise was about purity; Toyota's about reliability. The recalls demonstrated that the promises went undelivered, and reputation damage was inevitable.

A somewhat different example, with a different outcome, was the handling by supermarket chain Tesco of the horsemeat scandal that hit food manufacturers and retailers in 2013. For all those involved (Findus, Nestlé and many others were also managing this issue alongside less well known suppliers), this was a supply chain issue, and one which led consumers and stakeholders to question whether the companies could fulfil their purpose: to deliver in the product what it says on the package. As I told a fictional version of these events earlier in the book, it seems only fair to tell the true story of a well-managed issue-driven crisis.

Crisis over-management?

In January 2013, the British and Irish food industries were rocked by an adulterated meat scandal. The Food Safety Authority of Ireland (FSAI) announced that it had found equine DNA in beefburgers sold by supermarkets Tesco, Iceland, Aldi and Lidl. Following further testing, beef products sold by Ikea, Asda and Co-op and some manufactured by Findus were also found to contain horsemeat. The issue soon covered the whole European beef supply chain, with abattoirs, suppliers, manufacturers and retailers all under the spotlight.

In the public arena, the issue was one of food fraud rather than food safety. Concerns raised about a horse medication that could have an impact on human health if ingested never really took hold. Neither, surprisingly, did any sense of moral 'disgust' at the fact that many people could have eaten horsemeat (it is certainly not a meat on the menu of most Britons). This was a classic internal issue relating to performance: companies had failed in their most basic of duties of supplying the consumer with the product they promised.

Tesco, the biggest supermarket in the United Kingdom, was hit particularly hard. Tesco sits in the middle of the perceived price/quality supermarket scale, but 'higher' than other retailers who were implicated early. Tesco's Everyday Value range beefburgers were found to contain equine DNA with horsemeat accounting for 29.1 per cent of one burger tested by the FSAI, whilst a Tesco Everyday Value frozen bolognese contained up to 100 per cent horsemeat.

Tesco needed to act fast, and did. It immediately recalled the products and issued an unreserved apology in national newspapers. The full-page advertisements addressed customers directly and with humility: 'we and our supplier have let you down and we are sorry'[5] (neatly encapsulating the supply chain nature of the problem without seeking to outsource responsibility). Tesco mobilized senior executives, including Chief Executive Philip Clarke, and used social media to get its message across. Clarke took to Tesco's official blog to address the situation: 'If some of our customers are angry, so are we.'[6] The supermarket soon dropped two suppliers, Silvercrest and Comigel, when their beef products were found to contain horsemeat.

Tesco loyalty card customers received e-mails with the subject 'we are changing'. It repeated the apology and the commitment to change.[7] Tesco also launched *Tesco Food News*, a website focused on making the supply chain more transparent for consumers. It features a dedicated product testing section as well as a 'promises' section, making it easier for Tesco to be held accountable to its pledges. The supermarket also committed itself to sourcing more meat from the United Kingdom and Ireland.

The reaction to Tesco's crisis management was generally positive, with the company seen to have made a textbook response. But did Tesco go too far? Did it 'over-manage' the crisis? Tesco bore a disproportionate amount of the negative attention, primarily because it was so comprehensive in its crisis response. The company had two options: take ownership and control (but more of the negative attention); or seek to make the crisis an industry crisis by taking a less prominent or visible role in the crisis response. It chose the former, and essentially appointed itself as poster child for the crisis.

Tesco is the largest grocer in the United Kingdom. Its beef products were some of the first to be identified as containing horsemeat. The company rightly calculated that it was going to be the poster child for this crisis whether it liked it or not. By taking the action it did, it avoided the sort of reputation nightmare that the fictionalized version of this case study in Chapter 1 described.

On 5 June 2013, Tesco revealed its first fall in annual profits in 20 years, taking a 1 per cent sales hit. Whilst Tesco has managed to maintain its market share of just over 30 per cent, competitors who managed to escape involvement in the scandal, such as Sainsbury's, have seen a slight sales boost.[8] It may be that the decision to take a greater share of the responsibility for the industry-wide performance problem has harmed the chain in the short term. But the crisis could have been much worse. Crisis management is not just about tomorrow's headlines and till receipts. As the second section of this book will explain, it is about long-term recovery and an opportunity to change for the better. If Chief Executive Philip Clarke means it when he says 'we have changed', and Tesco is seen to have made improvements that its consumers will see and appreciate, he may well have played an excellent reputation 'long game'.

Challenges presented by 'reactive negative' internal issues

The challenges involved with managing this final subcategory of internal issue-driven risks to reputation are those most associated with crisis management. The first is *speed of response*, and showing control of a situation which is presenting the organization in a bad light. This may involve putting the right team together, and resourcing it. As the response will be about solving a problem, making decisions and making change, the team might involve operations, legal, HR, communications, quality control etc. Even if a crisis is not declared, the structures and processes of crisis management might be necessary to get on top of the situation.

Another challenge typical in this subcategory is *disclosure*: what to disclose, how to say it and when to do it. 'Do we need to go proactive on this?' is a question that is heard on many occasions when a reactive negative issue is being managed. The right answer is not just a matter of obligations. Even if there is no requirement to communicate with stakeholders, doing so might be the right course of action to show transparency, commitment to resolve a situation and control. As explained earlier, some teams do not have the luxury of asking this question: a whistleblower, customer or other stakeholder may already have drawn wide external attention to the issue.

Finally, a challenge is *taking and being seen to take the right actions* as well as expressing the right sentiments. When something goes so fundamentally wrong in the core of the organization, words are never enough. An apology is a prerequisite, but it is the actions that prove the remorse that are more powerful. Setting up internal investigations, suspending people, recalling products, stopping supply... all of these things are typical in the management of such issues.

Chapter summary

The internally driven issue is the most complex and varied of the four reputation risk categories examined in this book; hence the need for subcategories to understand where they come from, the characteristics they tend to display and the challenges they present.

The key lessons from this chapter are:

- Internally driven issues present extreme challenges because they arise from a performance failure.
- Some internal issues can be resolved before any external scrutiny or pressure is felt, whilst some are very public crises from the moment they are uncovered.
- Internal issues arise from positive and negative developments, and the organization can be on a proactive or reactive footing.

- Positives can be derived from internal issues, with Tesco providing an example of nimble operational, communications and strategic response to a performance issue.

Despite Tesco's success, it is generally very difficult to find opportunity when something has gone wrong with performance or is about to cast a cloud over a forthcoming positive development. But this is the heart of issues management: resolving risks that threaten the organization before they become crises. It requires the sort of capabilities – predicting, preventing, resolving – that the second half of this book covers.

Notes

1 Mervis, Ari [accessed 12 April 2013] 'A letter from our CEO to our Loyal Drinkers', *Victoria Bitter* [press release] www.victoriabitter.com.au/ 2012/09/a-letter-from-our-ceo-to-our-loyal-drinkers/

2 Staff reporter [accessed 12 April 2013] 'Soft drink is purified tap water', BBC News [online] http://news.bbc.co.uk/1/hi/uk/3523303.stm

3 Cope, Nigel [accessed 22 February 2013] 'Persil Power all washed up', *The Independent* [online] www.independent.co.uk/news/business/persil-power-all-washed-up-1574316.html

4 Staff reporter [accessed 27 February 2013] 'Terminal disgrace: Poor training and computer failings to blame for T5 chaos as flights fiasco to last into the weekend', *Mail Online* [online] www.dailymail.co.uk/news/article-547050/Terminal-disgrace-Poor-training-failings-blame-T5-chaos-flights-fiasco-weekend.html

5 Tesco [accessed 16 May 2013] 'An apology from Tesco' [press release] www.tescoplc.com/index.asp?pageid=17&newsid=728

6 Clarke, P [accessed 16 May 2013] 'Trust', *Tesco Talking Shop Blog* [online] www.tescoplc.com/talkingshop/index.asp?blogid=87

7 Clarke, P [accessed 16 May 2013] 'We are changing', *Tesco* [press release] www.network54.com/Forum/204096/thread/1361996016/last-1361996016/ Tesco,+we+are+changing

8 Griffiths, B [accessed 15 May 2013] 'Horsemeat scandal and intense competition from rivals sends Tesco sales into a slump', Mail Online [online] www.dailymail.co.uk/news/article-2334932/Horsemeat-scandal-intense-competition-rivals-sends-Tesco-sales-slump.html

06
Externally driven incidents

An incident that is not your fault can still put your reputation at acute risk. Acts of terror or sabotage, political uprisings, pandemic health scares and acts of nature are all incidents that require an operational and communications response. Many need a strategic crisis response too. There are plenty of examples of organizations that have mismanaged an incident over which they had no (or little) control, and have seen their reputations suffer as a result. Indeed, it is quite possible for an organization to mismanage itself into being the villain of a situation in which it is essentially a victim.

Perhaps the most memorable example of this victim-to-villain transition happened over two decades ago. In December 1988, a terrorist bomb detonated on Pan Am flight 103, killing all 259 people on board and 11 people on the ground in Lockerbie, Scotland. The tragedy was not caused by any performance or safety failure of the airline (although it was later criticized for lax screening procedures): Pan Am, an iconic American brand, was the victim of a terror attack. But the company came under fierce criticism for how it handled the crisis and especially how it handled the families of those who had lost their lives. The tragedy became a major reputational hit for a company already facing difficult times and undoubtedly played a part in its ultimate downfall soon thereafter.

The governing party in Spain suffered similarly after the March 2004 terrorist attack at Madrid's Atocha train station. Soon after the attack, police officials informed the government that explosives often used by Basque separatist group ETA were found at the blast sites which, along with other suspicious circumstances, led them to suspect ETA involvement. On the other hand, the Spanish Intelligence Service had concluded as early as the morning of the bombings that the attack was instigated by an Islamist terrorist group. They were, however, ordered by the government to deny the Islamist lead and insist that ETA was the only suspect.[1] The government went so far as to send messages to all Spanish embassies abroad, ordering them to uphold the ETA theory. President José María Aznar allegedly called a number of newspaper directors personally to ask for their support of this version.[2] This did not prevent some of the smaller Spanish outlets running with the news that Al-Qaeda was behind the attacks, a theory which was given almost immediate credibility when a van used and abandoned by the bombers was recovered containing not only detonators but also Islamic audio tapes.[3] It is perhaps politically understandable for a party which takes a hard line on ETA to want to lay the blame with this terror group. But the results spoke for themselves. An externally driven incident had been mismanaged; public opinion turned against the ruling Popular Party and the socialist opposition won a surprise victory at the following weekend's elections.

These sorts of incidents can also show organizations at their best: able to respond quickly and effectively, looking after their people, making the right decisions, doing the right thing. In stark contrast to the response of the Spanish government to Madrid's terror attacks, Mayor Rudy Giuliani became the hero of New York after the attack suffered by that city on 11 September 2001. So much so, he launched a credible presidential campaign from his hero status.

Externally driven incidents tend to have the following characteristics:

- They happen suddenly, or are fast-developing, and are high impact and high profile.

- Organizations affected are likely to be in crisis management mode immediately, responding to something that poses a direct threat to their people and/or their assets.

- The organization or organizations affected by the incident have little power to resolve it and are therefore managing effects rather than finding solutions. The organization may have a special and specific role to play (as did Roche, for example, when the Swiss healthcare company's Tamiflu brand was the 'solution' to the swine flu pandemic of 2008) but usually is one of many trying to manage a situation caused by others or by nature.

- There are likely to be many other actors involved, including police, other emergency services, security services, health authorities and governments. Externally driven incidents are true 'multi-stakeholder' events.

- Protecting people is likely to be the key to the response. This may be proactive (protecting people from a known threat such as an impending storm or health scare) or reactive (protecting/saving human life after an attack or in a volatile situation such as a riot).

- In addition to testing strategic crisis management capabilities, these incidents usually test the operational aspects of organizational resilience: emergency response, disaster recovery, incident management and business continuity. Business continuity is particularly relevant here, in that an organization may have to shut down facilities, encourage its people to stay at home (or explain why it is safe to return to work) and put other operational plans into place in order to be able to continue its operations.

However, despite these general characteristics, there are different types of externally driven incident, each of which has its own specific challenges. These are:

- An attack on you, or those in your care (eg piracy against one of your vessels, hijack of one of your aircraft, sabotage of one of your products).
- An attack on a wider group affecting you (eg a terrorist event which affects your people or assets).
- A political or social development endangering you or those in your care (eg a revolution, uprising or riot in which your organization or your people are caught up).
- A natural event (eg a health scare or weather event).

An attack on you, or those in your care

This is the externally driven incident that puts organizations most squarely in the spotlight in terms of response: as the direct target of a planned attack, organizations must protect their people, their customers, their assets and their business.

These sorts of attacks happen suddenly, but are not necessarily unpredictable. Many organizations have specific plans for situations such as kidnap, hijack and sabotage and will have rehearsed them in crisis exercises. The security department takes the lead on preparing for (and preventing wherever possible) such incidents but, as with any major incident, a cross-functional response is required if an incident occurs.

Many stakeholders – from the families of those potentially affected to the highest levels of government – have high expectations of how an organization responds to such adversity. In the early stages, there is sympathy for the plight of those affected and the organization at the centre of the attack. But this window is short. Any suggestion that the organization is mismanaging the response can turn sympathy into hostility very quickly.

This can be a difficult reality to face, especially when the incident is ongoing (such as a hijack or kidnap situation). The police, emergency services and negotiators will be seeking to take control, but the company must be seen to be taking the right actions and heard to be expressing the right sentiments. As the motivation behind the attack is often financial rather than political, the question of money is often uncomfortably juxtaposed with human life.

In situations such as product tampering or sabotage, the company is more of a decision-maker, in that logistical and supply chain decisions and solutions are needed. A product recall is a product recall, whether required because of a production fault or deliberate contamination. The Tylenol sabotage case study remains the standard for how to respond to such an incident, more than three decades after the crisis hit Johnson & Johnson in

1982. At first, three deaths from cyanide poisoning were associated with Tylenol capsules (Tylenol commanded 35 per cent of the US adult over-the-counter analgesic market, accounted for some $450 million of annual sales and contributed 15 per cent of Johnson & Johnson's overall profits[4]). Soon, as many as 250 deaths and illnesses in various parts of the United States were being linked to contaminated capsules. Although test results suggested the problem was limited to the Chicago area (ultimately Johnson & Johnson found no more than 75 contaminated pills, all from one batch) the company withdrew the product nationwide, thereby responding comprehensively to the worst-case scenario and allaying consumer fears. Seven people, all in the Chicago area, died but the brand survived and was even enhanced by the crisis. *The Wall Street Journal* wrote at the time: 'the company chose to take a large loss rather than expose anyone to further risk. The "anti-corporation" movement may have trouble squaring that with the devil theories it purveys.'[5]

Cyberattack – a new form of external incident

The threat of a malicious cyberattack or a seriously damaging cyber security breach has become one of the most talked-about potential externally driven incidents, after an increasing number of multinational companies have faced assaults on their databases, e-mail systems and websites. US President Barack Obama has declared that 'America's economic prosperity in the 21st century will depend on cyber security.'[6]

Cyberspace has been woven into the fabric of our lives. Huge volumes of data gathered from individuals and organizations are being saved on servers across the world. Almost everything we do depends on a digitized system of one kind or another, and the cyber era brings with it new risks and threats to both individuals and organizations. In the five years leading up to 2013, the volume of information and data that businesses generate has increased more than tenfold. Whether financial, or about people and systems, information is the lifeblood of any organization.[7]

The concepts of hacking, cyber spying and sabotaging have been around for decades. But with an ever-increasing number of interconnected systems, 24/7 media, and the hyperactive social media landscape, organizations are now at a much higher risk of cyberattack and having breaches publicly revealed. They must protect their data and intellectual property (IP) in order to survive and remain competitive. The pressure to do so is coming not just from clients and consumers, but also from investors. They have spotted the short- and long-term impacts that cyber security breaches have, and want companies to demonstrate their ability to protect their IP and defend their assets.

Corporate boards have begun to cite cyber security as a business-critical priority. It has moved from being the domain of the IT department to a strategic issue. The board needs to have an accurate picture of the potential impact on a company's reputation, share price, or ability to do business if sensitive internal or customer information held by the company were to be lost or stolen, and what the impact on the business would be if online services were disrupted for an undetermined period. At the start of 2013, US banks (TD Bank, Wells Fargo), technology companies (Apple, Facebook, Microsoft), and media outlets (*The New York Times, The Wall Street Journal, The Washington Post*) were all attacked.[8] The perpetrators disrupted online services, defaced public websites and stole supposedly protected information, including trade secrets, strategic plans, records of transactions and customer information.

Cyber security breaches can occur in different ways. An *internal cyber threat* could involve current or former employees stealing sensitive company information or sabotaging systems. It could also be involuntary: an organization can expose confidential information when an employee falls prey to a phishing attack or opens an attachment containing a virus. An executive at Coca-Cola was reportedly the victim of a phishing attack in 2009, allowing hackers to enter Coca-Cola's network, seeking specific information about a major upcoming acquisition of a Chinese firm, a deal that later fell apart.[9] According to the Corporate Executive Board (CEB) research, 93 per cent of workers knowingly violate policies designed to prevent data breaches, and senior executives are the worst offenders.[10]

'Hacktivism' is politically motivated hacking. Supporters conceal their identities and unite around a self-defined cause, with the aim of undermining an organization's authority. The most famous of these in recent years has been Anonymous and its various offshoots such as LulzSec and Ghost Shell. The movement and loose groups have gained notoriety and attracted significant media attention following successful attacks on the FBI and CIA, Booz Allen Hamilton, Sony, Microsoft and Saudi Aramco.

In 2013, US intelligence officials stated that *cyber espionage* had supplanted terrorism as the top security threat facing the United States. The developed world competes predominantly on its knowledge, innovation and experience. Due to the lack of regulation covering cyber security breaches, companies rarely disclose the theft of their IP. However, investigative journalism has uncovered theft of classified information on the development of the F-35 fighter from Lockheed Martin, for instance. One defence contractor reportedly had most of its research compromised in a three-year operation by hackers linked to China and Russia.[11] As a result, investors and shareholder groups are becoming increasingly concerned about the loss of competitive advantage following cyber security breaches and data theft.[12]

The rarest but potentially the most catastrophic threat is *cyber sabotage*. Governments have become concerned about cyber threats to a country's critical national infrastructure. Cyberspace has become essential to the functioning of most or all critical infrastructure.[13] The most high-profile example of an attack was the Stuxnet worm, which was discovered in the Iranian nuclear enrichment plant.

According to guidance published by the US Securities and Exchange Commission (SEC) public companies are not required by law to disclose cyber security breaches, unless there has been a significant material impact.[14] As a result, there are few first-hand accounts regarding the nature of cyberattacks and their actual impacts on a company's competitiveness, bottom line and long-term reputation. But cyber attacks pose a clear threat to companies' key information assets, and senior executives have responded by elevating cyber security to a board-level risk.

Piracy – the return of an old form of external attack

In recent years, whilst the cyberattack has been climbing the risk register, a form of attack that has been around for centuries has been making an unwanted comeback. The last decade has seen an upsurge in piracy in the Gulf of Aden off the coast of Somalia, an important international transit route.[15] Maritime piracy cost the international economy nearly $7 billion in 2011.[16] In 2009, the MV Maersk-Alabama became the first US-flagged ship to be captured by pirates in 200 years. The largest ransom, $11 million, was paid out for the Greek-owned MV Irene SL, hijacked in 2012.

An effort to curb the risk of piracy has seen an unprecedented degree of international counter-piracy cooperation. The most important development has been the growing use of armed private security guards on vessels, a measure which has helped reduce the threat considerably. As the International Maritime Bureau (IMB) notes, no vessel with armed guards has ever been hijacked.[17]

But piracy remains a threat. The communications challenges it presents are in many ways typical of the 'external attack', but there are also some unique challenges throughout the four-phase life cycle of a piracy incident.

Phase 1: incident and lack of information

In the immediate aftermath of a piracy attack, a shipowner will rarely be notified about the hijacking of one of its vessels through the usual chain of command. The news might come in from the pirates, or via families of the crew who have been directly contacted by the pirates. This immediately puts the vessel owner on the back foot, responding to a situation over which it has little control.

The first and most important communications role will be to establish contact with the families of the crew. This is done by the manning agent (the company that the ship operator has used to crew the ship), but families will expect direct contact with the shipowner and/or operator. They will know, or will soon find out, the entity from which the pirates are seeking payment, and are likely to put pressure on the company to solve the problem (by paying a ransom) from the very early stages. A crisis such as this cannot be outsourced to the different organizations in the value chain: the owner or operator will be the target and will need to establish ways of communicating with families of the crew.

A second early challenge will be communication within the shipping value chain. The vessel owner, vessel operator, cargo owner(s) and insurers/

reinsurers are the key stakeholders. If the cargo is a commodity like oil, then it may change ownership during the voyage. Establishing the stakeholder mix and contractual obligations is a potential early distraction when the communications function will be under pressure to communicate. There will also be close communication with the governments of countries whose citizens have been taken hostage. If American citizens are on board, the White House will often initiate a quick response and seek to take control. Since the Iranian hostage crisis of 1979–81, the United States is highly politically sensitive to its citizens being in such situations.

Phase 2: the long silence

After an initial flurry of activity, contact with the vessel may be lost for weeks or even months. There may be a media blackout at this stage, requested by the company or recommended by governments. Pirates seek the oxygen of publicity to ratchet up the tension (and the ransom demand) but most media will respect the desire of the companies involved and their families for a blackout. However, if families feel that the company is not doing everything it can to release their loved ones, they might decide it is in their interests to generate publicity to put greater pressure on the company to pay the ransom. Many simply will not be able to understand why multi-billion dollar companies are unwilling to part with a few million dollars to end a piracy situation.

The family response in this second phase will understandably be highly tense. Pirates will often attempt to get in touch directly with the families of hostages through social media. Families need constant reassurance and support; if families become 'enemies' of the shipowner/operator, the resulting conflict (and possibly publicity) is likely to make a bad situation worse.

This second phase is potentially a morale-sapping and frustrating experience. There will be much planning for resolution, with companies considering their (limited) options. Whilst both the United States and the United Kingdom have clear policies of 'no concessions to pirates', negotiations are not prohibited and are a matter for the company involved, not government. A US Presidential Order makes it illegal to pay known terrorists (and others) on a government list while the United Kingdom also prohibits the paying of ransom to terrorist organizations. When paying a ransom in the United Kingdom, a company must get clearance from the National Crime Agency to ensure the ransom is not classified as money laundering.[18] In Singapore, on the other hand, paying ransoms is completely illegal under the country's Kidnapping Act.[19]

Phase 3: the release

There are many challenges at the time of resolution, which usually comes many months after the taking of the ship. Ransom payment remains the most likely course of resolution, usually via a 'fee' paid to an intermediary who then concludes the negotiations and arranges for the release of the vessel and crew. Although the strategic aim of securing the release will have been accomplished, the crew needs to be repatriated, looked after and reunited with families. Families will want the crew returned immediately but law enforcement agencies, legal teams, forensic experts and others will want access to them first.

The media will also need to be managed at this stage, as the blackout no longer serves a purpose and journalists will be interested in the human-interest stories of returning hostages. Crew are actively discouraged from engaging with the media, partly because this will be an unusual and additional stress to them, but also because companies are concerned that any 'wrong message' they may give about the vessel and its preparedness for attack may threaten payment from the insurer.

Phase 4: the aftermath

Finally, there are challenges in the long term. A company may be dealing with the impact of a piracy situation for many years after the situation is resolved. Insurance claims and follow-up will take months, if not years, due to the sensitive nature of piracy incidents. Crew might seek damages: crew members of the MV Maersk Alabama, for example, are suing the vessel owner and operator for $50 million in damages after their ordeal.[20] In the long term, a company should also be prepared for dealing with issues such as post-traumatic stress disorder (PTSD). The communications challenge for one piracy incident may last for years.

An attack on a wider group affecting you

A piracy incident, like a cyberattack, is aimed at one organization for a specific reason: financial gain (piracy) or access to valuable information for the purposes of financial gain or causing disruption (cyberattack). A terror attack is less discriminate – the terrorist's aim is usually to disrupt society's functioning and/or effect political change rather than to destroy one company. There is some crossover with the subcategory above, however, as it is possible that one organization could be the sole unlucky victim of an attack aimed at a wider audience. The Pan Am flight 103 tragedy, described above, is an example of this.

The threat of terrorism is, sadly, ever present for organizations that have people and offices in a major metropolitan area, operate major assets or transport infrastructure or organize/sponsor major events. So much has been written and broadcast about the various terror attacks in this century (including New York, Washington, London, Madrid, Bali, Mumbai), there seems little value in repeating it.

For organizations, the key lies in predicting what could happen, remaining vigilant to help prevent attacks and preparing for the worst, all as part of a wider citywide or national resilience effort. If an incident of this nature does occur, operational matters will drive an organization's response. Although a crisis may be called at the highest levels of the company, it is likely that the key decisions are local and operational. But if there has been severe damage or potential damage to the organization's ability to function – by affecting people and assets needed for the operation of the business, for example – then strategic crisis management comes to the fore. This is the forward-looking, big-picture scenario planning that is required when the very existence of the business is potentially at risk.

From a communications perspective, the challenges are enormous. Communications professionals will find themselves in a situation where demand for information is extremely high – and often highly emotional – but where there is little information to give. It is likely that they will be learning as much from social media and anecdotal evidence as from official channels, and will therefore have to exercise extreme care with information use. They will be one of many responding organizations, seeking to coordinate information and communication. This will include first responders, government departments, embassies, other companies etc. Coordination may be hampered by operational and transport realities, for example: mobile phone networks might be taken down by the police, or public transport might be unavailable.

Although corporate 'victims' may be spared the scrutiny and pressure from the media associated with other forms of crisis, reputation damage can result from any perceived failure to protect and help employees, families, suppliers, contractors and customers. Reputation effects come from what you do, or are perceived to do, at the micro level – the small decisions that help people – as much as what you say. And, after the event, people will 'compare and contrast' the responses of different organizations: Company X showed 'amazing care and compassion' whilst Company Y 'straitjacketed itself in process'.

A political or social development endangering you, or those in your care

A third type of external incident is a sudden political or societal development which, whilst not targeted at you, puts those in your care at risk. As with the other forms of external incident, there is potentially chaos and confusion and you have little or no control over resolution. The characteristic that makes this situation different is that it is a highly politicized and volatile risk situation, usually in a developing market where infrastructure and information are not wholly reliable.

A sudden threat to the political status quo in a locality, country or region is something security departments should be planning against. There will also be the need for a robust human resources (HR) and communications response should the risk materialize. Organizations need to be nimble, be able to operationalize plans at short notice and scenario plan against the worst case.

Operating in remote parts of developing countries, the mining industry is familiar with this type of incident. The Marikana incident, which occurred in South Africa in August 2012, provides an example. The Marikana mine is operated by British-owned platinum producer Lonmin. On 10 August 2012, miners at the asset began illegal wildcat strikes over pay. The strikers wanted their monthly salaries tripled and walked out after Lonmin failed to meet with aggrieved workers. The strike escalated into violent clashes between police and strikers and, between 12 and 14 August, there were 10 fatalities: eight Lonmin employees and two policemen.

On 16 August, tensions escalated still further when strikers were fired upon by the South African Police Service (SAPS). There were a further 34 fatalities, making the incident the highest death toll incurred through police action in South Africa since the end of apartheid. The media labelled the incident a massacre. The police chief defended the action, claiming that officers had shot at charging, armed strikers out of self-defence. Lonmin released a statement from Chairman Roger Philimore who said the violence was 'clearly a public order rather than labour relations associated matter'.[21]

SAPS arrested and charged 270 miners in the aftermath of the incident, causing further outcry. The strikers vowed to continue, risking dismissal after Lonmin issued an ultimatum on 19 August to any striker who did not return to work by the following day. The ultimatum polarized strikers and mine managers as some deemed it disrespectful to their deceased colleagues. Lonmin extended the next-day deadline by 24 hours after South Africa's President Jacob Zuma announced a week-long mourning period. Lonmin later backed down from the ultimatum, fearing it could trigger further violence and agreed 'that no disciplinary action be taken against those unlawfully away from work who do not return this week'.[22]

As the strike continued, Lonmin launched a communications programme which aimed to keep the public and employees abreast of the situation. In a statement, Lonmin stated it was using channels such as 'leaflets, local radio, an SMS text system and word of mouth, and an emergency number for the reporting of any incidents of intimidation'.[23] The strike officially ended on 20 September, when the company agreed to raise wages and offered a bonus to employees who signed a new agreement.

Lonmin's share price fell 12 per cent between 10 and 17 August. In the aftermath, Lonmin established the Sixteen-Eight Memorial Fund, which aims to provide financial assistance to children of deceased employees to help them stay in education. Following the Marikana incident, President Jacob Zuma announced the establishment of a commission tasked with investigating, amongst other matters, whether 'by act or omission, the company directly or indirectly caused loss of life of damage to persons or property'.[24] President Zuma has stated that he believes Lonmin 'provoked' the strike and 'bears a wider responsibility'[25] for the incident, although he concedes that the company cannot be held solely responsible.

The Marikana incident was a tragedy that was directly related to the company involved, although Lonmin characterized it as civil unrest rather than a labour relations matter.

Some years earlier, in another part of Africa, another mining company faced a similarly volatile situation, but this time the violence was not linked to anything the company had done. Anvil Mining found itself caught up in civil unrest in the Democratic Republic of Congo (DRC) in 2004. But the real reputation threat came some time thereafter, when it was accused of complicity in what campaigners called the 'Kilwa massacre'.

Anvil, headquartered in Canada, had been operating the Dikulushi copper mine near a village called Kilwa in Katanga Province, DRC, since 2002. On 14 November 2004, a group of rebels briefly occupied Kilwa. The *Forces Armées de la République Démocratique du Congo* (FARDC), Congo's military, deployed troops on 15 November to quash the rebellion. The forces were successful, but a number of civilians were killed alongside insurgents in the process of supressing the uprising. In its quarterly report released in January 2005, Anvil praised the DRC government's response, stating that 'the government and military response on both provincial and national levels was rapid and supportive of the prompt resumption of operations'.[26]

The United Nations Organization Mission in the Democratic Republic of Congo (MONUC) carried out an investigation into alleged human rights breaches that took place during FARDC's intervention. The investigation concluded that summary executions, torture and illegal detention had been carried out by FARDC and that there was little combat. In all, the UN estimated 73 fatalities.

It emerged that Anvil Mining had provided the government troops with logistical support. In an Australian *Four Corners* television documentary, Anvil Chief Executive Bill Turner admitted that the company provided logistical support in the form of transport to the armed forces, but he denied the company played a part in the ensuing human rights abuses, claiming: 'we helped the military to get to Kilwa and then we were gone. Whatever they did there, that's an internal issue.'[27] Anvil released two media statements condemning allegations of the company's involvement in the incident. It stated that, 'given Anvil's previous experience with rebel activity in the Kilwa area, Anvil had absolutely no choice but to provide the transport required by the DRC Military'.[28] Anvil reiterated that the company 'had no knowledge of what was planned for the military operation, and was not involved in the military operation in any way'.[29]

The MONUC report, however, resulted in the arrest of three Anvil employees including the General Manager for Congo. In June 2007, the Anvil employees were found not guilty by a military court. But in a press release UN High Commissioner for Human Rights, Louise Arbour, expressed concern at the non-guilty verdict. Thereafter, Raid UK, a small UK-based human rights campaign group, published a report titled *The Kilwa Trial: A Denial of Justice*, which alleged that the 'proceedings were plagued with obstructions and political interference and documents serious flaws and irregularities in the trial of nine Congolese soldiers for war crimes and three employees of Anvil Mining for complicity in war crimes committed'.[30]

The matter was eventually ruled upon by the Canadian Supreme Court in November 2012, eight years after the incident. The Court dismissed an application by the Canadian Association Against Impunity (CAAI) to appeal against a ruling by the Quebec Court of Appeal, which had overturned a lower court's decision to allow the case to proceed in Canada. In a press statement, the CAAI pledged to continue the 'fight for justice' for the victims of the 'Kilwa massacre'.

The Kilwa incident is an example of how incidents involving political or social unrest do not just present short-term security issues. Anvil staff members were unaffected by the uprising itself and operations resumed quickly. But where there is political and social tension at the local and national levels, there is the possibility of long-term international legal and reputational implications for companies that – through no fault of their own – are perceived to be in some way involved. Although Anvil has never been found by a court of law to have acted wrongly, a quick Google search of the company's name brings up page after page of Kilwa-related information. The reputation 'tail' of such controversies can be a long one.

Leaving Libya

The following is a first-hand account, written by a colleague, of an externally driven incident. The Libyan uprising was a typical political/ societal event to which many companies with expat workers in the country had to respond.

Working as a consultant for Regester Larkin for eight years, I had much experience of advising people in the midst of stressful, emotional and unpredictable situations. I thought then that I would be prepared when I found myself caught up in the Libyan Uprising in 2011, when the Arab Spring arrived on my doorstep in my host town of Tripoli.

I had moved to Libya to accompany my husband on a two-year work placement with an international company. With a young family in tow, Libya was a great place to be: we were well looked after, the sun shone and there was a general feeling of security. The Gadhafi regime was ever-present but was a part of Libyan life that we came to be at ease with.

Security advice was not pushed on us by the company: we were encouraged, of course, to take sensible precautions such as having extra cash, petrol, water and food available to see us through any civil emergency or natural disaster. But life got in the way of this advice. Emergency food was 'borrowed' and the safe was raided to fund day-to-day living in a cash-only society.

Just as there was complacency amongst the expat community, the corporate approach to risk management was focused on the immediate and daily threats. Road convoys to the desert were considered high risk and monitored closely; potential for civil unrest less so.

When the Arab Spring spread towards us via Tunisia and then Egypt, there was a noticeable shift in mood amongst the local population. As the 'Day of Rage' was planned for the 17 February 2011, it was clear that this was unprecedented activity. Other muted signals, mostly from the local population, should have put us – and the country team – on high alert more quickly: Libyans began to criticize the regime openly, which was a marked change in attitude; fighting had erupted in the neighbouring suburbs; a jailbreak had apparently resulted in the release of a number of high-risk detainees as well as political prisoners; petrol purchases were monitored closely and buying petrol in drinks bottles, once common practice, was banned by the regime.

The warning signs were present. But it took time for a decision to be made to start selective evacuation. As the situation escalated, a curfew was imposed across the capital and roadblocks usually manned by uniformed police were taken over by plain-clothed armed guards. Options for exiting the country narrowed frighteningly quickly: companies and individuals had block-booked seats on the only regular flight out to the United Kingdom, leaving us with the decision to wait for a company-sponsored option, or run the gauntlet of an increasingly dangerous trip to the airport to try to buy our way on to overbooked flights to Malta, or Mali, or anywhere, with our store of cash.

Our last night in Tripoli was a sleepless one. With the sound of an approaching crowd, we were aware that tensions were running high and the situation was unpredictable. Telephone and internet communication was blocked and we had only BBC News coverage of protests in Green Square to keep us informed of the deteriorating situation.

Our eventual route out of the country should really have been a 'Plan B'. A UK airline was due to start its route to Tripoli on Monday 20 February and therefore had seats available. Although there was little confidence in this flight arriving, we headed via the back roads for an airport in chaos. Eventually we got through a nerve-wracking security check. Many colleagues were initially turned away because, in the haste to book flights, names had been misspelt and family members missed off the list.

After hours of delay we were on a flight, aware that many of our Libyan colleagues, friends and employees were left to manage in a worsening situation.

With hindsight, the experience underlined the importance of many of the basic principles of crisis management. Act quickly in unpredictable situations that have potential to escalate: look for the warning signs from a range of sources, not just official channels. Be realistic with scenario planning: is it really feasible to charter a plane? Make sure processes such as HR records and people in country lists are always up to date. Plan ahead and share responsibility with staff and families by introducing mandatory security training and standards for all who are dependent on the company for a way out.

A natural event

The final type of external incident-driven risk is different from the others in this chapter in that the volatility and threat are natural, not man-made. As discussed in Chapter 2, people feel differently about man-made risks than they do about natural ones, even though a weather event can wreak more havoc than a bomb, and a pandemic flu outbreak can kill many more than a revolution. Although the weather has no intent, it does not make it any less destructive.

Natural incidents can strike with no warning: an earthquake, for example, such as the one that led to the nuclear emergency in Fukushima, Japan in 2011. Or they can strike with some warning: severe storms are tracked minute by minute as they develop, change course and threaten communities. Some are predictable on a fairly regular basis: snow disruption during winter and storm activity in many climates during the summer. Others have happened and will happen again but nobody knows when: major flu pandemics, earthquakes and volcano eruptions. Some have consequences that take the world seemingly by surprise, such as the ash cloud created by the eruption of the Icelandic volcano, Eyjafjallajökull, which grounded air traffic and caused chaos in parts of Europe in April 2010.

Once again, responding to a natural event is more about impact management than it is resolution. Organizations cannot be blamed for the weather, but they can be criticized for not preparing for it or for responding poorly.

One challenge with this type of externally driven incident is the need to communicate to employees, customers and others around risk. The 'stay at home' or 'come to work' message of course has major business continuity and therefore commercial/financial consequences attached to it. But whether this is serious risk to life, or just disruption of service, the advice and support that an organization gives its internal and external stakeholders in these situations can build or erode trust.

Everyone is the 'victim' of an extreme weather event, but some organizations can come through such incidents as villains, whilst others emerge as heroes. The same incident, with the same amount of warning, presenting the same challenges can lead to different outcomes for different organizations depending on their ability to prepare themselves, their people and their assets for the event and on their ability to respond effectively.

The Incident Command System

During Hurricane Sandy, the US government and emergency services called upon the Incident Command System (ICS) to coordinate their response. The ICS is the joint operation of facilities, equipment, personnel, procedures and communications using a common structure and terminology. The system establishes a 'unified command' to manage the on-scene response to an incident.

Outside the United States, ICS is becoming a model for response to major incidents. New Zealand has a 'Coordinated Incident Management System', Australia uses the 'Australasian Inter-Service Incident Management System' and British Columbia in Canada has BCERMS (British Columbia Emergency Response Management System). The UN has also endorsed the system.

It was developed in the 1970s, following a series of fires in California. The lesson from the fires was that it was a lack of coordination, rather than a lack of resources or failure of tactics, that slowed the response. In the United States, with its highly devolved federal system, ICS ensures that the event, rather than the agency, is the focus.

One of the key features of ICS is a set of core roles. Two key roles are the Incident Commander (IC), a role that will always be filled when the unified command is established, and the Public Information Office (PIO). Any organization involved in the response may be asked to provide a PIO.

The agency with the most responsibility in managing the incident will appoint the lead Incident Commander. Participation and cooperation by all organizations (public and private) in the response are then expected under the Incident Commander's direction. The word of the IC is final in this command-and-control system.

The PIO communicates information to enable people to prepare for an incident and to make decisions during an incident to protect lives and property. This might include developing 'first hour' statements, engaging with media on the scene and providing counsel and support to other spokespeople.

Importantly, the ICS is not a substitute for crisis management. It deals only with the immediate scene and the two primary objectives of protecting lives and property. ICS works more closely with a company's emergency response teams than the strategic crisis management team (CMT). Unlike strategic crisis management, it does not look at reputation, long-term licence to operate or other impacts.

The 'heroes' and 'villains' of Hurricane Sandy

Sandy, which hit New York City on 29 October 2012, was the second costliest hurricane in US history, affecting 24 states, including the entire east coast. As of May 2013, estimated damages caused by Sandy were assessed to be over $53 billion.[31] Over six million people in 15 states were left without power after it struck the east coast. Two companies facing the same challenges emerged very differently.

Two weeks after Sandy hit, power company Consolidated Edison (ConEd) still had 3,900 customers without power.[32] ConEd was seemingly caught unprepared, leading customers and authorities to ask if they had sufficient response plans in place. New York Attorney General Eric Schneiderman subpoenaed the company, requesting plans and performance records on restoring power, communicating with customers without power and other aspects of the response.[33]

ConEd's poor operational response was compounded by poor communication. The company used social media to communicate with affected customers, but because of failings with their operational response, the platform backfired. Instead of providing accurate assessments of how long customers would be in the dark, ConEd tried to ease customers' minds about power restoration but only provided uneducated time estimates as to when this might be achieved. Over the course of its response, ConEd gave six different dates for power restoration and various different reasons for the delay,[34] which only made irritated customers angrier. While customers waited for their questions and complaints to be addressed, they used social media platforms to complain and share their negative stories about the company.

On the opposite side of the response spectrum was Atlantic City Electric in New Jersey. Atlantic City Electric had 220,000 customers affected by the storm – 90 per cent of those affected had power restored four days after Sandy hit, and the remainder had supplies restored within eight days.[35] The Company ranked first in overall effectiveness of handling the emergency amongst the 31 utilities impacted by Sandy, according to J.D. Power and Associates' 2013 Hurricane Sandy Responsiveness Study.[36]

Preparations at the company began before the storm hit, mobilizing employees, securing the services of contractors, making calls for out-of-state utility assistance, checking material inventories etc. Atlantic City Electric made automated calls to their customers enrolled in their emergency medical equipment programme. Through the crisis, Atlantic City Electric kept customers informed and updated through social media. It also updated its outage 'tracking' phone app and website, consistently issued press releases, held frequent press conferences and took part in many media interviews. Atlantic City Electric received 92,000 customer calls, 99 per cent of which were answered in less than 30 seconds.[37]

These two companies emerged from the same storm with different reputational outcomes. Both were hit directly by Sandy, and their core business – keeping the lights on – was impacted. But companies do not need to be directly affected by an event of this nature to get involved in the response. Some years before Sandy, Hurricane Katrina created almost unimaginable devastation and killed nearly 2,000 people. Whilst many organizations were criticized for how they handled Hurricane Katrina, Walmart emerged from it with an enhanced reputation.

Walmart builds reputation from Katrina

Walmart was – and is – an amazing corporate success story, but by the time of Hurricane Katrina in August 2005, it had in some ways become a victim of its own success. It was one of the biggest US corporations by revenue and employee numbers. But size and strength breed resentment, suspicion and distrust. At a time of anti-corporate campaigning, the public had come to view Walmart as destructive to local competition. Other criticisms levelled against Walmart included putting unfair cost pressures on suppliers, using overseas 'sweatshops' to produce goods, treating employees poorly and damaging the environment. Walmart's profits were starting to decline.

Walmart has an Emergency Operations Centre (EOC) in Arkansas that monitors developments in the United States which might adversely affect the company – from customer and employee injuries to natural disasters. The EOC can utilize its customer database to study consumer purchase patterns in hurricane-prone areas. In preparation for a storm, customers buy water, torches, generators etc. Afterwards they buy mops and chainsaws.[38]

On 28 August 2005, Hurricane Katrina, having wreaked havoc in Florida, changed course and headed towards New Orleans. In preparation for the hurricane, New Orleans Mayor Ray Nagin had ordered a mandatory evacuation from the city. Walmart's meteorology experts had already noticed (before the National Weather Service) that Katrina had changed course and, in response, the company had rerouted materials originally dispatched to Florida. Walmart also mobilized additional resources in some distribution centres in nearby states.

In further preparation measures, Walmart's senior executives had called a meeting in which store managers were given authority to make on-the-ground decisions. Walmart's Chief Executive, Scott Lee, was reported as saying: 'A lot of you are going to have to make decisions above your level. Make the best decision that you can with the information that's available to you at the time, and, above all, do the right thing.'[39] Scott added 'I want us to respond in a way appropriate to our size and the impact we can have.'[40]

The hurricane caused extensive damage. The confirmed death toll was 1,836.[41] Despite the government's declaration of a health emergency along the Gulf Coast, criticism began to mount over the delay in getting aid to affected people by the Federal Emergency Management Agency (FEMA). Meanwhile, Walmart had managed to reach hurricane-hit areas before government relief arrived and had begun to distribute essential items to those affected. Walmart's efficiency became part of the story. By September 13, all but 13 of the facilities that had been shut down were operational again and Walmart had offered 97 per cent of its displaced employees jobs elsewhere.[42] Alongside its $3 million donation in essential items, the company made a cash donation of $17 million to the relief effort, the largest corporate cash contribution at the time. Walmart was careful about the way it communicated its actions, avoiding self-aggrandizing advertising. Instead the company made local employees available for media interviews, adding to the 'community feel' of the response.

In the aftermath of Hurricane Katrina, Walmart was widely commended for its logistical efficiency and disaster planning abilities.[43] Senior figures including former presidents George HW Bush and Bill Clinton praised the company's response while the *National Post* ran an article entitled 'In Walmart We Trust', which outlined the relief efforts of the company.[44] Writing in The *Financial Times*, reputation expert Daniel Diermeier stated that 'the Katrina response re-energized the beleaguered company, which received credit for exploiting core competencies: knowing what customers want and getting it to them fast and efficiently'.[45] Marketing experts agreed that Walmart's actions had resulted in both short- and long-term reputation uplift, especially amongst its customer base. As one analyst said, 'they're going to remember Walmart was there'.[46]

Walmart's size, which some had come to view as a liability, was precisely what saved the day in the aftermath of Hurricane Katrina. Rather than apologizing for this, Walmart was able to successfully leverage it for the greater good and to boost its faltering reputation.

Chapter summary

As with the Walmart example described above, it is often by the most basic of needs, the smallest of measures and the most personal of touches that corporate responses are judged in externally driven incidents. Making sure employees can be paid or have access to basic nutrition, finding ways to update people who may have had the usual communications channels shut down, ensuring the customer service experience is a positive one even in the most difficult of circumstances. Walmart succeeded because it offered its goods and services – the things that made it successful – as part of a community-based response.

The key lessons from this chapter are:

- An incident that is not your fault can still damage your reputation if it is not well managed.

- External incidents can be non-physical (cyberattack) as well as physical; man-made as well as natural.

- External incidents almost always require operational as well as strategic and communications responses.

- Managing an external incident is more about managing impacts than solving problems.

- Companies can rarely be perceived as victims even when they are directly attacked, but they can be 'villains' if their response is seen to be poor.

- Companies can be seen as valuable citizens if they bring their organization, skills and power to the aid of people in the wake of an external incident

External incidents test an organization's preparedness and its ability to respond. They test its resilience, its resolve and its humanity. In reputation terms, organizations are starting from a position of relative strength. The incident itself is not their fault. But failing to be prepared organizationally for what is to a greater or lesser extent predictable, failing to protect people against worst-case scenarios, failing to communicate about a developing situation and failing to respond operationally and emotionally to potentially devastating situations can be as reputationally damaging as any other risk.

A Chief Executive of a major company hit by a weather event admitted to me afterwards that they had made mistakes that others had not and that they did not meet some of their employees' basic human needs. Because of this, the incident hit the company harder than many of the other issues and incidents that had happened over the years. 'I had internal hate mail for weeks after the event, and I never want that to happen again.'

Notes

1 European Strategic Intelligence and Security Center (17 March 2004) *Briefing Note, Post Incident Report: Attacks on Madrid*

2 Democracy Now! [accessed 16 May 2013] 'Remembering March 11: The Madrid Bombings and Their Effect on Spanish Government, Society and the Antiwar Movement' [online video clip] www.democracynow.org/2004/11/23/remembering_march_11_the_madrid_bombings

3 Staff reporter [accessed 17 May 2013] 'Spain's PM vows to catch bombers', BBC News [online] http://news.bbc.co.uk/1/hi/world/europe/3502218.stm

4 Regester, Michael and Larkin, Judy (2005) *Risk Issues and Crisis Management*, Kogan Page, London

5 *The Wall Street Journal*, 'The Tylenol Trouble'

6 Obama, President Barack [accessed 11 June 2013] 'Remarks by the president on securing our nation's cyber infrastructure', *The White House* [speech] www.whitehouse.gov/the_press_office/Remarks-by-the-President-on-Securing-Our-Nations-Cyber-Infrastructure

7 The Corporate Executive Board Company, *Maximizing the Business Value of Information: New Principles for Using and Securing Information*, Washington DC: CEB [pdf] www.executiveboard.com/exbd-resources/pdf/executive-guidance/eg2013-q1-final.pdf

8 Worstall, Tim [accessed 10 June 2013] 'The Biggest Cyber-Attack Ever Is Slowing Down The Internet', *Forbes* [online] www.forbes.com/sites/timworstall/2013/03/27/the-biggest-cyber-attack-ever-is-slowing-down-the-internet/

9 Robertson, Jordan [accessed 10 June 2013] 'How a Coca-Cola Exec Fell for a Hacker's E-mail Trick', *Bloomberg* [online] http://go.bloomberg.com/tech-blog/2012-11-06-how-a-coca-cola-exec-fell-for-a-hackers-e-mail-trick/

10 McCarthy, Bede [accessed 11 June 2013) 'Staff undermine cyber security efforts', *Financial Times* [online] www.ft.com/cms/s/0/01f936e6-a365-11e2-ac00-00144feabdc0.html#axzz2fR6MWZpy

11 Riley, Michael and Elgin, Ben [accessed 11 June 2013] 'China's Cyberspies Outwit Model for Bond's Q', *Bloomberg* [online] www.bloomberg.com/news/2013-05-01/china-cyberspies-outwit-u-s-stealing-military-secrets.html

12 Elgin, Ben, Lawrence, Dune and Riley, Michael [accessed 10 June 2031] 'Coke Gets Hacked And Doesn't Tell Anyone', *Bloomberg* [online] www.bloomberg.com/news/2012-11-04/coke-hacked-and-doesn-t-tell.html

13 Clemente, Dave [accessed 10 June 2013] 'Cyber Security and Interdependence: What is Critical?', *Chatham House* [pdf] www.chathamhouse.org/sites/default/files/public/Research/International%20Security/0213pr_cyber.pdf

14 US Securities and Exchange Commission [accessed 11 June 2013] 'CF Disclosure Guidance: Topic No. 2' [online] www.sec.gov/divisions/corpfin/guidance/cfguidance-topic2.htm

15 Bellingham MP, Henry [accessed 10 June 2013] 'Tackling piracy: UK Government response', *Foreign and Commonwealth Office* [speech] www.gov.uk/government/speeches/tackling-piracy-uk-government-response

16 Contact Group of Piracy off the Coast of Somalia [accessed 7 June 2013] 'Background' [online] www.thecgpcs.org/about.do?action=background

17 Guled, A and Straziuso, J [accessed 6 June 2013] 'Party over for Somali pirates? Attacks way down', *Associated Press* [online] http://news.yahoo.com/party-over-somali-pirates-attacks-way-down-163001992.html

18 Staff reporter [accessed 6 June 2013] 'Government "approves ransoms to Somali pirates"', *The Week* [online] www.theweek.co.uk/uk-news/44374/government-approves-ransoms-somali-pirates

19 Singapore Government Attorney-General's Chambers [accessed 7 June 2013] 'Kidnapping Act' [online] http://statutes.agc.gov.sg/aol/search/display/view.w3p;page=0;query=DocId%3A%2266f8915c-6e5a-406a-810a-e074ea9b3c80%22%20Status%3Ainforce%20Depth%3A0;rec=0

20 Harries, Paul [accessed 7 June 2013] 'Crew of US ship rescued from Somali pirates sues owners for $50m', *The Guardian* [online] www.theguardian.com/world/2012/may/26/crew-ship-rescued-somali-pirates-sues

21 Lonmin [accessed 1 May 2013] 'Lonmin Statement on Marikana' [press release] www.lonmin.com/downloads/media_centre/news/press/2012/Lonmin_Statement_on_Marikana_-_16_08_12_-_FINAL.pdf

22 Lonmin [accessed 1 May 2013] 'Statement on Marikana and Covenants' [press release] www.lonmin.com/downloads/media_centre/news/press/2012/Marikana_and_Covenants_update_-_21_08_12_-_FINAL.pdf

23 Lonmin [accessed 1 May 2013] 'Statement on Marikana and Covenants' [press release] www.lonmin.com/downloads/media_centre/news/press/2012/Marikana_and_Covenants_update_-_21_08_12_-_FINAL.pdf

24 Zuma, President Jacob [accessed 30 April 2013] 'Appointment of Judicial Commission of Inquiry on the Marikana Tragedy', *The Presidency Republic of South Africa* [speech] www.presidency.gov.za/pebble.asp?relid=6649

25 Starkey, Jerome [accessed 30 April 2013] 'UK company provoked massacre of miners, says Zuma', *The Times* [online] www.thetimes.co.uk/tto/news/world/africa/article3747915.ece

26 Neighbour, Sally [accessed 1 May 2013] 'The Kilwa Incident', *ABC Four Corners* [online] www.abc.net.au/4corners/content/2005/s1384238.htm

27 United Nations Organization Mission in the Democratic Republic of Congo (MONUC) [accessed 30 April 2013] *Report on the conclusions of the Special Investigation into allegations of summary executions and other violations of human rights committed by the F ARDC in Kilwa (Province of Katanga) on 15 October 2004'* [pdf] http://raid-uk.org/docs/Kilwa_Trial/MONUC_report_oct05_eng_translated_by_RAID.pdf

28 Anvil Mining [accessed 30 April 2013] 'Anvil Confirms Denial of Unfounded Allegations' [press release] www.anvilmining.com/files/2005June212005Allegations.pdf

29 Raid UK [accessed 1 May 2013] 'Anvil Mining Limited and the Kilwa Incident Unanswered Questions' [pdf] http://raid-uk.org/docs/Kilwa_Trial/KI_Briefing_20-10-05.pdf

30 Raid UK [accessed 1 May 2013] 'Anvil Mining Limited and the Kilwa Incident' [online] http://raid-uk.org/work/anvil_dikulushi.htm

31 United States Department of Commerce National Oceanic and Atmospheric Administration's National Weather Service [accessed 12 June 2013] *Hurricane/Post-Tropical Cyclone Sandy, October 22-29, 2012* [pdf] www.nws.noaa.gov/os/assessments/pdfs/Sandy13.pdf

32 Gandel, Stephen [accessed 11 June 2013] 'How ConEd Turned New York City's lights back on', *Fortune* [online] http://finance.fortune.cnn.com/2012/11/12/con-ed-hurricane-sandy-2/

33 Hakim, Danny [12 June 2013] 'Schneiderman Subpoenas Utilities Over the Storm', *The New York Times* [online] www.nytimes.com/2012/11/15/nyregion/schneiderman-subpoenas-con-edison-and-lipa-over-storm.html?_r=0

34 Fanelli, James [accessed 11 June 2013] 'SI Lawyer Sues Con Ed After Sandy Left Him Without Power for 17 Days', DNA Info New York [online] www.dnainfo.com/new-york/20130115/annandale/si-lawyer-sues-con-ed-after-sandy-left-him-without-power-for-17-days

35 Schneider, Mike [accessed 12 June 2013] 'Atlantic City Electric President Defends Utility's Response to Hurricane Sandy', NJTV, December 14, 2012 [online video clip] www.njtvonline.org/njtoday/video/atlantic-city-electric-president-defends-utilitys-response-to-hurricane-sandy/

36 JD Power & Associates [accessed 11 June 2013] *2013 Hurricane Sandy Responsiveness Study* [online] www.jdpower.com/content/press-release/93IMBM9/2013-hurricane-sandy-responsiveness-study.html

37 Worrell, Carolina [accessed 11 June 2013] 'Tristate Power Companies Surge Ahead With Upgrades', ENR New York [online] http://newyork.construction.com/new_york_construction_projects/2013/0610-major-tristate-power-companies-surge-ahead.asp

38 Levenson, Eugenia and Leonard, Devin (2005) The only lifeline was the Wal-Mart, *Fortune*, **152**(7), pp 74–80

39 Horowitz, Stephen (2009) Wal-Mart to the Rescue: Private Enterprise's Response to Hurricane Katrina, *The Independent Review*, **13**(4), pp 511–28

40 Barbaro, Michael and Gillios, Justin [accessed 12 April 2013] 'Wal-Mart at Forefront of Hurricane Relief', *The Washington Post* [online] www.washingtonpost.com/wp-dyn/content/article/2005/09/05/AR2005090501598.html

41 Staff reporter [accessed 15 April 2013] 'Timeline: How the hurricane crisis unfolded', BBC News [online] http://news.bbc.co.uk/1/hi/world/americas/4211404.stm

42 Levenson, Eugenia and Leonard, Devin (2005) The only lifeline was the Wal-Mart, *Fortune*, **152**(7), pp 74–80

43 Barbaro, Michael and Gillios, Justin [accessed 12 April 2013] 'Wal-Mart at Forefront of Hurricane Relief', *The Washington Post* [online] www.washingtonpost.com/wp-dyn/content/article/2005/09/05/AR2005090501598.html

44 Cosh, C [accessed 15 April 2013] 'In Wal-Mart We Trust', *National Post* [online] www.nationalpost.com/opinion/columnists/story.html?id=b65bd77e-511f-4e00-88a7-a53a2a5ea4ca&k=68939

45 Diermeier, Daniel [accessed 15 April 2013] 'Case Study: Walmart', *Financial Times* [online] www.ft.com/cms/s/0/b28b8dcc-5580-11e0-a2b1-00144feab49a.html#axzz2elxtMIf3

46 Bhatnagar, P [accessed 12 April 2013] 'Wal-Mart redeems itself, but what's next', *CNN Money* [online] http://money.cnn.com/2005/09/09/news/fortune500/walmart_image/

07
Internally driven incidents

A sudden and self-inflicted incident that puts your people, a community or the environment at risk is the stuff of nightmares for any organization. Senior leaders dread the knock on the door, the phone call or the interrupted meeting to tell them that the facility has exploded, the ship has capsized or the plane has crashed and that people have lost their lives.

The internally driven incident is the sudden, catastrophic failure perceived to be of the organization's own making. It might be predictable – an airline can of course predict that one day it might have to deal with an aircraft crash – but it comes without warning. In so doing, it puts the organization under the public spotlight. It is not surprising that it is this sort of incident that has dominated crisis management thinking over the years.

It is important to note, however, that an incident does not need to be physical. A sudden technical failure that wipes out corporate knowledge or systems, impairing the ability of the organization or its customers to do business, is as much an internally driven incident as an oil spill. It may not have the arresting visibility, human tragedy or environmental impact of a physical incident but it can have reputational and other consequences that are just as serious.

At the operational level, for physical incidents, the emergency response and/or incident management teams (IMTs) swing into action. Their role is to save lives, prevent damage to the environment and protect assets. These operational teams will – or certainly should – have detailed plans for managing such incidents which will involve external organizations such as the coastguard, police and fire service.

At the management level, there may be two responses to a physical or non-physical incident. One level will concern operational or business continuity. This essentially looks at how the impacts of the incident can be managed to keep the business or operation functioning. How do we fulfil contracts, switch production, maintain supply and protect the business?

At the senior management level, a decision will be required about whether the incident constitutes a crisis and, if so, at what level of the organization. If it is decided that the incident represents a threat to the wider strategic objectives, reputation or existence of the organization, a Crisis Management Team (CMT) will be assembled. Not all incidents are crises. A fire that breaks out in a factory, hurting nobody and having minimal impact on the organization's ability to go about its business is unlikely to be declared a crisis. What identifies a crisis is not the nature of what has happened but what is at stake – reputation, the bottom line and the licence to operate – and the immediacy of the threat.

There is much crossover between this chapter and the last. In the immediate aftermath of some incidents it may not be known whether it was internally driven (a catastrophic safety or system failure) or externally driven (a physical or cyber terrorist attack) but this does not matter as it should not affect the response. Indeed, all major incidents should be treated the same in terms of organizational response, whatever the cause. They should focus on protecting people, the environment and assets; in the short term, what caused the incident is secondary.

There are no subcategories in this chapter. All internally driven incidents tend to have the following characteristics:

- As with externally driven incidents, they happen suddenly, or are fast-developing, and are high impact and high profile. If they are serious, the organization that has had the incident is likely to invoke its crisis procedures immediately.

- With physical incidents, it is possible that there will be a complex value chain involved. An incident on an oil rig, for example, may involve contractors, rig owners and other specialist suppliers, as well as the operators of the field. Not all of these organizations will necessarily invoke their crisis procedures, but they will be involved in the operational response and are stakeholders of the organization(s) at the centre of the crisis.

- Unlike with externally driven incidents, where organizations are primarily managing impacts rather than addressing the cause, the organization affected may have the power of 'resolution'. Examples of this would be an ongoing oil spill (BP's efforts at finding resolution to the 2010 Deepwater Horizon oil spill were front-page news for weeks) or a system failure, where the organization itself needs to solve the technical problem to get itself and its customers back up and running as quickly as possible.

- There are likely to be many other actors involved, such as emergency services, regulators and governments. Unlike with externally driven incidents, however, the perception is that they are helping you manage *your* problem rather than leading a coordinated response to something caused by others.

Ten safety incidents that shaped crisis management today

A list of past crises that fall into the internal incident category reads like a catalogue of the most famous corporate disasters of all time. Some of the following list may seem like ancient history, but nearly all of these incidents had a profound effect on the organization that experienced them, the general public's view of that organization and industry regulation. Many also led to improvements in incident and crisis management that have informed best practice today.

1. Bhopal – getting to the scene of the incident

Bhopal was the worst industrial accident in history. The incident happened on 3 December 1984, when 45 tonnes of methyl isocyanate escaped from the Union Carbide plant in Bhopal, India. Thousands were killed immediately as the gas drifted over densely populated neighbourhoods. The final death toll is estimated to be between 15,000 and 20,000. The injured numbered in hundreds of thousands, suffering respiratory problems, eye irritation or blindness.

The company's Chairman, Warren Anderson, flew immediately from the United States to Bhopal against the advice of his lawyers who realized that he was likely to be arrested on arrival. He was. But he understood the need for the most senior company official to go to the scene of the tragedy. Union Carbide tried to compensate the victims but Indian bureaucracy hampered these efforts and many of the victims received no compensation.

2. Piper Alpha – major incidents require media and relative response capabilities

On the night of 6 July 1988, the oil production platform, Piper Alpha, operated by Occidental Oil in the UK North Sea, was destroyed by an explosion and fire. The disaster killed 167 men. Lord Cullen, who led the inquiry and wrote the report on the disaster, concluded that Occidental Oil had not provided adequate training to make its work permit system effective, that monitoring of the system was inadequate and that communication was poor.[1] The report's recommendations changed the way offshore operators in the North Sea have to prepare their safety cases before they are allowed to operate.

In the immediate aftermath, the company set up two media response centres, one in London and one in Aberdeen. This caused difficulties, as Aberdeen always had information ahead of London. The media began playing the two off against each other to test consistency. Occidental Oil had no Relative Response Team (RRT) in Aberdeen, so the local police took the role of informing families about injuries as well as fatalities (under UK law, it is always the role of the police to inform families of fatalities, but not of injuries). As the police were performing both roles, the process was slow, causing much consternation to families and fuelling negative media stories. This incident reinforced the importance of coordinated, centralized media and relative response centres.

3. Exxon Valdez – if you don't act, regulators and politicians will

On 24 March 1989, Exxon's *Valdez* oil tanker hit rocks in Prince William Sound, Alaska. Ten million gallons of oil leaked from the vessel into the natural habitat. The disaster became instant world news, but the media response from Exxon was slow and minimal. When the Chairman did give an interview sometime after the spill, he was unprepared and unimpressive. He did not visit Alaska until a fortnight after the event. When he did go, his visit was kept secret from the media.

New legislation was imposed requiring all new ocean-going tankers to be built with double hulls[2] – at huge expense to the oil tanker and oil and gas industries. The new legislation appeared to be a knee-jerk, political reaction. But when industry fails – and is seen not to be doing the right thing in terms of crisis response – governments have to be seen to enforce change.

4. Pan Am – companies cannot be victims

Although this was an 'external incident', it deserves a place in any list of crisis management 'game-changers'. On 21 December 1988, a terrorist bomb on board Pan Am Flight 103 exploded above the town of Lockerbie in Scotland; 243 passengers, 16 crew and 11 people on the ground in Lockerbie were killed. Pan Am seemingly decided that it was not going to communicate about the disaster because it was the 'victim', not the 'villain'. By distancing itself from the terrorist atrocity, the company believed the airline's name would not be associated with it. But if the media are not fed by the organization at the centre of a crisis, they will go elsewhere... and will become suspicious.

It was later discovered that all US airlines that flew the same route had received a bomb threat. The threat named the route and two dates between which a bomb would be placed on a US airline. A concerned Pan Am looked at its passenger list, which showed that the families of US diplomats were booked on the flight to fly home for Christmas. Pan Am called the embassies to warn them of the bomb threat, and the diplomats removed their families from the flight. When it became known that only an elite group of people had been given this privileged information, there was outrage. Far from being the victim, Pan Am had become the villain.

5. Swissair – families can forgive if you help them remember

Swissair Flight 111 was en route to Geneva from New York when it crashed near Peggy's Cove on the Nova Scotia coast on 2 September 1998. All 229 crew and passengers on board were killed.

Whereas Pan Am, perhaps as part of its 'victim' strategy, had provided no help to fly relatives to Lockerbie, nor any assistance to those that made the journey themselves, Swissair organized for families to be flown from Geneva to Halifax and to stay in accommodation near Peggy's Cove. Each family was given $5,000, not in compensation, but simply to take care of immediate needs. Unlike the anger that Pan Am's (lack of) relative response had generated, which led family members to start holding their own press conferences, there was comparatively little negative publicity from the families of the Swissair victims.

6. Herald of Free Enterprise – never speculate

On 6 March 1987, the *Herald of Free Enterprise*, a cross-channel ferry operated by Townsend Thoresen, left Zeebrugge in Belgium for Dover in England. Before the vessel had passed through the harbour it filled with water and turned onto its side. The tragedy claimed the lives of 193 passengers and crew.

Shortly afterwards, the company's Chairman speculated about the cause of the accident, saying that the ferry had hit the harbour wall on its departure. Thereafter the company gave few interviews, stating it had to deal with the operational aftermath. The company's lack of communication prompted deeper investigation, which soon established the ferry had not hit the harbour wall but had left Zeebrugge whilst still closing its bow doors. The media discovered that Townsend Thoresen always operated its vessels in this way for a quicker turnaround time. Accusations of a 'cover up' were compounded by accusations of corporate greed.

Shortly before the tragedy, Townsend Thoresen had been acquired by the bigger shipping line, P&O. The acquisition had been made partly because of the goodwill associated with the Townsend Thoresen name. After the tragedy, Townsend Thoresen vanished as an entity altogether.

7. Deepwater Horizon – the spokesperson matters

Eleven oil platform workers died on 20 April 2010 when an explosion and fire rocked the Deepwater Horizon oil rig in the Gulf of Mexico. By the time the well was sealed, in September 2010, an estimated 4.9 million barrels of oil had leaked into the Gulf.

The communications response came to be characterized by some on-screen errors made by BP's Chief Executive, Tony Hayward. Pictures of the BP boss enjoying himself on the waters of the Solent in the United Kingdom were described by White House Chief of Staff, Rahm Emanuel, in an interview with ABC News as 'just another in a long line of PR gaffes and mistakes. I think we can conclude that Tony Hayward is not going to have a second career in PR consulting.'[3] For a full case study on the Deepwater Horizon incident, see Chapter 12.

8. British Midland – reputations can be built with a good crisis response

On 8 January 1989, a British Midland Boeing 737 flying from Heathrow to Belfast crashed near the M1 motorway in the United Kingdom, killing 47 people. Airline Chairman, Sir Michael Bishop, offered himself openly and immediately for media enquiries. On his way to the scene of the accident, he gave live interviews from his car phone, with almost no knowledge about the situation. He told of his concern and pledged to keep the media updated. British Midland suffered little commercial damage, due in large part to the leader's decision to communicate quickly in the face of adversity.

9. Hudson River – crises need heroes

On 15 January 2009, US Airways flight 1549 landed in the Hudson River in New York after a bird strike resulted in the loss of thrust from both engines. All 155 passengers and crew on board the flight were able to evacuate without any fatalities after the pilot successfully executed an emergency water landing. The incident was dubbed the 'Miracle on the Hudson' by the media.

The airline chose to focus on and leverage the heroic actions of the crew members aboard Flight 1549. US Airways praised the actions of its 'five outstanding aviation professionals',[4] including pilot Captain Chesley Sullenberger, who had performed well in the face of catastrophe. The crew members, widely celebrated in the media, became the faces of the 'Miracle on the Hudson'. Whilst the story may have been very different had there been fatalities, the crisis showed that the crisis 'narrative' is to some extent in the gift of the organization at its centre.

10. Texas City – crisis management is about actions as well as words

On 23 March 2005, hydrocarbon vapour ignited at BP's Texas City Refinery. Fifteen people were killed and 170 injured. BP initiated an effective crisis communications response, with the most senior people in the organization heard to be expressing the right sentiments. Chief Executive Lord Browne visited the scene, and the media praised his and the company's response.

But it soon became apparent that the refinery had a poor safety record leading up to the explosion. The acute incident therefore became a chronic issue: BP's safety record and performance. A US government report blamed 'systemic lapses' by BP's management and budget cuts which knowingly left Texas City with 'unacceptable deficiencies in preventative measures'.[5] Good crisis communications can buy time, but it cannot alone save reputation.

All of the above were major physical/safety incidents. An example of a non-physical incident was the sudden collapse of Royal Bank of Scotland Group's (RBS) customer banking systems in 2012.

RBS Group systems failure

The 'worst computer system outage the UK financial system has ever seen'[6] happened on 19 June 2012. A routine system update to the software which handles the payment processing system for banks of RBS Group suddenly failed, resulting in a backlog of payments in and out of customers' accounts. The incident affected customers across the group, including, RBS, NatWest and Ulster Bank customers.

The problem remained unresolved and the effects were still being felt by customers some days later, creating a build-up of anger and frustration. NatWest and RBS resumed normal services 10 days after the IT problems began, whilst Ulster Bank's recovery took a little over a month, prompting accusations that RBS Group was treating Ulster Bank customers as a lower priority.

The immediate response was, as one commentator described it, 'textbook'.[7] RBS Group was seen to be doing everything it could to solve the problem and manage its impacts, and it was heard to be saying the right things. Chief Executive Stephen Hester made a clear and unequivocal apology: 'I am very sorry for the difficulties people are experiencing. Our customers rely on us day in and day out to get things right, and on this occasion we have let them down. This should not have happened.'[8]

The bank also quickly reassured customers that it would help resolve all problems arising from the incident. Hester said: 'Where our customers are facing hardship or difficulty we can and will help them... I also want to reassure customers that no one will be left permanently out of pocket as a result of this.'[9] This help took the form of parachuting in extra staff to extend weekday opening times and to open branches on Sundays. Social media were also used to disseminate the message. NatWest's Twitter account tweeted: 'If you urgently need cash and can't get to a branch, please tweet us or call us.'[10]

The bank launched a detailed investigation to be overseen by independent experts and wrote to Members of Parliament, stating that bonuses for senior management would be affected.[11] At a time when the banking industry was in reputational crisis, RBS Group showed humility and contrition. But the good response – actions as well as words – could not compete with the anger at the fact that the incident had happened in the first place and that the impacts of the crisis were being felt by customers for many days.

Just as with any serious incident, the media carried many human-interest stories after the banking system collapsed. But, whereas with physical incidents these stories are about tragic loss of life and injuries, these stories were about inconveniences. This does not necessarily make it easier in crisis management and crisis communications terms. In some respects, managing an indignant and inconvenienced customer base and outraged media is just as difficult as managing a situation of grief.

Some of the human-interest stories were serious, others less so. A man who was granted bail at a court had to stay in remand as the money was unable to be transferred. Many people were unable to do their usual post-payday grocery shopping or pay their rent. Doctors in Mexico 'threatened to turn off a dying girl's life support system because a payment from NatWest had stalled'.[12] One customer's inability to access money meant that her daughter's birthday proceeded without a birthday cake and a trip to a theme park. One woman tweeted that she had missed her flight home from Italy as she couldn't check out of the hotel.[13]

These impacts made for great copy, and RBS Group must have been reading the stories in full knowledge that there was nothing it could do to stop them, except work hard to resolve the impacts as soon as it could. The company did, it seems, step in to solve problems effectively. Stephen Hester promised that customers would be reimbursed for the cost of fines or late payment fees incurred as a result of the delays. RBS Group even promised to work with credit agencies to make sure no credit ratings were affected. An incident of this nature, however, is not easily forgiven. Like the internally driven issues discussed in Chapter 5, it is seen as a failure – this time acute/catastrophic rather than chronic – of the organization's basic duty: to make customers' money available to them when they need it.

An interesting aspect of this crisis was the spreading of speculation about what had gone wrong. A theory that one untrained operator in India pressed one wrong key and caused the whole incident took hold very quickly. This rumour appears to have originated on 25 June, when *The Register*, an online science and technology news site, revealed that the software that caused the problem was run from India. 'At least some of the support staff for that software had been outsourced to India – as recently as February,'[14] it stated, despite also quoting an RBS spokesperson saying 'the software error occurred on a UK-based piece of software'.[15]

The following day, *The Register* followed up with another exclusive: a source (someone who had worked at RBS 'for several years') told *The Register* that an 'inexperienced operative' had made a 'major error'.[16] *The Register*'s article was picked up by the major national newspapers the following day and the term 'inexperienced operative' was suddenly on all journalists' lips. Britain's largest workers' union, Unite, spotted an opportunity to further its anti-offshoring agenda. 'RBS management has slashed 30,000 staff, cut pay and decimated the pensions of those dedicated staff who are now working hard to resolve the problems,' it said.[17] The *Daily Mail* happily jumped on the bandwagon: 'Such outsourcing is a betrayal of the UK – and a lethal blow to our ambition to be a modern, technology-savvy economy capable of competing with the rest of the world.'[18]

Stephen Hester responded, stating again: 'The IT centre in Edinburgh is our main centre, it is nothing to do with overseas.'[19] And a letter from Hester to the Chairman of the House of Commons Treasury Select Committee also explained the genesis of the problem as an Edinburgh-based team doing maintenance on the system. But the rumour was well-established, and too politically interesting to counter. Because of the impacts on, and anger of, customers, RBS Group was not in a position of strength to take on this rumour. It therefore persisted throughout the life cycle of the crisis.

Communications and the internal incident

The communication challenges associated with crises triggered by internal incidents are those most familiar to students of crisis management and, as this is the most rehearsed form of crisis in simulation exercises, to corporate executives. It would be logical to assume that this is the most reputation-threatening form of crisis for an organization – something catastrophic has happened that is, or is seen to be, the organization's own fault and which has potentially devastating consequences for people and/or the environment. There should be anger, blame and reputation damage.

But, in fact, the dynamics of how people respond to an incident like this are more nuanced. Chapter 1 imagined different airlines with different reputations facing a horrific internal incident – a plane crash. It argued that people might make different assumptions about the cause of the crash based on the airlines' different brand propositions and reputations. But what is also true is that, in the very early stages of the crisis, if you are watching this tragedy unfold on your TV screens or online, you are unlikely to make immediate judgements about the company involved. The first feeling you would have is shock. You feel a sense of empathy for the people involved: the injured, the relatives of the dead arriving at the airport, the emergency services battling to save human life. You would be hoping for the best and wanting everyone to come through the crisis.

At this early stage most people do not feel anger: they are too caught up in the human emotion of the tragedy to start apportioning blame. Furthermore, were the media to give the airline representative a serious grilling about safety when bodies were still being taken from the burning wreck, most would think this inappropriate. At the beginning of any major physical crisis, the public is almost always rooting for the company involved, whatever their reputation. This cannot be said of crises emanating from internally driven issues.

But this window does not last long. Shock and empathy can turn to anger and blame in two ways. First, if it transpires that the incident was caused by some sort of negligence. This, however, is usually some way down the line, something that comes out in the inevitable inquiry. Second, anger comes if the company is perceived to be managing the crisis badly. Preventing shock turning to anger and reputation damage is a key goal for any incident-driven crisis, but is particularly acute for the internally driven incident: 'not only did they cause it, they didn't respond to it well'.

What does 'managing the crisis badly' look like in the early stages of an incident? There are many answers to this question, but some of the most obvious failures are:

- Failure to help and support those impacted by the crisis – customers, passengers, employees, relatives, affected communities etc.
- Failure to acknowledge the gravity of the situation quickly enough.
- Failure to explain what has happened and keep people updated.
- Failure to take the right actions quickly and decisively enough, and show that you are in control of the situation.
- Failure to express the right emotions about the situation you have (or are perceived to have) caused.

All of the above involve communications. Chapter 14 looks at how organizations should respond to a crisis once it has occurred, and argues that crisis response is about actions and words working together. It is about being seen to do the right thing, and being heard to say the right thing.

For the communications professional, there are many challenges associated with the internal incident.

The first challenge is *speed of response*. Something has happened and it is highly likely that it is already known about and being talked about in the traditional media or in online social networks. The need to start communicating is immediate, despite the fact that the details of what has happened – let alone why it has happened – are likely to be unknown for some time to come.

Another challenge is *calling the crisis*. Whether or not the incident constitutes a crisis by the organization's definition may seem trivial in the early stages: it is an incident that needs dealing with, whatever the organization chooses to call it. But crisis structures and procedures (both general and communications-specific) are there for a reason: to help an organization make, enact and communicate decisions quickly and effectively. Communications should be involved in discussions about whether the crisis procedures should be invoked and, if in doubt, should encourage the organization to convene its crisis team to decide how the response should best be managed.

An obvious challenge is *managing the media*. As with any crisis, the media interest is likely to be intense. If it is a physical incident, the pressure is perhaps greater as there is something for the media to see and a place for journalists (including 'citizen journalists' armed with smartphones) to congregate. And if this is an internally driven incident, perceived to be caused by you, it feels like they are descending on you and you alone like the proverbial swarm of locusts.

External coordination is vital in these incidents. This applies to the crisis management and communications response as well as the operational response. Whilst one organization may be at the crisis epicentre, there are potentially many others that have invoked their own crisis procedures to deal with impacts or to support the response. This requires coordination: joined-up thinking, acting and communicating wherever possible. But this coordination can turn into confrontation if there are immediate and open disagreements between different organizations in the supply chain, for example.

Internal coordination can be just as challenging. A big company response to a major incident will likely involve hundreds of employees across different businesses, functions and geographies. This all needs coordination so the company acts together and speaks with one voice.

A further challenge in this sort of incident is *stakeholder outreach*. In any crisis, you need friends. In most situations, stakeholders are keen to help and provide support where they can. But friends can be hard to come by if the early stages of the response do not go well. Organizations managing major incidents should make sure that stakeholders are informed, their needs understood and their offers of support are heard. The stakeholder list starts long and grows longer, and is neglected at the organization's peril.

Any crisis requires *long-term thinking*. This is the job of the CMT: thinking about the big picture, the commercial impacts and the reputation recovery. But this can be more difficult when the crisis is sparked by an internal incident: the temptation can be to delay any big-picture thinking until the immediate situation is resolved.

A key challenge, which the communications function needs to be aware of, is *ensuring a people-focused response*. These sorts of incidents have impacts on people. It may be that people have died or been injured; it may be that their homes or their businesses have been impacted. Ensuring that protecting people is at the heart of the response – short and long term – is vitally important; communications professionals need to work with human resources and others to this end.

Being people-focused may seem obvious, but not every organization facing an incident gets this right. One that did not was cruise company Costa Cruises, and its parent company Carnival Corporation, which lost the cruise liner Concordia off the coast of Italy in January 2012.

The Costa Concordia

On 13 January 2012, the Costa Concordia cruise ship hit a granite outcrop off the Island of Giglio, Italy, during a detour from the pre-programmed cruise route. The collision, which tore the ship's hull, resulted in the lower compartments flooding, causing the Concordia to list and putting all passengers and crew on board at risk. At this time the captain, Francesco Schettino, notified Costa Cruises' Chief Crisis Unit Officer of the subsequent blackout, but did not raise the alarm to say the ship was in distress.[20] As the ship began to list, passengers suspected that something was seriously wrong despite the captain's assurances that the problem was due to a minor electrical outage. Passengers began to contact relatives, and it is through this communication that the news of the incident reached the Italian Coastguard, who contacted the Costa Concordia.

Captain Schettino initially downplayed the seriousness of the situation, rebuffing the Coastguard's attempts to offer help: 'It's all ok, it's just a blackout, we are taking care of the situation.'[21] It was almost an hour after the collision when the captain finally admitted that help was needed, but still the order to evacuate was not given. According to eyewitness accounts, crew members eventually started to load the lifeboats without permission. Under pressure from the Italian Coastguard, Captain Schettino eventually issued an order to abandon ship. The heavy listing angle of the ship delayed evacuation procedures and many of the passengers were unable to board lifeboats. Fatalities would later be found at muster points, wearing life jackets. During the evacuation, Captain Schettino left the damaged ship, claiming he tripped into a lifeboat before the last survivors had been rescued. Despite numerous orders by a senior Coastguard official for the captain to return to the ship and coordinate the evacuation, Schettino failed to do so. In the media he became known as 'Captain Coward'.[22]

After rescue crews searched the wreckage for weeks, 32 people were confirmed dead. Captain Schettino was arrested on the grounds of multiple manslaughter, failure to assist passengers in need and abandonment of his ship.

Costa Cruises' first press statement came at 01.00 on 14 January, four hours after the initial incident and during the evacuation (which the release claims started 'promptly'[23]). The first expression of 'sorrow' came at 17.30 on 14 January, when the President of Costa Cruises stated: 'I want to express our deep sorrow for this terrible tragedy that devastates us.'[24]

Costa Cruises is only one brand in the family of brands owned by Carnival Corporation. It is perhaps understandable that Carnival wanted the brand, rather than the corporation, to front the crisis. But Carnival is well known, as was its then Chief Executive, Micky Arison. It was hardly surprising, therefore, that people looked to Carnival for action and words. Carnival's initial response came through press statements released on the company's official website. The first statement came a full 24 hours after the incident. The company stated that it was 'committing full resources to provide assistance and ensure that all guests and crew are looked after'.[25]

Micky Arison declined to appear before the media. Instead, he communicated his condolences through his personal Twitter account as well as through a second Carnival statement. 'Where is Micky Arison?' asked *The Wall Street Journal*, as commentators began to criticize the usually highly visible billionaire for not flying to Italy.[26] 'He wants to distance himself from this disaster,' said one 'longtime acquaintance', quoted in the same article. 'Carnival drops as CEO oversees shipwreck response from Miami,' ran the Bloomberg headline on 17 January.

Incidents such as a cruise ship sinking are people incidents, and the response should be a people response. But many of those impacted – the customers and employees of Costa Cruises and their families – have not been impressed with Costa Cruises' response or that of Carnival. The relative response operation was seen as uncoordinated, contact details were not widely disseminated by the company and, in the absence of official information (Costa Cruises' website crashed at one point due to high traffic), family members resorted to unofficial channels (such as Facebook groups) in order to swap information.[27] This uncertain information flow exacerbated, rather than allayed, families' concerns. Additionally, because parent company Carnival took too long to offer 'assistance and counselling' to family members,[28] many families had already self-funded trips to Italy, resulting in further confusion.

Further down the line, the treatment of the survivors and the families of those on board seemed unchanged. An important part of post-crisis support is to help with the grieving process and to provide opportunities for families and survivors to remember the incident and the victims. But Costa Cruises did just the opposite. In the days leading up to the one-year anniversary of the incident, the company sent a letter to all passengers who had survived the disaster asking them not to travel to the island of Giglio for a ceremony organized to remember those that had lost their lives, due to 'logistical reasons'. Many survivors did return, however, to thank those on the island who had offered them support. The letter from Costa Cruises had heightened their anger, and gave them another opportunity to express their feelings about the cruise line and how it had handled the incident. One survivor said that the company 'has had an inhumane and unacceptable attitude from the start' and accused Costa of trying to encourage families to attend other ceremonies instead: 'They tried to buy our silence by offering us €125 to go to Paris.'[29]

Costa Cruises and Carnival Corporation pursued a strategy of placing full and immediate blame on Captain Schettino. The day after the tragedy, a Costa Cruises press statement said: 'While the investigation is ongoing, preliminary indications are that here may have been significant human error on behalf of the ship's Master, Captain Francesco Schettino, which resulted in these grave consequences.'[30] Costa suspended and later dismissed Schettino. This is not unusual: the 'duty of care' an organization has to an employee involved in such an incident is one thing, but this can be achieved whilst action is seen to be taken in the form of suspension or dismissal.

Placing the blame may have seemed a sensible strategy – early information seemed to implicate the captain, and the media were already vilifying him as 'Captain Coward'[31] – but it is a dangerous strategy and one that was unlikely to impress the survivors, employees, families and other stakeholders of the cruise company. The vehemence with which Costa Cruises sought to lay all the blame on one individual seemed inappropriate, and risked portraying it as a company unwilling to accept responsibility. Who, after all, hired Schettino? Who trained him? Who managed him? Who prepared him for incidents?

Captain Schettino responded as one would expect someone to respond if they have been assigned the entire blame for a major tragedy: he bit back. He criticized the crew and claimed that Costa had encouraged him to steer close to the shore as a way of generating publicity for the brand. The very public conflict between company and captain made for interesting and damaging media coverage over many weeks.

Compounding its inappropriate response, when entering into a public conflict with the discredited captain, Costa sought to present itself as the victim and Schettino as the villain. Furthermore, in April 2013, Costa Cruises asked an Italian court to consider it a victim of the disaster, saying it too wants to seek damages. 'After the poor victims, Costa is the most damaged party having lost a 500 million euro ship,'[32] its attorney stated. This ongoing manoeuvring and attempt to be cast as the victim, rather than the villain, is surprising to say the least. Clearly this is legal positioning but, whatever the courts of law say, it seems Costa has been found guilty in the court of public opinion, at least in the eyes of the survivors and the families of those that lost their lives.

In June 2013, Mickey Arison stepped down after 34 years in the top job at Carnival. In terms of other impacts, Costa Cruises Chief Executive, Pier Luigi Foschi, admitted that sales suffered after the Concordia accident but was quoted in an Italian newspaper as saying: 'We have been annihilated in the media. Our brand has been massacred.' He went on to describe the media treatment of Costa as 'an attack... for the most part unfair and unverified'.[33] Those affected by this terrible tragedy see it rather differently.

Chapter summary

As the crises described in this chapter show, there is a reason why internal incidents are the most chosen category of crisis for training and simulation exercises. They are dramatic, often visual, and put an organization in the public spotlight for something catastrophic that endangers others and which is perceived (either immediately or in time) to be their fault.

The key lessons from this chapter are:

- Internal incidents include the 'classic' fires, explosions, crashes and spills, but can also include non-physical incidents, such as a sudden, catastrophic system failure.
- These incidents may also involve a complex value chain of contractors and suppliers, and a multitude of other organizations that have invoked their own crisis procedures.

- There is sometimes a short window of shock and empathy after a tragic physical incident, but this does not last long, especially if the organization involved is perceived to be responding poorly.
- Internal incidents are almost always 'people' incidents and the response needs to be people-focused.

The goal of any incident-driven crisis is to deal with the incident and its impacts quickly and effectively, meaning that the crisis response can be stood down as soon as possible and the recovery can begin. The worst-case scenario – which, as we shall see later, the crisis team should be thinking about – is that what seems to be an isolated incident ignites a much larger narrative about the organization's safety culture or operational integrity. Journalists and commentators like patterns and they like to draw generalizations from specifics. Whilst of course lessons must be learned and improvements made to 'ensure this never happens again', there is still such a thing as a terrible accident that is not a symptom of a wider corporate failing.

Notes

1 Cullen, Lord William [accessed 4 February 2013] 'Review: Lord Cullen – what have we learned from Piper Alpha?', Finding Petroleum [speech transcript] www.findingpetroleum.com/n/Review_Lord_Cullen_what_have_we_learned_from_Piper_Alpha/044b5113.aspx

2 Exxon Valdez Oil Spill Trustee Council [accessed 7 March 2013] 'Spill Prevention and Response' [online] www.evostc.state.ak.us/facts/prevention.cfm

3 Emanuel, R [accessed 14 June 2013] '"This Week" Transcript: Rahm Emanuel', ABC News [interview transcript] http://abcnews.go.com/ThisWeek/week-transcript-rahm-emanuel/story?id=10962588

4 Lawson, Cole [accessed 14 June 2013] 'From tragedy to triumph for US airways' [online] www.colelawson.com.au/NewsandBlog/PublishedArticles/USAirwaysaccidentPR/tabid/117/Default.aspx

5 US Chemical Safety Board [accessed 14 June 2013] 'CSB Investigation of BP Texas City Refinery Disaster Continues as Organizational Issues Are Probed', CSB News [online] www.csb.gov/csb-investigation-of-bp-texas-city-refinery-disaster-continues-as-organizational-issues-are-probed/

6 Worstall, Tim [accessed 6 March 2013] 'RBS/NatWest Computer Failure: Fully Explained', Forbes [online] www.forbes.com/sites/timworstall/2012/06/25/rbsnatwest-computer-failure-fully-explained/

7 Peston, Robert [accessed 6 March 2013] 'Is outsourcing the cause of RBS debacle?', BBC News [online] www.bbc.co.uk/news/business-18577109

8 Hester, Stephen [accessed 5 March 2013] 'Message to Customers from Stephen Hester RBS Group Chief Executive', *RBS Group* [press release] www.rbs.com/news/2012/06/message-to-customers-from-stephen-hester-rbs-group-chief-executive.html

9 Staff reporter [accessed 6 March 2013] 'RBS chief apologises for NatWest banking problems', BBC News [online] www.bbc.co.uk/news/uk-18566048

10 NatWest Help (@Natwest_Help) [accessed 6 March 2013], *Twitter* [tweet] https://twitter.com/NatWest_Help/status/217948296751226880

11 Furness, Hanna [accessed 6 March 2013] 'RBS computer failure "caused by inexperienced operative in India"', *The Telegraph* [online] www.telegraph.co.uk/finance/personalfinance/consumertips/banking/9358252/RBS-computer-failure-caused-by-inexperienced-operative-in-India.html

12 Staff reporter [accessed 5 March 2013] 'RBS-NatWest Computer Failure Keeps Man In Jail Cell', *The Huffington Post* [online] www.huffingtonpost.co.uk/2012/06/26/rbs-natwest-computer-failure-keeps-man-in-cell_n_1626627.html

13 Monk, Ed and Oxlade, Andrew [accessed 6 March 2013] 'RBS-NatWest bank meltdown rolls on: Chaos to hit millions all weekend, customers STILL can't get wages – and it may last until next week', *This is Money* [online] www.thisismoney.co.uk/money/saving/article-2163048/NatWest-RBS-banking-problems-Millions-wages-meltdown-enters-second-day.html

14 Leach, Anna [accessed 5 March 2013] 'RBS collapse details revealed: Arrow points to defective part', *The Register* [online] www.theregister.co.uk/2012/06/25/rbs_natwest_what_went_wrong/

15 Leach, Anna [accessed 5 March 2013] 'RBS collapse details revealed: Arrow points to defective part', *The Register* [online] www.theregister.co.uk/2012/06/25/rbs_natwest_what_went_wrong/

16 Leach, Anna [accessed 5 March 2013] '"Inexperienced" RBS tech operative's blunder led to banking meltdown', *The Register* [online] www.theregister.co.uk/2012/06/26/rbs_natwest_ca_technologies_outsourcing/

17 Treanor, Jill, Insley, Jill and Wainwright, Martin [accessed 6 March 2013] 'RBS boss says outsourcing not to blame for computer glitch', *The Guardian* [online] www.theguardian.com/business/2012/jun/25/unite-attacks-rbs-slashing-jobs

18 Brummer, A [accessed 5 March 2013] 'The real scandal at RBS is how it sacked thousands of British workers – and sent their jobs abroad', *Mail Online* [online] www.dailymail.co.uk/debate/article-2165765/Natwest-meltdown-The-real-scandal-RBS-sacked-thousands-UK-workers-sent-jobs-abroad.html

19 Furness, Hannah [accessed 6 March 2013] 'RBS computer failure "caused by inexperienced operative in India"', *The Telegraph* [online] www.telegraph.co.uk/finance/personalfinance/consumertips/banking/9358252/RBS-computer-failure-caused-by-inexperienced-operative-in-India.html

20 Stabe, Martin, Bernard, Steve and de Sabata, Eleonora [accessed 8 April 2013] 'Timeline: The Costa Concordia disaster', *Financial Times* [online] www.ft.com/cms/s/0/5e95fb2a-644e-11e1-b30e-00144feabdc0.html#axzz2fR6MWZpy

21 Staff reporter [accessed 8 April 2013] 'Cruise disaster: timeline of how the Concordia disaster unfolded', *The Telegraph* [online] www.telegraph.co.uk/news/worldnews/europe/italy/9019049/Cruise-disaster-timeline-of-how-the-Concordia-disaster-unfolded.html

22 Weathers, Helen and Evans, Rebecca [accessed 8 April 2013] 'Captain Coward had his eye on English dancer: After claims he was distracted by a woman on the bridge, passengers and crew reveal Casanova antics of crash skipper', *Mail Online* [online] www.dailymail.co.uk/news/article-2089680/Costa-Concordia-Captain-Coward-Francesco-Schettino-eye-dancer-Domnica-Cemortan.html Reguly, Eric [accessed 8 April 2013] '"Captain Coward" forever linked to cruise ship disaster', *The Globe and Mail* [online] www.theglobeandmail.com/news/world/captain-coward-forever-linked-to-cruise-ship-disaster/article554460/

23 Costa Cruises [accessed 5 April 2013] 'Costa Concordia – update' [press release] www.costacruises.co.uk/B2C/GB/Info/concordia_statement.htm

24 Costa Cruises [accessed 5 April 2013] 'Costa Concordia – update' [press release] www.costacruises.co.uk/B2C/GB/Info/concordia_statement.htm

25 Carnival Corporations [Accessed 5 April 2013] 'Carnival Corporation & plc Statement Regarding Costa Concordia' [press release] http://phx.corporate-ir.net/phoenix.zhtml?c=200767&p=irol-newsArticle&ID=1648204

26 Esterl, Mike and Lublin, Joann [accessed 5 April 2013] 'Carnival CEO Lies Low After Wreck', *The Wall Street Journal* [online] http://online.wsj.com/article/SB10001424052970204624204577177131752006116.html

27 We are searching for our Loved Ones who went missing in Costa Concordia accident [accessed 5 April 2013] *Facebook* [online] www.facebook.com/groups/232027703542759/?fref=ts
Costa Concordia photos and videos to help locate and remember the victims [accessed 5 April 2013] *Facebook* [online] www.facebook.com/groups/313410032042126/?fref=ts

28 Pietchmann, Patti [accessed 8 April 2013] 'Costa and Carnival confirm commitment to support victims of Concordia disaster', *Examiner* [online] www.examiner.com/article/costa-and-carnival-confirm-commitment-to-support-victims-of-concordia-disaster

29 Staff reporter [accessed 5 April 2013] 'Outrage as Costa Concordia survivors are asked to stay away from anniversary event', *Mail Online* [online] www.dailymail.co.uk/travel/article-2260771/Costa-Concordia-anniversary-Survivors-outrage-asked-stay-away-wreck.html

30 Costa Cruises [accessed 5 April 2013] 'Costa Concordia – update' [press release] www.costacruises.co.uk/B2C/GB/Info/concordia_statement.htm

31 Weathers, Helen and Evans, Rebecca [accessed 8 April 2013] 'Captain Coward had his eye on English dancer: After claims he was distracted by a woman on the bridge, passengers and crew reveal Casanova antics of crash skipper', *Mail Online* [online] www.dailymail.co.uk/news/article-2089680/Costa-Concordia-Captain-Coward-Francesco-Schettino-eye-dancer-Domnica-Cemortan.html

32 Staff reporter [accessed 5 April 2013] 'Concordia ship owner seeks victim status in wreck', Associated Press [online] http://news.yahoo.com/concordia-ship-owner-seeks-victim-status-wreck-151425680–finance.html

33 Staff reporter [accessed 5 April 2013] 'Costa battles media onslaught, Concordia scams', *Seatrade Insider* [online] www.seatrade-insider.com/news/costa-concordia/costa-battles-media-onslaught-concordia-scams.html

08
Interrelated risks

Life is not as simple as a four-box matrix. This concluding final chapter of the first half of the book looks at how risks in one category can trigger or escalate risks in another. Figure 8.1 shows how this can happen.

FIGURE 8.1 How risks create/enhance other risks

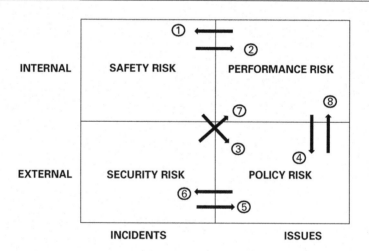

1. An unresolved internal issue leads to internal incident

For example, concern about ageing assets might be seen as an internal issue that needs to be addressed, but if a major incident were to happen involving one of these assets it would potentially create a crisis that goes far beyond the management of the incident. It would show a company that was aware of its safety shortcomings but had failed to address them.

2. An internal incident creates a longer-term internal issue

Similarly, an incident, or series of incidents, although minor in themselves and not deemed crises, could lead to a much longer-term 'perceptions of safety culture' issue for the company. This is arguably what has happened to BP in the United States since 2005 – after incidents including the 2005 Texas City Refinery explosion, the 2006 pipeline leak in Alaska and the 2010 Gulf of Mexico disaster, it is managing a long-term issue about perceptions of its safety processes and culture.

3. An internal incident triggers an external issue

For example, a crisis triggered by a safety incident becomes a major political and societal issue which a wider industry needs to respond to over time. This happens regularly, when plane crashes, oil spills, maritime accidents etc lead to societal/political outrage which then needs to be managed as an issue over time, potentially leading to stringent (and sometimes unnecessary) regulation.

4. An internal issue becomes an external issue

A mismanaged issue could not only lead to a crisis, it could lead to a longer-term externally driven issue that an entire industry must deal with, whilst the original 'offender' remains the poster child. This is what happened to the UK newspaper industry after News International's phone hacking crisis. After enormous external political and societal interest, the entire industry was targeted for regulatory change.

5. An external incident triggers an external issue

This could happen, for example, if a major weather event leads to concerns about general societal (and by extension organizational) preparedness. A riot or uprising that affects an organization could become an externally led NGO or political 'outrage' issue. This is essentially what happened to Anvil Mining when it was accused of helping the army of the Democratic Republic of Congo suppress an uprising.

6. An unresolved external issue leads to an external incident

This scenario may seem entirely beyond the control of the organization, but is a risk nonetheless. Externally driven issues such as labour rights could result in riots or uprisings to which the company would need to respond. Another example would be environmental demonstrations becoming violent.

7. An external incident triggers an internal issue

This happens frequently. Something beyond the company's control happens and, however it is managed, leads to issues being raised about customer contact, information, culture etc. This is what happened to the US electric companies as described in the Chapter 6 case study.

8. An external issue amplifies an internal issue

If a bubbling societal issue puts the spotlight on a particular industry, the first company in the sector to experience a difficult internal issue will be managing it in a context of high scrutiny and cynicism. Now is not a good time to have an internal issue in the banking sector, for example. Trust in the sector is low, and even those issues that might be ranked fairly low down the risk matrix could be the trigger for a crisis.

A crisis on a scale of the Fukushima nuclear disaster in Japan can cut across almost the whole model.

The international fallout of the Fukushima disaster

On 11 March 2011, the most serious nuclear crisis since the 1986 Chernobyl disaster began at the Tepco Fukushima Daiichi nuclear plant. It was only the second disaster in nuclear history to be classified a Level 7 on the international nuclear event scale.[1] When three reactors at the plant went into meltdown following earthquake and tsunami damage, the errors of one company sent shockwaves throughout the global nuclear power industry.

It emerged during the investigation that Fukushima's reactors were not built to withstand earthquakes and resultant tsunamis, due to a design fault that made back-up power systems vulnerable to flooding. Furthermore, Tepco was accused of ignoring earthquake resistance standards revised and issued by the Nuclear Safety Commission in 2006. Neither were reactor checks carried out by the organization to ensure they adhered to the new standards. Such errors brought the issue of nuclear power plant safety into question.

The Fukushima incident ballooned from being a regional single-company problem to becoming a global industry-wide issue. Following the turning tide of public opinion and the growing safety concerns, the global nuclear industry and countries with nuclear power facilities were forced to re-examine the safety of nuclear power. EU Energy Commissioner Gunther Oettinger said in the immediate aftermath: 'Fukushima has made me start to doubt.'[2] Germany took immediate action and on 14 March – just three days after the disaster – closed plants pending a review of plant safety.

India, France, the United Kingdom and the United States all stated that they would review and carry out any necessary upgrades to plant safety. On 30 May 2011, Germany imposed a total ban on new nuclear power plant construction and pledged to decommission all reactors by 2022.[3] Spain and Switzerland have also banned the construction of new plants.

Meanwhile, energy companies are dealing with the consequences of an incident they did not cause. A number of nuclear power developments have been abandoned in light of the Fukushima disaster. In September 2011, Siemens announced its intention to withdraw entirely from the nuclear industry as a response to the Fukushima nuclear disaster. In 2012, German utilities companies E.ON and RWE abandoned the joint Horizon project to build two new plants in the United Kingdom.

Some crises are far too big to fit into a four-box matrix, but the categorization system is nonetheless useful in understanding how in the case of Fukushima the incident became an issue. The trigger was a weather event (external incident) but the scale of the disaster was augmented by the company's own safety performance (internal incident). The investigation led to questions of overall corporate capability and performance (internal issue) and it led to impacts for many organizations across the world when it became an emotive political and societal issue (external issue).

Reputation risks are unpredictable in nature and consequence, so categorization systems provide only guidelines rather than rules. All the categories present their own challenges but, as we shall see in the second half of this book, the basic principles of managing risk through the reputation risk life cycle remain the same.

Notes

1 Process Industry Forum [accessed 23 July 2013] 'Top 10 Nuclear Disasters' [online] http://blog.processindustryforum.com/energy/nucleardisasters/

2 Staff reporter [accessed 23 July 2013] 'Spiegel Interview with Energy Commissioner Oettinger: "Fukushima Has Made Me Start to Doubt"', *Spiegel Online* [online] www.spiegel.de/international/europe/spiegel-interview-with-energy-commissioner-oettinger-fukushima-has-made-me-start-to-doubt-a-754888.html

3 Staff reporter [accessed 23 July 2013] 'Germany: Nuclear power plants to close by 2022', BBC News [online] www.bbc.co.uk/news/world-europe-13592208

09
Managing reputation risk through the life cycle

The first half of this book looked at reputation, the changing external context in which reputations are managed and the various categories of reputation risk that organizations face. The second half looks at how organizations can manage reputation through the life cycle of a risk, from spotting issues on the horizon through to helping the organization recover, change and prosper after a major crisis.

Figure 9.1 shows that, as explained in earlier chapters of this book, crises can come from incidents or issues. Incidents can be *predicted*, actions can be taken to try to *prevent* them and actions can be taken to *prepare* for them. But they still happen. Issues can also be predicted and, sometimes, prevented; they can also be *resolved* through good issues management. However, a trigger can escalate them into a crisis. Whether a crisis is caused by an issue or an incident, it needs *response* at a time when pressure and scrutiny are high. Finally, organizations need to *recover* from a crisis.

The life cycle starts with *predicting* reputation risk. For communications professionals, this is primarily about issues identification; predicting incidents is more the responsibility of the health, safety and security functions. The activities covered under *predict* include:

- **Horizon scanning,** both in the short and long term. This means having a capability in place (process and competence) for understanding where external policy and societal debates and issues are heading and where they might conflict with internal change, developments, policies or practices.

FIGURE 9.1 The risk life cycle

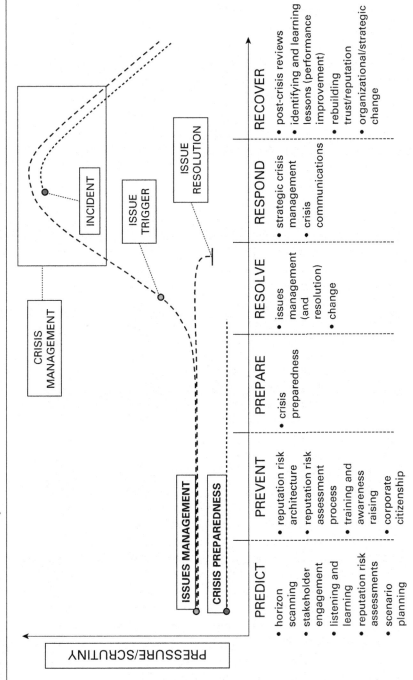

- **Stakeholder engagement,** because the best way to spot what is on the horizon is to have constructive relationships with those stakeholders who initiate or contribute to issues.
- **Listening and learning,** from stakeholders but also from past experience both within the organization and from others in the industry or indeed in other sectors.
- **Reputation risk assessment** to understand, quantify and prioritize issues so that actions can be put in place to address or resolve them.
- **Scenario planning,** taking the identified reputation risks and thinking through in detail how they might develop over time, understanding what will trigger certain scenarios, what might escalate the risk and what the impacts might be were the risks to materialize.

The second stage of the life cycle is *preventing* reputation risk. Again, in terms of incident-led risks, this is headed by Health, Safety, Security and Environment (HSSE) functions. For issue-driven risks, this stage is about interventions and controls that ensure reputation is factored into key decisions, strategies and plans. This is therefore about performance more widely. The best way to prevent issue-driven reputation risks is to have exemplary financial, corporate, environmental and social performance. The activities covered under *prevent* include:

- **Reputation risk architecture,** which is the structure within an organization that ensures reputation risks and opportunities are factored in to key decisions and strategies. This might involve, for example, a reputation risk subcommittee of the board empowered to consider the reputational implications of commercial decisions, and/or a reputation advisory group consisting of internal (executive and non-executive) and external members.
- **Reputation risk assessment process,** standardizing the way in which the organization considers and makes decisions about risks within this architecture.
- **Training and awareness raising,** against standards, policies, codes of conduct etc. This is the 'soft' intervention that sits alongside the 'hard' intervention of compliance, which together help create the right behaviours.
- **Positive initiatives,** such as corporate citizenship. Whilst not necessarily reputation building in and of themselves, such initiatives can help prevent reputation risks by creating a positive, mutually beneficial and listening environment both within the organization and between the organization and the communities and societies in which it operates.

The third stage is *preparing* to face risks. Even the best risk-prevention measures will minimize rather than eliminate risk. All organizations therefore need to be prepared for the worst. Indeed, a company's senior leaders and stakeholders – including board members and investors – should demand assurance from the organization that it is 'ready for anything'. This *prepare* phase includes all crisis preparedness (both general and communications-specific) activities such as:

- **Preparing leaders,** to take a senior role in a crisis.
- **Preparing structure,** to ensure the organization can enter into a crisis modus operandi where decision-making powers and limitations, escalation and roles and responsibilities are documented.
- **Preparing people,** through training and exercises, to fulfil their roles.
- **Preparing procedures,** including useful guidance, tools and templates, that help people fulfil their roles and work as part of a wider response.
- **Building relationships and goodwill,** both of which are invaluable in a crisis.

The fourth phase is *resolving* risks to reputation. This is where communications and other functions need to work closely with the business to manage identified issue-driven risks down a benign curve. The activities included under *resolve* are:

- **Developing and operating an issues management capability,** including structures with clear ownership and processes as well as competence.
- **Devising strategic issues management strategies,** and executing them with the right communications and other actions.
- **Changing.** As described in Chapter 4, issue resolution sometimes requires change, whether in response to something that has been driven externally (societal, political issues) or something that is internal.

The next phase is *responding* to live crises. Whether a sudden incident has struck, or an issue has suddenly escalated, a crisis has been called. The *respond* phase may include incident management, emergency response, business continuity management and other operational responses but, for the purposes of this book, I focus on **crisis management,** at the senior strategic level, and **crisis communications.**

Last, but certainly not least, comes an important but sometimes overlooked aspect of the reputation risk life cycle: *recovering* from a crisis. However deep and intense the crisis, and however long its 'tail', there is always a point at which a senior leader stands the crisis response down. But whilst most of the organization returns to some sort of 'business as usual', the immediate aftermath of a crisis is a crucial time. It is the time that will see the organization rebound – possibly even stronger than before – or struggle to recover reputation, market share and/or share price. This crucial *recovery* phase includes:

- **Post-crisis reviews,** which document how the crisis was managed (and sometimes why the crisis happened in the first place, although this is often treated quite separately for legal reasons).

- **Identifying and learning lessons,** by implementing change to crisis preparedness (structures, processes and training) to ensure that the output of the post-crisis review is taken on board and that the organization is in a better place to manage any future crises.
- **Rebuilding trust,** with both internal and external stakeholders.
- **Changing the organization** more fundamentally. Leaders can use the 'crisis dividend' – the window of opportunity a crisis presents – to achieve wider change in the organization.

The next six chapters look at each of these six phases in greater detail.

10
Predicting reputation risk

Almost every reputation risk is predictable. There are very few issues or incidents that a company can genuinely look back on and say: 'There was absolutely no way of predicting that.' The severity of the risk, the speed at which it develops and the complicating factors associated with it can all be surprising or alarming. The risk itself, however, has usually been thought of by someone, somewhere.

Any organization can compile a simple reputation risk register against all of the four categories explained in Chapters 4 to 7. A consumer goods company can predict, for example, that one day it might face massive disruption from a weather event or act of sabotage (an external incident), a major safety failure at a facility that causes death and injury (an internal incident), a scandal or controversy emanating from behaviours or governance failures (an internal issue), or questions around the environmental sustainability or societal impacts of its products or operations (an external issue). A cross-functional and cross-business team with enough whiteboards could cover a lot of ground on such a reputation risk register fairly swiftly.

A good *predict* capability, however, is more complex. It involves anticipating risks to reputation as early and as completely as possible, understanding how, when and why they might develop, and assessing the impacts they might have on the organization if they develop in certain ways. This assessment must then be factored into the organization's strategic decision-making and operations to prevent the risk from happening, prepare for it, resolve it before it becomes a crisis, or respond to it if prevention and mitigation fail.

Predicting incidents is important. Organizational resilience starts with knowing what could happen of a sudden and potentially catastrophic nature. But predicting major physical or systematic incidents is not something in which the corporate affairs department has a significant role. This is usually led by HSSE.

This chapter therefore focuses on the area where communications professionals have a bigger, often leading, influence: how organizations can predict the emergence, development and impact of issues; whether internally or externally driven. There are three elements to this:

1 **Being a listening and engaging organization** – having a finely tuned reputation risk radar for externally driven issues.
2 **Being reputation-conscious as an organization** – having a similar reputation risk radar for internally driven issues.
3 **Analysing the predicted risk and assessing potential impacts.**

The external reputation risk radar and horizon scanning

If having a finely tuned external risk radar is the objective, then horizon scanning is the capability that delivers it.

Horizon scanning helps an organization to identify emerging strategic, operational and reputation risks/opportunities in the short to medium term. It is primarily an 'outside in' capability which brings developing trends and issues into the organization for consideration, analysis and – importantly – action. Some organizations look further ahead to predict societal, political, economic or other changes that may take place over decades. But the time frame usually associated with horizon scanning is up to one or two years.

As part of a horizon scanning capability, organizations should be constantly monitoring the outside world for information on current or possible issues. They should be monitoring a range of sources, with the media only being the most obvious. Large organizations have many sources, both internally and externally, from which to get this information.

But this should be much more than monitoring: reading source material and sharing interesting articles do not constitute horizon scanning. Monitoring only tells an organization second-hand what others are saying and doing. Hearing directly what others have to say on emerging matters is better. And better still is engaging: talking to stakeholders to encourage a shared understanding of what their, and your, agendas and concerns are. Good stakeholder engagement, therefore, is a prerequisite to good horizon scanning.

'Stakeholder engagement' is an unfortunately ugly piece of corporate-speak, which describes something that is fundamentally important to any organization: listening to, talking to and understanding the people who have an impact on your business. It is a part of good crisis preparedness, as it builds the understanding, goodwill and relationships that are crucial to an organization in time of crisis. When things go wrong, you need friends and support.

It is equally important in managing issues, and indeed managing day-to-day business. Any company knows that if it does not listen to its customers, then its products and services are unlikely to meet with their approval. Similarly, if a company does not listen to its stakeholders – governments, regulators, employees, communities and others – its conduct and decisions (and sometimes by extension its products and services) are unlikely to meet with their approval. Companies need to respond to and manage this stakeholder demand as much as they need to manage customer demand.

Stakeholder engagement helps a company see itself, and the world in which it operates, as others see it. It helps spot issues and opportunities it might not otherwise have identified. It helps companies understand issues as others understand them, develop strategies to address them and, where necessary, change what they do and how they do it.

The communications function is often expected to take a lead in stakeholder engagement, or at least to provide the framework in which stakeholder engagement takes place. But the engagement itself is something that should be taking place across the wider organization: site managers meet with local communities; senior executives meet with politicians; technical experts may be members of professional societies. This is all to be encouraged as just part of doing business.

Horizon scanning therefore draws on an organization's stakeholder relationships and engagements as well as written sources. It also needs to draw on the knowledge and expertise that companies have across businesses, geographies and functions. All of this together represents the 'information in'.

However the information comes in, some structure and process are required to turn it into analysis, predictions and actions. This may seem dangerous – imposing some sort of stakeholder engagement process risks over-engineering what to a certain extent should come naturally – but companies need structure and process to make things happen, to avoid duplication (and in this case the giving of mixed messages) and to share information.

Structure and process, as long as they are easy to navigate and not too onerous, can also give confidence that the organization will listen to the information that is being generated and that somewhere, somehow, this might make a difference. This is where the *predict* stage is best seen in the context of the wider reputation risk management process. 'Information in' is often of a higher quality when there is confidence amongst employees in the organization's ability to assess the information in terms of reputation, commercial and financial impacts (information analysis) and its ability to escalate the information through the organization for action (information up).

The ability to predict reputation risk thus becomes part of a wider organizational capability, requiring the right structure, process, competence, accountability and culture. For example, the organization might have a formal issues management system, one component of which is an issues identification and prioritization tool. The system might require regular meetings to assess new developments, discuss emerging issues, decide whether certain issues are rising up or falling down the stakeholder agenda, assign ownership to issues that are identified as high risk, approve mitigation strategies and check progress towards issue resolution. The information going in to this meeting and the wider system is thus seen as meaningful. It may be a short 'issues update and horizon scan' report, or it might be presentations from topic experts, but at least it provides a forum for the 'information in' to make a difference.

The internal reputation risk radar

Predicting risks to reputation from internal issues is subtly different. Because reputation risk ultimately plays out in the outside world, it still requires knowledge of stakeholder opinion and developments. But the source of the risk is an internal development rather than an external trend. It is the difference between 'How will this action/decision be received by stakeholders?' (internal) and 'What are the issues out there that we are seeing stakeholders focus on?' (external).

There is some crossover. For example, 'access to short-term (and often high-interest) credit for those on low incomes' may be considered an external issue for a financial services provider. The company should be monitoring the issue; analysing the positions certain stakeholders are taking on it; assessing the strength of feeling; looking at other markets to see how similar issues have developed elsewhere; talking to stakeholders to hear their concerns and to discuss the issue in the round. The internal issue equivalent might be 'launch of our payday loan product'. This is a different, and more immediate, route into the same issue and the same reputation risk/opportunity. It could also be seen as an internal 'trigger' for the wider external issue.

The internal risk radar is about reputation self-assessment: having the capability as an organization to predict which key decisions, new products or services, strategies and other courses of action present a reputation risk. In an ideal world, reputational impacts (positive and negative) would be 'in the room' at all levels of the business all of the time, but this is not a realistic aspiration. This is therefore something to which management – and senior management in particular – needs to be finely attuned.

Using the payday loan example above, the key question would be: how early in the development of a new product – which may potentially be commercially very beneficial for the company – should reputation risk be brought into the decision-making process? The wrong answer to that, of course, would be that there is some sort of reputational 'final hurdle' for new products to overcome just before launch. This would leave the people in product development who had worked long and hard developing a new product feeling resentful that the 'reputation police' had intervened at the last minute to reject their hard work. The best answer would be that such a new product idea would never even make it off the flipchart into development because everyone involved instinctively understood that it would present a risk to the reputation of the organization that no senior manager would ever allow to be taken. The truth lies in between, but the role of the communications function should be to push for early reputational thinking wherever possible.

Take another example from another industry: a chemicals company develops a new material that protects fabrics against wear and tear and which will have multiple consumer product uses. The process for creating it, however, is highly energy intensive. The company predicts that this may become a reputation risk given its recent efforts to boost its green credentials and the similar needs of its customers, the companies who would buy the product to turn it into consumer products. The challenge here is more nuanced. The company has created – or believes it can create – something that is potentially of huge benefit to the end consumer, by giving longer life to everyday products. It is something that allows its customers to make more durable products for their consumers. The invention may be transformational in its financial benefits for the company, but it may be seen as an unacceptable development for stakeholders concerned about energy intensive industry.

What does this mean for early internal risk identification? Does early prediction risk stifling a culture of innovation? Does the possibility of having an innovation 'spiked' because of possible reputation risk mean that product developers or strategists are in fact more likely to keep their ideas under wraps until, perhaps, they have gone so far down the development road that it would be perceived as too costly and destructive to turn back?

The key to answering these problems is trust. Throughout the organization, people need to trust that there are mechanisms for considering reputation risk alongside other risks and benefits. This requires some 'soft' and 'hard' interventions:

- **Process** that helps put reputation on the agenda of early stage product development or strategy meetings.
- A **structure** that allows predicted risks to be escalated quickly and which people trust will fairly balance all the commercial, financial and reputational risks and benefits of the course of action.
- **Competence** of people who are tasked with predicting the risks and helping make the decisions.
- A **culture** which values reputation and encourages reputation red flags being raised.

This is the beginnings of a reputation risk infrastructure that Chapter 11 looks at in more detail.

Some companies are purposefully 'disruptive' in their product development, and create reputation risk through the innovation that drives them. Google, for example, has invented many new products and ideas that are controversial by their very nature. Google Streetmaps and Google Glass, which were both launched amidst concerns about privacy, presented the company with issues to manage. But nobody inside or even outside the company would want these ideas stifled by over-exuberant reputation risk thinking. Google's philosophy is that it develops the ideas and lets society debate their merits and the safeguards required in adoption. This may work for a technology company, but is not so easy in other industries.

Analysing risk

Predicting that something could happen is fairly meaningless unless it is accompanied by an assessment of what it would mean if it did happen. To use one of the examples above, the chemical company would doubtless want to understand in some considerable detail the potential impacts – financial and commercial – of the reputation risk associated with its new invention so that it can weigh these up against the clear commercial benefits.

Scenario planning, now a standard part of crisis and issues management, is also a useful exercise in the early stages of the reputation risk life cycle. Once a risk is predicted, it helps develop the assessment of the risk. It can be done as a workshop or as analytical deskwork. There are various ways of conducting a scenario planning exercise, but the outcome should be the same for each: an understanding of what it would look and feel like for the company if a risk develops in a certain way, and what the impacts of this would be.

Scenario planning

The model I have developed for scenario planning is a variation on the familiar bow-tie model. See Figure 10.1.

The model shows the triggers and escalating factors which could lead to a scenario (in this case, the 'worst-case scenario'). It then shows the possible impacts that this worst-case scenario could have on the organization. The model suggests action: triggers must be mitigated (or resolved) and the impacts must be prepared for.

In a scenario-planning workshop, looking at a worst-case scenario, for instance, this model is best used as follows:

1 Be very clear about the *subject area* to be covered. Is this scenario planning for a particular course of action or decision, for the effects of something that has already happened or been decided, or for a developing external issue?

2 Discuss and agree the *worst-case scenario*. In a reputation risk context, the workshop is usually convened with a negative mindset, so it is best to draw out participants' worries and concerns from the start. If this got really bad, participants should be asked, 'What might that look and feel like?' Often, at this point, people start to contribute

FIGURE 10.1 Scenario planning model

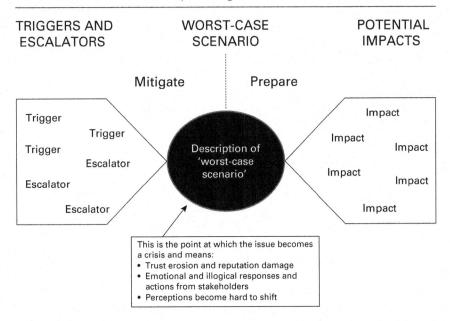

triggers or impacts. 'There may be a consumer death' may be tragic, but the death is a trigger rather than a scenario. It is best to park these triggers for now. Similarly, 'Sales of other products may fall' is an impact. The worst-case scenario should be a statement such as 'The company name, as well as the product, is embroiled in a high-profile product disaster.'

3 Discuss the *impacts*. Whilst the worst-case scenario might sound bad enough in itself, it is important to think through what that could actually mean for the company. This is the impacts conversation. If the company was, and was seen to be, in this worst-case situation, what would be the consequences on its operations, business, share price, relationships etc? The impacts identified might be, for example: sales of other products suffer; new contract X might be impacted; the decision to Y might have to be revisited; senior management in Z operation might be vulnerable; new regulation might be proposed; the wider corporate strategy might be called into question etc. It is important in this part of the conversation that participants focus on impacts that are 'realistically bad' rather than completely catastrophic. For instance, 'The company goes into administration and we all lose our jobs' is not necessarily helpful as an impact in a scenario planning session like this.

4 Next, the *triggers* parked earlier should be discussed. Triggers are the events that could, either independently or more likely in association with other triggers or escalating factors, lead to the worst-case scenario, unless they are avoided or mitigated.

5 Finally come the *escalators*. These are the factors that can multiply the effects of the triggers. This is a useful conversation to have separately as it helps to explain the 'perfect storm': the mix of events that turns what may seem like a minor trigger event into a major reputation-threatening scenario.

If the scenario planning is part of a wider issues strategy workshop, the discussion should then move to answering questions such as:

- What can we do to avoid or manage (prevent and/or resolve) these triggers?

- How can we ensure we become aware of escalating factors that may evolve?

- Can we quantify the cost of the worst-case scenario and the potential impacts?

- How could we manage the impacts to minimize this cost (being ready to respond)?

Prevention, resolution and response are covered in later chapters.

Figure 10.2 envisages (in fairly basic form) how the scenario plan might look for the fictional chemical company issue already used in this chapter.

The model can also be used to generate a best-case scenario. This is particularly helpful when, as with our fictional chemical company, there is a clear potential win from the course of action under consideration or the

FIGURE 10.2 Chemical company 'worst-case' scenario

FIGURE 10.3 Chemical company 'best-case' scenario

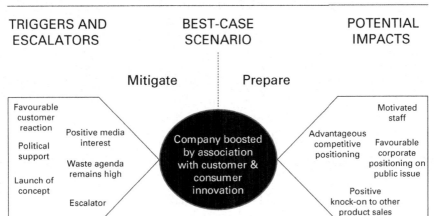

developing external issue. The best-case scenario essentially becomes the issue management objective.

Figure 10.3 is the 'best-case scenario' for the chemical company.

Scenario planning is sometimes a stand-alone activity, but more often is part of a wider reputation risk assessment process. Many corporate decisions are worthy of a reputation risk assessment of some description, and many organizations have reputation risk infrastructure to help bring reputation risk to the table at the right time in the right way. The communications function is often involved in developing the assessment.

Organizations mature in reputation risk have standard processes and templates for use across businesses or geographies, helping those tasked with carrying out the reputation risk assessment to present something familiar and comparable. The guide below is the basic structure I recommend using, whether the end product is a 100-page reputation risk analysis of a major global strategic move or a 10-slide presentation on an early idea.

Reputation risk assessment

1 The **introduction** should be a simple explanation of what the reputation risk assessment is for and how it should be used. As with scenario planning, it is important to set this out so there is no confusion about what is, and is not, in scope. It is also recommended to set out the opportunity early on so there is a shared understanding that the course of action is potentially a very positive one, commercially if not reputationally.

For example: 'The business is considering investing in a new joint venture in Country X with local Company Y. The new arrangement will bring us access to an important developing market with an emerging middle class able and keen to buy our products; it will also start a new relationship with Company Y, which adds potential value to our wider portfolio. As well as these commercial benefits, it is recognized that the strategy to enter this market and enter a Joint Venture (JV) with this company may bring reputation risk in the short, medium and long term. This assessment looks in detail at the reputation risks and opportunities attached to this particular course of action. It will feed into the overall decision-making about the commercial, financial and reputational risks and benefits of the opportunity.'

2 Next, the **context** should set the external scene in which this risk should be considered. It explains stakeholder and public positioning, the nature of the debate, the link issues it touches upon etc. For non-communications audiences this is usually the most illuminating part of the reputation risk assessment, and therefore the most detailed. Aspects of this section are:

● An analysis of the debate (or debates) as it currently stands externally. How high up the agenda is it? Is the public interested, or is it a limited-audience debate? Is it international? Does it play out differently in different markets?

● An assessment of how the debate might develop (independent of the organization's decision).

● An assessment of stakeholder interest – perhaps in the form of the familiar interest/influence and/or interest/stance stakeholder matrix. Who is interested? Why? How high is it on their agenda? Are they engaging on it? With whom? Where do our competitors/peers stand? This is where stakeholder mapping comes in: showing how different stakeholders interact and influence each other on a particular issue.

● An overview of short- and long-term milestones: potential flashpoints in the issue/controversy that might affect the company's strategy.

● Comparison with similar issues that the organization or others may have faced in the past, how they played out and how they were managed. This is often helpful, as it brings to life through examples something that at this stage seems theoretical.

3 An outline of the **reputation opportunity** should come next. Although this document is usually commissioned in the context of a negative ('we know this will be controversial; can you help us understand just what that might mean'), there is almost always some potentially positive reputational impact, however small. It is worth starting with

this to ensure reputation is not just seen as the negative part of the equation, stacked up against the commercial and financial positives. In the new market entry and new JV example, this might include: 'This decision is an opportunity to demonstrate our commitment to getting high-quality products to a wider number of people; it is a good example of a company creating jobs and wealth through international opportunity.'

4 The **reputation risk register** is the heart of the assessment. Often presented in a spreadsheet, this is the long list of things that could happen with reputational consequence if the company were to go ahead with the proposed course of action. It shows primarily what might be perceived and what stakeholders might say or do at different stages. The spreadsheet or list may contain some sort of scoring mechanism to show the highest risks in terms of impact or likelihood.

5 The **scenario planning** section may be in the same format as that recommended earlier in this chapter, covering the short, medium and long term. Using the same market entry/JV example, this might include:

- Short term – risks associated when the decision is announced, such as: becoming the poster child for a volatile issue, thereby giving NGOs and media a new hook to discuss a developing controversy; unexpectedly negative customer, stakeholder and/or political reaction.

- Medium term – risks associated with gaining formal and societal approvals to enter the market and set up the JV, such as: public opposition in and outside the market putting pressure on an immature regulatory regime; legal challenge; media campaign.

- Long term – risks associated with long-term operations (safety, environmental and social performance and consequences of failure) and with possible future actions of the host market or the JV partner.

Remember that the 'impacts' aspect of the scenario planning is an opportunity to join up the reputational and the commercial/financial risks and opportunities. Something that has a reputation impact leads to other impacts, such as customer choice or other stakeholder action.

6 The **reputation strategy** section starts the conversation about how the identified reputation risks can be mitigated. Although in the context of this book we are still in the *predict* phase rather than *resolve* or *respond* phases of reputation risk management, reputation risk assessments are, in my view, incomplete without at least initial thoughts on how the risks would be mitigated or managed. Senior decision-makers need to understand the risk, but also consider whether they have confidence in their organization's ability to manage that

risk down a benign curve or respond to a sudden escalation. This is a core requirement in answering the question: 'Is this a risk worth taking?' Risks that are high, but are still seen to be manageable through a competent team delivering a reputation strategy, may still be risks worth taking.

7 Finally, the **reputation risk assessment**. It is rarely appropriate for this document to make a firm recommendation on a go/no go decision, but a clear summary – perhaps with an overall reputation risk rating – will help decision-makers. For example: 'This assessment concludes that the reputation risk of entering Country X is Medium, and that doing so through a JV with Company Y pushes the risk to Medium/ High. There are, however, clear opportunities to manage this risk successfully, at least in the short term. The debate about Country X is fluid, with many stakeholders seemingly supportive of bringing it into the international community. Negative sentiment towards Company Y is softening. What remains clear is that Country X will be a reputationally risky place to do business for the foreseeable future.'

Lessons from the past

Part of reputation risk assessment involves understanding lessons from the past. This chapter started with the contention that 'almost every risk is predictable'. This is largely because almost everything has happened before, in one form or another. True, every situation is unique and has its own combination of context, facts and interested parties to make it so, but there are usually fairly direct comparisons that can be drawn between any new challenge that presents itself and challenges faced by your organization or others in the past.

When companies see other organizations – even their fierce competitors – go through incident-driven crises, there is usually a sense of 'There but for the grace of God go we.' There is humility and empathy, and sometimes there may be ways in which the company provides support to its peer or competitor as it responds to the crisis. When a company sees a competitor going through an issue-driven crisis, the temptation may be to delight in the competitor's fall from grace and to reap the benefits of the commercial impacts of the crisis. The first questions to ask, though, should be: Could this happen to us? What products/services of ours could suffer a similar fate? Could protestors/consumers/stakeholders turn their fire at us?

There is always the danger that a company will say: 'We run our business better than they do theirs' and, of course, a company wants its employees to have a sense of pride in its people, services and products. But leaders should look at issues that others are experiencing and consider internal studies into their own resilience: Are we doing everything we can to prevent that from happening to us? Could we resolve the issue better than (or as well as) they did? As an example, it is unlikely that many companies currently paying negligible UK tax are rejoicing in the controversy being managed by Starbucks, Google, Amazon and others. More likely, they are turning their energies to their own tax arrangements and thinking about how they can prevent or resolve this issue before reputation risk comes to them.

Learning from the internal past is often as hard as learning lessons from elsewhere. Keeping experiences in the corporate memory is difficult as people move on or up. It is not unusual to see almost carbon-copy issues developing: the same issues emerging in the same part of the same company, with the response seemingly not drawing on the lessons learned from the previous experience. This is why it is so important for every major issue or crisis to have a formal 'lessons learned' exercise afterwards, something to which I return in Chapter 15.

Companies need to spend more time remembering what has happened to them or others before. As an example, the ongoing debate about the risks and benefits of fracking (hydraulic fracturing) is very similar to the debate about genetically modified (GM) foods which reached its peak in the mid-1990s.

Will fracking succeed where GM failed?

The merits and risks of 'fracking' – the technology used to extract gas and oil from shale – are one of the major industry/society debates to emerge in recent years. Similar to other debates such as climate change, obesity and globalization, fracking is a highly politicized issue in which industry, NGOs, politicians, regulators and society at large all have a voice and interest. Whilst it is a relatively new issue, it is following a very familiar path.

In the mid-1990s, GM foods were being hailed as a breakthrough technology with the potential to solve world hunger. Stock in Monsanto, the agriculture and biotechnology company at the forefront of GM technology was high. Although some international NGOs, such as Greenpeace and Friends of the Earth, had expressed concerns over GM foods, their campaigns had gained little traction in the United States.

When Monsanto sought to expand into Europe, however, it encountered a backlash it had not predicted and was not prepared for. A debate that Monsanto had hoped would be about eradicating famines became one about 'playing God' with nature and creating 'Frankenstein foods'. It was a classic failure of risk communication and strategic issues management. Political support, which had started strongly, dissipated quickly. Sensing the prevailing public mood, thanks in large part to an orchestrated media campaign and NGO activism, food manufacturers and retailers also withdrew support.

Nearly 20 years later, genetic modification remains highly controversial in Europe, and only two EU-grown GM products are approved for human consumption. In February 2012, German chemical giant BASF announced it was moving its plant biotechnology activities from Germany to the United States, blaming a lack of political and consumer acceptance for GM in Europe.[1] Monsanto, the company that became almost a household name (for the wrong reasons) in the 1990s, announced in July 2013 that it was scrapping attempts to win approval to grow new types of GM crops in the EU.[2]

In the last few years, advances in extracting gas and oil from shale have been revolutionary in the United States, turning the country from an importer of natural gas to a potential exporter in a matter of years, bringing down energy prices and stimulating the economies of many states. The technology for extracting energy from shale formations is known as 'hydraulic fracturing' (or 'fracking'). It is not new; the energy industry has been fracturing rock to access energy sources for decades, but is being applied in a new way. The benefits – energy security and wealth creation – are self-evident. And there are substantial shale gas reserves in Europe.

Concerns have been raised – on both sides of the Atlantic and indeed elsewhere – over the potential public health and environmental impacts of fracking. (This is a term I imagine the industry wishes, in retrospect, it had moved away from when it could. Whilst the industry always preferred the softer 'fraccing', campaigners understandably changed the spelling, and groups with media-friendly names and slogans such as 'Frack Off' were born). A documentary film, *Gasland*, which became famous for scenes in which householders' water taps could apparently be set ablaze, supposedly due to gas in the aquifer, was nominated for an Academy Award in 2010. A feature film, *Promised Land*, starring Matt Damon and following the familiar formula of 'big company versus local community', was released in 2012.

In the United Kingdom, shale gas was a highly salient political issue for some months after earth tremors were recorded between April and May 2011 in Lancashire, the only region in the United Kingdom where test drilling was taking place. A report published in November 2011 found that fracking for shale gas was the 'likely cause' of the tremors.[3]

Although arising in very different sectors, there are clear similarities between these two issues. Both are a new application of an existing technology; both are positioned as solutions to major problems; both have attracted concerns about risk to the environment and health; both were received (reasonably) well in the United States, before making the move to Europe. What specific lessons can and should the fracking industry take from the GM foods issue of 20 years ago?

Lesson 1: what works in one market might play differently in another

The first lesson is about corporate awareness of differences in the political and societal context. Monsanto was, it seems, not aware that European consumers (and their elected representatives) are far more suspicious of sudden leaps of progress than Americans, especially when the proponents are big US corporations. The United States, with its vast plains of agricultural production, had a different attitude to food 'progress' than Europe, home of the subsidy to small farmers and the Common Agricultural Policy. Europe had at the time experienced a number of food-related health scares, and food safety was high on the political agenda. The industry failed to address these fears in its communication strategy. A Deutsche Bank report to investors put it surprisingly bluntly: 'Hearing from unsophisticated Americans that their fears are unfounded may not be the best way of proceeding.'[4]

Similarly, in the United States, the shale revolution has been primarily welcomed as progress – an all-American solution to the problem of importing energy from unstable regimes. Much of the shale gas being developed in the United States is in states suffering from the post-2008 recession; the resulting job creation was more than welcomed at state and, later, federal levels.

Crucially, the United States has space, whilst European countries have much denser populations and planning regimes that empower local authorities. In the United States, surface landowners also have rights over the resources found beneath their land, whereas this is not the case in Europe, where rights are exercised by central government. Landowners therefore do not have the same incentive to invite explorers on to their properties.

Lesson 2: on perceived environmental risks, you need to understand how NGOs work

The GM foods issue was a perceived food safety and environmental impact issue, but there were also strong anti-corporate undertones. Many people were genuinely concerned about the environmental effects, but the strength of ill-feeling towards Monsanto in particular reflected a resentment of wealthy American corporates making money from tampering with nature.

Activist NGOs habitually use 'Trojans' – arguments that are designed to whip up public outcry – to win their debates when their own agendas are somewhat different. This is even more the case with fracking. Most national or international NGOs in Europe are opposed to fracking fundamentally because it is a method of extracting fossil fuel, which they believe deflects attention from the need to switch to renewables. But this argument is not a winning one in tough economic times. So the arguments they use to generate negative public perceptions are more basic: fracking causes earthquakes; fracking pollutes water supplies; fracking is visually intrusive etc. Focusing on localized risks provokes outrage and weakens the chances of industry winning the all-important 'public acceptance'. Without public acceptance, projects will struggle to gain the necessary permissions and face delays, policymakers will come under pressure to oppose fracking and investors' patience will be tested.

Lesson 3: concerns need to be heard and addressed head-on

At the start of the attempted introduction of GM foods to Europe, there was a sense from its supporters that the perceived benefit of the technology was enough to override what they believed to be unfounded concerns. This was 'hero' technology. Safety and responsibility, whilst of course not completely overlooked, were not part of the early proactive communication campaign. A failure to listen and respond to public concerns meant fears went uncalmed and safety allegations unanswered. Monsanto's US Chairman, Bob Shapiro, encapsulated this by saying later: 'Because we thought it was our job to persuade, too often we have forgotten to listen.'[5]

This lesson has clearly been learned by shale gas explorers. There is recognition that developing and espousing best safety practice as a priority message protects the reputation of the industry. In the United States, Shell, Chevron and Consol Energy have joined forces with the US Environmental Defense Fund and the Clean Air Task Force to create the Center for Sustainable Shale Development. It aims to set standards for shale gas performance, monitored by independent consultants. Producers will be able to apply for certification. Although it is currently limited to the Appalachia region, the organization aims to promote 'rational dialogue' at a national level.[6] In the United Kingdom, trade body the Onshore Operators Group (UKOOG) recently issued 'UK Onshore Shale Gas Well Guidelines' setting out best practice.[7] And industry is encouraging the creation of sensible regulation. Regulation is a good thing when novel technologies are being considered: public confidence in a sound regulatory regime helps to manage concerns.

Lesson 4: a coalition of support must be built with the value chain and government

Although many governments, notably in the United Kingdom, were initially supportive of the GM foods industry, they were ultimately forced to reverse their positions due to the adverse public reaction. When political support started to ebb, so did the support of retailers and food manufacturers. Monsanto and others had failed to create a strong coalition of support. A number of top European food manufacturers and retailers – including Unilever, Nestlé, Tesco and McDonald's – pledged that their products would become 'GM-free' over the course of 1999.[8]

Proponents of fracking seem to have identified this lesson too. The industry in Europe has notably slowed its pace – in operations and communications – essentially inviting politicians to take the lead, which they are starting to do for all the aforementioned reasons (such as energy security and economic development). In July 2013, the UK government proposed tax breaks for firms involved in the shale gas industry. Chancellor of the Exchequer, George Osborne, speaking about the tax cut, said that he wanted 'Britain to be a leader of the shale gas revolution'.[9] The UK government is also leading on community acceptance. The newly unveiled Department of Energy and Climate Change (DECC) community incentives package outlines an engagement charter to foster communication between communities and industries and introduces the concept of financial community incentives.[10] But not all governments are leading the way: 'As long as I am president, there will be no exploration for shale gas in France,' President Hollande told French television in July 2013.[11]

But, setbacks aside, in introducing a 'new' technology with major benefits but perceived risk, the shale gas industry has at least recognized it needs to be 'joined at the hip' with governments.

Lesson 5: there must be a positive case, well made

There was a very strong case for GM foods, and there still is. Improving crop yield in developing countries and helping to solve hunger are a pretty good message. But it was not well made. Many positive messages that could have been better promoted, such as the potential cut in pesticide use of one million gallons per year, went practically unnoticed. The agenda of the debate was elsewhere: on risk, corporate profit and environmental damage.

The positive case for shale gas extraction is being well made, and crucially not just by the companies involved or their trade associations. A coalition of political and academic support is growing, but there is a way to go yet. The 'shale debate' is currently nascent and fragmented: nascent because shale gas is at such a formative stage in terms of its potential contribution to the global energy mix (outside the United States); fragmented because there is no single argument that has become the core 'battleground' for opposing views. This presents the opportunity for the shale gas operators and advocates to address public concerns proactively, and to frame the debate in positive terms. As the case of GM food shows, once the debate has become polarized, a technology is viewed as 'toxic', and trust in the industry is eroded, it becomes difficult for companies or governments to address concerns and make the positive case. For now, it is still a debate that can be shaped, and won, by proponents.

Who's learning from whom?

The sheer length of time that the GM industry has been out of favour in Europe is a lesson to any industry looking to introduce a technology that is, or is perceived to be, new. The shale industry knows it needs to tread carefully, and has seemingly learned lessons from the past. But the reception it received is (was) entirely predictable, and the battles ahead will follow patterns similar not only to GM foods but to other industries too.

In June 2013, the UK Prime Minister David Cameron said in a speech: 'It is time to look again at the whole issue for GM food. We need to be open to arguments from science.'[12] It is nearly 20 years since the controversy peaked; 20 years of waiting for the issue to be sufficiently 'detoxified' for such a senior endorsement. Proponents of GM foods have another shot at convincing Europe. The shale industry is learning the lessons from the past and, whilst there are many bumps in the road ahead, is in a much better position. Perhaps the question now is: Will the GM food industry learn the lessons of the shale gas 'revolution'?

Chapter summary

Predicting reputation risk, and having the ability to assess how it could develop and impact an organization, is the first part of good reputation risk decision-making and management.

The key lessons from this chapter are:

- The communications function has a significant coordinating or leading role to play in predicting and assessing the potential impacts of issue-based reputation risks.

- Large organizations have many internal and external sources from which to get good information; having the capability to turn this 'information in' into useable analysis of reputation risk is the key to good horizon scanning.

- Stakeholder engagement – listening to and understanding stakeholders – is a prerequisite to good horizon scanning. It is better to engage with stakeholders directly rather than just read about their views in the media.

- In addition to the external reputation risk radar (horizon scanning), organizations should have an internal reputation risk radar to identify and assess the possible reputational consequences of decisions, launches, strategies or other courses of action.

- Scenario planning – whether undertaken as a workshop or deskwork – helps develop the assessment of an identified reputation risk, whether it is an internally or externally driven issue.

- A full reputation risk assessment ensures the reputation lens is applied to identified risks; it should include a recommended reputation strategy to show how identified and assessed risk can be mitigated. Risks that are high but are still seen to be manageable through a competent team delivering a reputation strategy may still be worth taking.

- As very few reputation risks are entirely new, organizations must learn the lessons from the past – both from within their organization and from peers/competitors. As with the shale gas case study, it is one thing to identify lessons, another to learn them and to manage issues accordingly.

As we shall see in chapters to come, predicting and assessing reputation risk need to be part of a wider infrastructure that provides confidence that what is predicted and analysed can be prevented or resolved.

Notes

1 Trager, Rebecca [accessed 18 April 2013] 'BASF pulls out of Europe over GM hostility', *Royal Society of Chemistry* [online] www.rsc.org/chemistryworld/ News/2012/January/basf-pull-out-gm-crops-biotech.asp

2 Staff reporter [accessed 17 April 2013] 'Monsanto drops GM crop plan in EU', BBC News [online] www.bbc.co.uk/news/business-23356054

3 Staff reporter [accessed 17 April 2013] 'Fracking tests near Blackpool "likely cause" of tremors', BBC News [online] www.bbc.co.uk/news/uk-england-lancashire-15550458

4 Brown, Alex [accessed 17 April 2013] 'DuPont Ag Biotech: Thanks, But No Thanks?', *Deutsche Bank* [pdf] www.biotech-info.net/Deutsche.pdf

5 Vidal, John [accessed 18 April 2013] 'We forgot to listen, says Monsanto', *The Guardian* [online] www.theguardian.com/science/1999/oct/07/gm.food

6 Crooks, Ed (20 March 2013) 'Energy groups address US fracking fears', *Financial Times* [online] www.ft.com/cms/s/0/c8209ae2-91ab-11e2-b839-00144feabdc0.html#axzz2elxtMIf3

7 United Kingdom Onshore Operators Group (UKOOG), *UK Onshore Shale Gas Well Guidelines: Exploration and appraisal phase* [pdf] www.gov.uk/government/uploads/system/uploads/attachment_data/file/185935/UKOOGShaleGasWellGuidelines.pdf

8 National Centre for Biotechnology Education Genetically-modified food [accessed 18 April 2013] 'What *was* in the shops?', *University of Reading* [online] www.ncbe.reading.ac.uk/ncbe/gmfood/shops.html

9 Staff reporter [accessed 19 July 2013] '"Generous" tax breaks for shale gas industry outlined', BBC News [online] www.bbc.co.uk/news/business-23368505

10 Regester Larkin Energy (July 2013) *The Shale Report*, London: Regester Larkin

11 Staff reporter [accessed 15 July 2013] 'Shale gas ban in France to remain, says Hollande', BBC News [online] www.bbc.co.uk/news/business-23311963

12 Hope, Christopher [accessed 14 June 2013] 'David Cameron: It is time to look again at GM food', *The Telegraph* [online] www.telegraph.co.uk/news/worldnews/g8/10121599/David-Cameron-It-is-time-to-look-again-at-GM-food.html

11
Preventing reputation risk

Only a minority of reputation risks that have been predicted and assessed can then be entirely prevented.

Internal incidents cannot be eliminated from the risk register. Although 'zero harm' should certainly be the safety goal of any organization, accidents can and do happen as a result of process safety failures (mechanical or operational fault) and personal safety failures (human error or negligence). For some organizations there is an upside to safety risk management: contractors to global companies (such as rig operators in the oil industry) seek competitive advantage from their safety performance. But good safety practice can only minimize, rather than prevent, the occurrence of internal incidents and the reputational damage they can cause.

External incidents cannot be prevented. Organizations cannot control the weather, and have no control over political or social disturbances in which they get caught up. They can, of course, have excellent vigilance for possible terror or other attacks. But, as occasional tragic events show, some of those intent on causing harm or disruption will succeed.

For both categories of incident, the task of risk minimization lies with operational experts in the health, safety, security and environment department(s). Whilst everyone in an organization should take responsibility for safety and vigilance, the communications function has no special role here.

External issues cannot be prevented as, by definition, they arise from external stakeholders such as NGOs and politicians. The reputation risks associated with them can be managed through excellence in predicting, assessing and resolving issues. Theoretically, an external issue could be spotted so far on the horizon that swift action or change could essentially prevent the issue becoming a risk. Whilst this is rare, it is certainly true that the earlier an external risk is predicted, the easier it is to manage down a benign curve, or even to turn it into competitive advantage. This is covered in Chapter 13 on issue resolution.

That leaves risks deriving from *internal issues*. As we saw in Chapter 5, internal issues can come from a range of sources but, for the purposes of this chapter, this can be simplified to 1) poor performance and 2) bad decisions.

In terms of performance, if all employees of an organization were performing to an exemplary standard, demonstrating the right attitudes and behaviours at all times and making no mistakes, then the majority of internal issues would be prevented. But this is an objective that can never be reached, despite all the codes of ethics and standards to which employees are required to adhere and despite the compliance and audit functions set up to implement, monitor, police and improve them. In decision-making, despite the declarations by senior leaders about how important reputation is to their organization, good businesses still make bad reputation decisions.

The focus of this chapter is on what interventions can prevent bad reputation decisions. Or, to express it more positively, what can be done to encourage good reputation-conscious critical decision-making throughout an organization? This is usually about not doing, rather than doing, something. Once a certain course of action – however commercially beneficial – has been identified as a reputation risk and the potential impact has been assessed as high, it can be stopped in its tracks: do not launch the product, do not approve the campaign, do not enter the market, do not sign the contract. This is classic risk avoidance.

It is rarely this black and white, however. Reputation is important but it cannot, and must not, be a complete block to progress or to hard decisions that need to be taken for the right reasons. An organization that needs to restructure should do so if it is the right thing to do, whether or not reputation damage is a probable or possible consequence. An organization that knows its new innovation will meet with some controversy and opposition should go ahead if it feels, on balance, that the reputation risk is worth taking for the greater good of the company, its customers and society.

These are consciously made reputation risk choices. The problem arises when decisions do not have the reputation lens applied early or thoroughly enough, or at all. This is usually because the correct reputation risk structure and controls are either missing or not properly functioning. But it can also be because the emotional or 'soft' interventions are missing, or the culture in which decisions are made is not sufficiently sensitive to reputation.

With this in mind, this chapter on reputation risk prevention covers:

- **Reputation risk architecture and process.** This is the 'hard' or 'rational' intervention: the structures and controls within an organization that ensure a reputation lens is applied to key decisions and strategies.

- **Reputation awareness, leadership and training.** This is the 'soft' intervention to encourage the right attitudes and behaviours required in an organization for implementing the reputation risk process and performing to high standards.

- **Corporate citizenship.** Because 'good' companies tend to manage reputation better than 'bad' ones, this section also looks at citizenship as a concept that, if properly understood and implemented, can help create an environment in which reputation risk can in theory be prevented.

Reputation risk architecture – 'hard' intervention

A risk management initiative is deemed to be successful if the likelihood and consequence of the risks are affected (ie they are prevented or mitigated) and/or better strategic decisions are made. The same is true of reputation risks.

Reputation risk architecture refers to the internal structures, escalation procedures, processes, roles and responsibilities that together, when functioning well, ensure that a reputation lens is applied to key corporate decisions at appropriate levels.

Whilst it needs to be proportionate to the size and nature of the organization (a mid-size professional services firm may convene an occasional Reputation Council to consider client or conflict issues, whereas a multinational mining company may have a complex structure across its businesses, functions and geographies), most medium or large companies should have some sort of formal architecture in which reputation risks are considered. The following are typical roles and responsibilities of different bodies at different levels, escalating from the bottom up.

Individual decision-makers

The primary responsibility for assessing reputation risk associated with key decisions rests with the individual decision-makers in the business, geography or function. It is they who are closest to the decision, and it is therefore their responsibility to identify and assess any risk attached to it. They may be able to avoid or accept the risk at this point, or they may decide that it should be escalated through the structure. They should have access to guidance (both written and through training) on how to exercise their judgement in this regard. It is important to stress that here, and through the rest of the architecture, it is unlikely that the reputation decision will be black and white. There may be reputation upsides and downsides (with different audiences) to consider. But usually the positive decision to go ahead with a certain course of action will be reputationally more risky.

Business/function committee

The first escalation beyond an individual decision-maker is most likely to a reputation risk committee at a business, functional or geographic level.

This may be a committee that meets on a regular (say, quarterly) basis with a set agenda, or it may be more ad hoc. If it meets on a regular basis, it may also have the responsibility for building a reputation-risk-aware culture. It is likely, in fact, that this committee exists for wider purposes and reputation risk represents an additional (but important and permanent) agenda item. If it is an ad hoc committee, however, it should have 'permanent members' to ensure that, when it does meet, there is some continuity of conduct and treatment of risk. Either way, the committee should have a 'Terms of Reference' document and should produce minutes of decisions taken and judgements associated with those decisions. If the committee decides that the risk needs escalation, it may have some leeway within the architecture to decide where the decision goes next. It may be appropriate to take further soundings, or it may be appropriate to escalate straight to the next level within the structure.

Organization-wide reputation risk management committee

Depending on the size of the organization, there may be a committee (specifically dedicated to reputation risk, or convened to discuss wider risks and cross-business matters) that exists to join up operational level managers before further escalation to senior executives. This will bring valuable cross-organizational thinking into something that, until this point, has escalated through one part of the organization only. If the risk makes it this far through the structure, it clearly has some momentum: the biggest blocker to appropriate consideration of reputation risk is often the attention and scrutiny that come with inviting other parts of the organization to participate in a decision that has thus far remained within a silo.

Reputation Council

The next escalation is to some form of executive-level Reputation Council, which is likely to be a subcommittee of the organization's Executive Committee (ExCo) or at least will operate under its auspices. In organizations that do not have the organization-wide reputation risk management committee as described above, this body will perform the joining function between units. But it will also have more senior responsibilities, including setting, improving and monitoring the effectiveness of the reputation risk architecture and processes. In many cases, the Reputation Council will make the final decision on risks referred to them, including taking the ultimate risk prevention decision. The Reputation Council will report its decisions and justifications to the ExCo and, if appropriate, the board or a sub-committee of the board. If it remains undecided, or wants its decision to be actively ratified by a higher body, then the final escalation takes place.

The board and/or ExCo

These two bodies can be considered together as, if a decision on a reputation risk has reached these heights, it is likely that both the ExCo and the board will become aware and have some involvement. Integrating reputation risk management, and risk management generally, into the culture and everyday operation of the organization requires leadership, commitment and clarity of accountability from the top of the organization. The board of a plc has overall responsibility for risk management, and reputation should be incorporated into this role as a regular part of the agenda. The board's role should be to ensure reputation risk management is embedded into all processes and activities. If a particular risk decision has escalated this far, the board has ultimate authority to make a decision. In practice, the board is likely to rely heavily on the advice and briefing of the ExCo and/or its Reputation Council.

External reputation advisory group

Finally, and usually separately from the formal architecture, there may be an advisory group that has been established to discuss reputation matters or risks. This group will often comprise board members together with external experts or stakeholders. The role of this advisory group will rarely be to participate in go/no go decisions on matters where reputation risks have been identified, but to provide insights and act as a 'sounding board'.

The potentially complex architecture described above needs to be overseen and managed to ensure it is being properly used and is fulfilling its purpose. The audit function will perform the mechanics of this oversight, whilst the Reputation Council will have more expert guidance on what improvements might be made. This may be supported by functional expertise: some large organizations have a dedicated reputation risk management function which documents risk policies and structures, coordinates all of the above activities and escalations, helps ensure compliance and compiles content (risk information and reports) for the Reputation Council and/or ExCo/board.

This reputation risk management functional expertise usually has a hard or dotted line to the communications function. Communications should also be represented on many of the committees within the architecture. Indeed, the communications function is often the glue that binds the architecture together as it is this function that generally brings the most advanced reputation thinking into business decisions. Crucially, however, communications must not position itself as the 'naysayer'. It rightly expects other functions and businesses to understand and factor reputation into key decisions, but these other functions and businesses have an equal expectation for communications to understand and consider the commercial, strategic and other benefits of a decision. Just as business people can make bad decisions when reputation thinking is not in the room, communications people can make naïve assessments when business thinking has been marginalized.

Behavioural change through 'soft' interventions

The above reputation risk architecture represents the 'hard' or rational intervention in preventing reputation risk. But any structure and process still needs the softer interventions – leadership, culture, competence – to be effective. The objectives of soft interventions in reputation risk prevention are to encourage better performance or behaviours that prevent the risk from arising in the first place, or which help ensure risks are taken responsibly through the formal architecture described above.

Figure 11.1, which also featured in Chapter 2, shows that systems and process intervention can guide behaviour but are not the sole determinant of behaviour. Ultimately, people, not processes, manage risks.

The following are some of the key principles of this 'soft' or emotional intervention in reputation risk prevention:

- Tone from the top. Senior leaders must be the champions of reputation, creating a culture where it is acceptable to make decisions or change plans with reputation in mind. They should also explain, if it is not commercially or otherwise sensitive, when they have made a decision on reputation grounds.

- In a similar vein, leaders should be open about keeping lessons from the past – good and bad – alive in the organization, in order to inform future decision-making. Bad decisions that led to bad reputation outcomes should not be buried, but discussed and understood throughout the organization. Good decisions should be kept in the corporate memory.

FIGURE 11.1 Behaviour in the corporate context

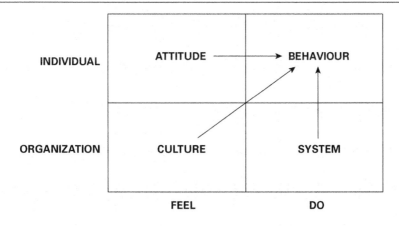

- Training on reputation risk can include everything from simple online training modules for new joiners to reputation risk workshops for managers and experiential training (exercises) for senior decision-makers.

It is not easy to find good case studies to demonstrate risk prevention or avoidance. Successful reputation risk prevention usually means a course of action has been spiked before it reached the public domain, and companies are not keen to discuss reputational near misses.

One of the examples from the previous chapter – the new market entry with a new JV partner – was a fictionalized version of a real reputation risk, which for illustrative purposes I will build on here. A client was considering a new JV with a smaller company in an adjacent sector and was weeks away from sealing a deal that would have brought significant commercial benefits and positioned both partners as leaders in an emerging technology. But it was recognized that the technology had its detractors and that the larger company would become the poster child for this and possibly wider issues.

The reputation risk discussion had started in the communications function, through the functional representative on the project team, and escalated to the project steering committee which invited views from others. The team conducted a full reputation risk assessment, devised a risk mitigation strategy and conducted crisis exercises to ascertain whether it was ready for the worst.

Importantly, it was recognized that this was not a reputation 'zero sum game'. There were risks associated with a 'no go' decision because some stakeholders (shareholders in particular) would perceive weakness and fear at a time when the company needed to show innovation and investment. Framed positively, there was a reputation upside in going ahead with the joint venture.

When this work was completed, the final decision was pushed up to the reputation subcommittee of the board who took soundings from others, including external sources. The decision was taken by the board, on the advice of the subcommittee, not to go ahead with the deal – the reputation risk was deemed too severe, despite the suggested mitigation actions. Developments since have proved to the company that it was the right decision. A reputation risk was prevented.

Corporate citizenship

The concept and practice of corporate citizenship need to be covered somewhere in a book about reputation, issues and crisis management. Indeed, corporate citizenship is so fundamental to successful management of reputation risk that it could be covered in almost any section. I have chosen to cover it here because, as the embodiment of the values, culture and purpose of an organization, it can play a large part in preventing reputation risks from arising or developing unchecked. Corporate citizenship is, thankfully, re-entering the corporate lexicon after having been sidelined for a few years by the term corporate social responsibility (CSR).

CSR, as a term, is framed negatively. The phrase comes from an assumption that there is something potentially or actually wrong with companies and their contribution to society. It suggests that corporate entities are not intrinsically socially responsible, requiring instead a programme of activities and promises to make them palatable to the world. By buying in to this concept, companies are endorsing the external mindset that they need to somehow make up for the fact that, without CSR, they are bad news.

Whereas CSR makes being a good business sound like a chore, corporate citizenship is framed more positively and describes more accurately the desired positioning of companies in wider society. Good companies should behave like good citizens. They should obey the law wherever they find themselves in the world. They should be respectful and helpful neighbours. They should think about, and be sensitive to, wider society's needs as well as their own. They should respect the opinions of others. They should feel free to speak out when they have an opinion.

Citizenship, if framed correctly and actively endorsed by the senior leadership, captures the wider purpose of the organization, its values and its ambitions. A familiar construct would be for a company to state that, as a good corporate citizen, it wants to deliver a return to its shareholders in a way that also delivers a positive value to specific communities where the company operates as well as wider society. It ties the corporate wellbeing to a wider wellbeing and is a catch-all for good financial performance, social performance, environmental performance, community investment and thought leadership.

The concept of good financial and corporate performance is once again key. The danger of phrases like corporate citizenship (and certainly CSR) is that they become interchangeable with ethics and doing 'good'. But doing well is just as important for a company as doing good. Indeed, you cannot do good without doing well, and there is no point in an organization being a loveable failure.

Can good corporate citizenship prevent reputation risks? Not in itself. But it can, and does, create the goodwill and stakeholder engagement that help a company understand its value and position in wider society. It helps companies – from individual employees to the entire enterprise – feel involved and interconnected with the outside world. It creates a feeling amongst an organization's employees that there is a world out there in which the organization is a citizen. It fosters positive attitudes and cultures which in turn drive behaviours as much as, if not more than, structures and processes. Bad decisions are taken in vacuums; better ones are taken in a positive internal culture and supportive external environment of mutual respect and understanding.

Chapter summary

Prevention is better than cure. The best reputation management is therefore to develop capability amongst the leaders and managers who make the decisions that can have reputational consequences.

The key lessons from this chapter are:

- Preventing reputation risk focuses on internal issues – eliminating or at least minimizing poor performance and bad decisions. To put it more positively: what can be done to encourage good reputation-conscious decision-making?

- Reputation risk prevention requires 'hard' interventions – structure and process – and 'soft' interventions – awareness raising, training and tone from the top – to encourage the right reputation behaviours.

- Corporate citizenship can be considered part of reputation risk prevention, not because it buys external support but because it helps create goodwill and stakeholder engagement that help an organization understand its value to wider society, and the value of reputation.

Reputation risk prevention can come from mitigation as well as risk avoidance. A company that habitually closes down opportunities whenever a reputation risk is spotted is unlikely to grow and prosper in the long term, and indeed would gain a reputation amongst some key stakeholders for being overly cautious and driven by a fear of failure rather than a desire to succeed.

What is more likely is that a reputation risk that has been predicted and assessed is deemed to be a risk that needs to be managed, or preferably resolved, in a way that does not undermine commercial imperatives or opportunities. This is issues management, which is covered in Chapter 13.

Before that, I look at the phase that accepts that serious and acute risks to reputation will sometimes materialize despite all efforts to prevent or mitigate them: crisis preparedness.

12
Preparing for acute reputation risk

Most of the work done in the name of crisis management is in fact crisis preparedness.

All organizations recognize that it is impossible to eliminate the emergence of issues or the occurrence of incidents that could become crises. 'Are you ready to face the worst?' is a question that boards ask, regulators ask, governments ask and investors ask. They want to know that an organization and its senior management are in an advanced state of crisis preparedness.

This chapter looks at how an organization can become 'crisis ready', focusing on strategic crisis preparedness at the top of the organization and within the communications function.

As this is the first of two chapters specifically devoted to crisis management (the other being Chapter 14 on crisis response), it is perhaps helpful to restate the definition of a crisis and of crisis management. According to *PAS 200: Crisis management: guidance and good practice*, a crisis is an 'abnormal, unstable and complex situation that represents a threat to the strategic objectives, reputation or existence of an organization'.[1]

My definition of crisis management, from Chapter 3, is: 'making, implementing and communicating strategic decisions under exceptional circumstances of intense scrutiny, acute pressure and high organizational risk'. It is not the same as incident management, emergency response or business continuity. All of these operational response capabilities are vital; but crisis management sits above them at the highest strategic level. This echoes *PAS 200*'s contention that '[crises] develop in unpredictable ways, and the response usually requires genuinely creative, as opposed to pre-prepared solutions. Indeed, it is argued that pre-prepared solutions (of the sort designed to deal with more predictable and structured incidents) are unlikely to work in complex and ill-structured crises. They may, in fact, be counterproductive.'[2]

Crisis preparedness is therefore about preparing *people* to face extraordinary challenges. This involves educating, training, coaching and exercising. But in order to make, implement and communicate good decisions in a crisis, people need a framework (structure) and rules/guidance (policy and process). They also need support and goodwill wherever they can find it, internally and externally.

With this in mind, this chapter looks at how an organization can become 'crisis ready' by:

- preparing its policy;
- preparing its leaders;
- preparing its structure;
- preparing its procedures;
- preparing its people; and
- preparing its culture and relationships.

The first question, however, is: Who is doing the preparing?

Who should own and manage crisis preparedness?

Crisis management as a discipline exists in an organization primarily as a preparedness function. In some organizations, the crisis management function (whether it is a special unit or a specified accountability within an existing unit or division) has a role to play in a crisis – usually as the guardian of the policy and process rather than a decision-making role – but its main purpose is to prepare the organization for the worst.

Crisis management as a function does not always have a happy home. This is because a true crisis could arise in any part of a business, could have consequences for the entire organization, and requires a cross-business and cross-functional response. It is potentially all-encompassing. But someone must own it and someone must take responsibility for driving preparedness.

In terms of ownership, the more senior the better. If the Chief Executive or Chief Operating Officer is seen to take ownership of the organization's crisis management capability – writing the foreword to the crisis manual and reporting to the board on crisis preparedness, for instance – this is a powerful statement of the importance attached to strategic crisis management.

Senior ownership is the easy part. Finding the right home for driving crisis preparedness is more difficult.

The crisis preparedness function is usually found either in corporate affairs or in Health, Safety, Security and Environment (HSSE). When found in corporate affairs, it tends to be driven by reputational resilience; when found in HSSE, it tends to be driven by operational resilience. In large engineering firms, or other companies that have major physical risks, crisis management is more likely to sit within HSSE alongside incident response, emergency response and business continuity. In consumer goods, healthcare,

FIGURE 12.1 Categorization of crises

	INCIDENTS	ISSUES
INTERNAL	SAFETY RISK	PERFORMANCE RISK
EXTERNAL	SECURITY RISK	POLICY RISK

financial and service companies, it is more likely to sit in corporate affairs. This seems to make sense in the context of the categorization model described in the first section of this book and simplified in Figure 12.1.

If an organization perceives its biggest risks to be from incidents (whether internally or externally driven), crisis preparedness tends to have a more operational focus; if its risks are more likely to come from issues, corporate affairs will take the lead.

But the danger with this dichotomy is that it risks crisis management capability being ghettoized in one function or another when it should be strategic and high level. Companies that have evolved their crisis management capabilities from their incident management capabilities, and failed along the way to demerge the two, can fall into the trap of turning something that is strategic and emotional into something that is over-processed and rigid. Companies that have come to crisis management from a pure communications perspective can wrongly believe that crisis management is about spin rather than substance.

But the decision on where to house crisis preparedness should rest on pragmatism rather than purism. The pragmatic questions to ask are:

- Which function is most strategic in its outlook and makeup?
- Which function is most likely to drive a cross-functional approach to crisis management?
- Which function has the best appreciation of the organization's entire risk landscape?
- Which function has the strongest support within the wider organization?
- Which function has the best access to senior decision-makers?

- Which function has the global reach and resource to ensure implementation of crisis preparedness?
- Which function is most representative of the organization's culture?
- Which function will ensure compliance and can 'get things done'?

It is unlikely that the answers to all these questions will be the same. The best overall answer, therefore, is that crisis preparedness is genuinely cross-functional: corporate affairs and HSSE should work together alongside other functions, such as HR, risk and legal to drive crisis preparedness. Those organizations that have dedicated crisis preparedness functions should ensure that they are staffed with people from different functional backgrounds. In order to signal that crisis management is strategic, vitally important and transcends functions and businesses, this dedicated function should report directly to the office of the Chief Executive.

But even a dedicated crisis preparedness function reporting to the Chief Executive is likely to have a 'dotted line' to another function. If it does, I would recommend, on balance, that crisis management is housed in corporate affairs. The corporate affairs function usually enjoys close proximity to senior leadership and has the ability to access and influence the wider organization. It also has higher levels of emotional intelligence (remember that crises are emotional, illogical and unstructured) and can better identify strategic threats and issues of which operational functions will have little knowledge or experience.

Most importantly, corporate affairs is rarely where a crisis is caused, but always where it is *felt*. As the focus of strategic crisis management is managing impacts rather than finding tactical solutions, it follows that preparedness should find its home nearer the consequence than the cause.

What does a crisis-ready organization look like?

Most of the rest of this chapter looks at the different components of how an organization – and its communications function – can become 'crisis ready'. It is perhaps helpful to establish from the start what I believe to be the key principles of crisis management which guide an organization's preparedness activity. They are:

- Crisis management is a distinct component of an organization's wider resilience framework.
- Crisis management requires strong, effective leadership in both preparation and execution.
- Crisis management requires a clearly defined structure delineating powers between different teams.

- Crisis management requires procedures that guide an organization's crisis response.
- Crisis management requires trained, skilled professionals to fulfil specific responsibilities.
- Crisis management requires a culture that values reputation and the importance of external goodwill and relationships.

1. Preparing policy

Principle: crisis management is a distinct component of an organization's wider resilience framework.

Crisis management policy should explain how the organization thinks about and prepares for crises as a distinct component of a wider resilience framework.

The crisis management policy should have a clear definition of a crisis, such as the one used in the introduction to this chapter. Every organization needs to know what constitutes a crisis because a crisis management modus operandi should not be invoked lightly. A senior leader must declare that the organization is in crisis in accordance with procedures (see below); to do so, he/she must have a definition to work with. One client once told me at the start of a crisis management improvement project: 'If the boss says it's a crisis, it's a crisis.' This is not enough.

A crisis is an exceptional, unusual and severe situation. It is not something that happens every day, despite what the fraught communications department might sometimes think. So the definition should reflect this. Also, it is better to focus the definition on consequences rather than causes. At the moment of crisis declaration, it does not matter what has caused the situation; what matter are the severity of the situation, the potential impacts on the commercial, financial and reputational interests of the business and the need to manage it strategically.

The following are some examples of crisis definitions from companies in different sectors and of different sizes:

- 'An exceptional occurrence that has the potential to: threaten human life or public health; significantly impact or threaten our assets or financial position, or viability of the business; result in potentially significant material liabilities; attract undue government and/or regulatory scrutiny and/or media attention; cause widespread damage to the environment; damage the reputation of our company, our products and/or threaten our licence to operate.'
- 'An unstable and abnormal situation which presents extreme difficulty, complexity and potentially profound reputation and/or business consequences.'
- 'A crisis is an event or potential event that impacts or threatens the continuity of the business, the response to which is beyond the

normal "business as usual" structure and requires executive interventions for decision-making and coordination.'

- 'A crisis is an incident (either a situation or event) that has the potential to impact the wider organization in terms of safety of life, continuity of business or damage to reputation; where there is a degree of complexity so that it is unclear what action should be taken; or where extraordinary resources are required to bring the incident under control and manage it to a satisfactory outcome.'

- 'An acute situation, with ongoing consequences, which: threatens (actually or potentially) the organization's licence to operate; has an actual or potential negative impact on the organization's share price; is perceived by external stakeholders to significantly threaten (actually or potentially) the safety or wellbeing of people, the environment, the organization's reputation and/or its financial viability; requires a strategic response and the deployment of additional resources (human, capital, equipment); falls outside normal business continuity, emergency response and disaster recovery arrangements.'

- 'A crisis is an abnormal situation which presents intense difficulty, complexity and danger. A crisis can have profound knock-on effects on reputation and/or profit. A crisis may be characterized by an issue or incident that threatens the safety of our personnel or members of the public; can significantly impact our reputation or business operations; may ultimately endanger our licence to operate.'

All of these definitions are similar, all focus on the impact rather than the cause and all stress the 'extreme' nature of crisis management.

After defining a crisis, the second key purpose of a crisis policy should be to explain how strategic crisis management fits within the wider resilience framework. Crisis management is not the same as emergency response, incident management, business continuity or issues management. But the policy should explain how these operational functions relate to crisis management, and should make reference to other procedures. Figure 12.2 explains the difference between strategic crisis management and operational response to a situation.

FIGURE 12.2 Strategic and operational response matrix

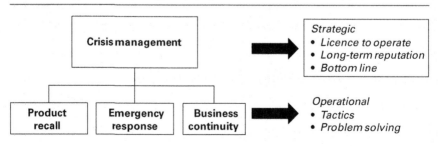

One author has previously referred to the 'hostile takeover' of crisis management by business continuity planning.[3] His contention is that the strategic capability of crisis management is degraded if it is subsumed into operational business continuity functions. According to *PAS 200*, business continuity 'does not subsume crisis management, nor is it subordinate to crisis management'[4] but rather is a complementary activity. This may be true in preparedness, but in a real crisis the strategic nature of crisis management necessarily sits on top of any other management function. Where there are multiple teams managing the same situation, the Crisis Management Team (CMT) must have sight of – and ultimate authority over – all other teams.

2. Preparing leaders

Principle: crisis management requires strong, effective leadership in both preparation and execution.

Leadership guru John Kotter has written that leadership defines a vision of what the future should look like, aligns people with that vision, and inspires them to make it happen despite the obstacles.[5] This is true of leadership at any time, and certainly true of crisis leadership.

Crisis management requires creative decision-making, not blind rule-following. Leadership therefore makes a huge difference to a crisis response, and leaders must be properly prepared to fulfil their role.

There are different leadership roles in a crisis. The focus of this section is situational leadership: how leaders adapt to lead a CMT. But crises also require wider organizational leadership and public leadership. The first is about leading an organization in crisis, maintaining the support and confidence of colleagues. The second is about maintaining confidence and support outside the organization, playing the role of corporate figurehead and, potentially, spokesperson.

Not all leaders will have the skills and experience to play all roles equally well. This is not a sign of weakness in a leader, merely an acceptance of reality. Some will play the organizational and public leadership role effectively, inspiring confidence and trust whilst leaving others to lead the CMT. Others will be better utilized running the crisis response and allowing others, where possible, to continue business as usual and take the more visible leadership roles. Indeed, anyone who has been involved in a major crisis will know that combining the role of spokesperson and CMT leader is often too much to ask.

There is not only one leader in a crisis. In fact, many senior executives and managers will take on some sort of leadership role. As well as being part of a CMT, they may be leading their functional or business support teams. The head of communications, for instance, may be leading a team of many dozens of people – often the largest team activated in a crisis – whilst also playing his or her part on the wider CMT. And, if the crisis involves multiple geographies, businesses or other 'tiers' of a crisis management structure, it is easy to see how a large number of people will be expected to demonstrate crisis leadership.

Leadership of a crisis team is different from peacetime leadership. It is a different skill and style. There is no 'right' sort of leadership or leader, but a crisis needs decisiveness and direction. A good leader must know what he/she wants the end of the crisis to look like and must be able to persuade the team that it is worth achieving and can be accomplished, despite what may seem at the beginning to be a dire situation.

Crises cannot be managed by consensus, but neither can they be managed by a strident leader whom nobody is following. A collaborative, if not consensual, leadership style is often seen as the critical skill at the strategic response level. It is easy to list out the attributes one might look for in a crisis leader – motivating, providing direction, staying strategic, listening, thinking long term, being decisive, allowing creativity, delegating etc – but the danger is this becomes just a list of 'nice-to-haves'. The way to prepare leaders is not to try to mould them into an ideal, but to help them better understand and appreciate their styles and skills. This will help them deploy their strengths and recognize their shortcomings, and adapt themselves and their teams accordingly.

Preparing leaders for a crisis therefore involves auditing, testing and refining leadership skills amongst a potentially large group of diverse people. Leaders should be aware of the role they might be expected to play, and should be comfortable with it. Their skills should be assessed in exercises and improved through coaching.

Leadership matters perhaps more than anything else in a crisis. It is often easy to tell fairly early in a crisis (whether it is an exercise or the real thing) how it is going to pan out by observing the leadership on display. Some leaders relish the opportunity, whilst others dread it. Some have the humility to understand it is not their forte, and decide to focus their attentions elsewhere; others do not.

What is certain is that leaders will not succeed just because they are senior. They need to be prepared to perform well through good training which focuses on self-awareness of strengths and weaknesses. A mature crisis-ready organization will have a bank of leaders able to take on a crisis leadership role in their function, business or geography or at the most senior level.

3. Preparing structure

Principle: crisis management requires a clearly defined structure delineating powers between different teams.

Crisis management structure must empower the right people and teams at the right levels to make, implement and communicate decisions. It is the framework which enables successful crisis management.

In this context, preparing structure includes:

- deciding what entity can declare a crisis;
- setting the powers of different entities (teams) in a crisis;

- codifying how crisis management is escalated through an organization, and how different teams work together; and
- codifying the composition of an individual CMT.

A crisis management structure must be clear, intuitive, effective, aligned with internal cultures and practices, reflective of best practice and resilient. As each crisis is unique and all crises are fast-moving, this structure needs to be adaptable. But at the same time there must be a clear demarcation of powers and limitations.

The first structure question is: 'Who can have a crisis?' A crisis can, as we have seen, come from many different sources and erupt in different parts of a business. But invoking the crisis manual should be a very formal declaration on behalf of an entity that is empowered to do so. Some organizations have a one-tier crisis management structure in which the term 'crisis' is reserved for the most senior group management only. This is unusual but has the benefit of simplicity and reserves the emotive term 'crisis' for only the most serious of global threats. Others have a two-, three- or even four-tier crisis structure in which a business unit, a country, a region and/or a site can also call a crisis. The current trend is to reduce complexity, with many global organizations now moving to a two-tier structure based on geography: a crisis is either limited to a country/region or is global.

Crisis structure should also be clear about who has the power to call a crisis at the different levels. In the above two-tier structure based on geography, for instance, a 'group crisis' might be declared by the group Chief Executive whilst the country crisis is declared by the country Managing Director, both of whom should have one or two alternates if he/she is not available.

A clear escalation model is crucial in a crisis structure. It is also sometimes misunderstood. Rarely, if ever, does one crisis team 'take over' the responsibilities of another. The different levels have different roles and responsibilities. For example, if a country crisis has been declared, but is then deemed to have escalated beyond the country's borders, it might be declared a group crisis. But this does not mean that the group crisis team takes over from the country crisis team. It means that, whilst the country crisis team continues to manage the crisis at its level, a group crisis team has formed to consider implications and actions on a global scale. It would be madness to stand down the country crisis team which is, after all, closest to the matter.

The key is to set the right mandates: authority to make decisions but also an understanding of when to consult more senior bodies or individuals who may in turn declare a crisis at a higher level. The principle of 'inform one level up' should apply. Even a group CMT will need to inform or defer to the board on certain matters. The crisis structure should explain these powers and limitations.

The decision to declare a crisis at a higher level should be intuitive and, once again, based on possible impacts and outcomes rather than events or causes. Setting rigid escalation criteria – such as 'up to five people killed is a level 2; six or more is a level 3' – is not a good idea. There are also cultural considerations in escalation. Some cultures see escalation as a sign of failure. Others seem happy to declare crises – and inform up – to show they are in control. The design of the structure cannot really take account of this, but it is worth noting. What is more worrying is if there is a fear of declaring a crisis because of a lack of trust in the structure or in colleagues. If one crisis team is avoiding escalation because they think 'they'll only make it worse', then either the structure or the culture is broken.

Structure should specify the composition of a CMT at any level. The basic formation, and role descriptions, of a CMT should be the same across the organization, so that people in different teams at different levels can liaise with their counterparts and know how other teams are operating. This is the thinking behind the ICS system used in the United States (see Chapter 6). Crisis teams should be formed by roles, not named individuals. A structure that specifies that John Smith will perform a particular role will fall at the first hurdle if John Smith is, for whatever reason, unavailable.

Importantly, structure must take into account any joint venture, special regulatory or other arrangements that may exist. This is often a gap in crisis structure, as companies focus on getting their own houses in order rather than worrying about others. But in modern global business there are complex value chains. A shipping disaster, for example, might mean that the crisis structures of the shipowner, the ship operator, the cargo owner(s) and national regulators are operationalized. If they gel together, it makes things a whole lot easier.

Structure sometimes needs to be overhauled: this might be in light of organizational changes, after a merger or acquisition, after an internal audit into organizational resilience or after a real-life crisis. In the past year, the company I run has helped three organizations to overhaul their crisis structures: one needed to change in light of a crisis that exposed its weaknesses and lack of reputation thinking in what was a business continuity-driven structure; one needed to change from a three-tier to a two-tier structure to reflect a changing global business model; one needed to change because exercises had shown that its structure was overcomplicated and it needed to shift crisis accountability to country rather than business managers. It is sensible to reflect every so often, and certainly after real crises, on whether the crisis structure currently in place is the right one.

4. Preparing procedures

Principle: crisis management requires procedures that guide an organization's crisis response.

The structure is the framework in which people and teams manage crises. Procedures are there to provide them with some rules and guidance.

Crisis procedures are not procedures in the sense familiar to those in business continuity or incident response. Crisis procedures – or a 'crisis manual', which I think is a more helpful term – should be a handful of pages long.

It is not a step-by-step guide as to what to do next in any given situation, but a set of rules within a working framework in which good decisions can be made, implemented and communicated.

The manual will likely cover mobilization, roles and responsibilities, access to resource, crisis team composition, escalation etc. Some of this has been covered in the section on structure above. The section below contains some typical sections from a crisis management manual.

Developing the crisis management manual

The following are some sample sections of a typical crisis manual, to provide a sense of the content and style of this important, but simple, document.

Declaring the crisis

In many circumstances, the decision to declare a crisis will be a judgement call made on incomplete information. If uncertainty exists, the principle of prudent overreaction should be applied: a CMT can be established, can consider the situation and, if appropriate, can then stand down. It can reconvene should the issue or incident escalate. In the event of a crisis being declared, leadership of the CMT will fall to XXX or XXX. On occasion authority to lead the CMT may be delegated. Responsibility for notifying the Executive Committee (ExCo) and the board lies with XXX.

CMT composition

The composition of the CMT is determined by the CMT leader and should reflect the nature of the crisis. Roles should be allocated on a functional rather than personal basis. Each function should have a primary member and at least two alternates that have been specifically trained and have the requisite experience (crises can be prolonged and people are not always immediately available).

The CMT's 'core' membership is:

- CMT leader;
- coordinator (assisted by a secretariat and information managers);
- legal; and
- communications.

Other roles that may be required include:

- human resources (HR);
- finance;
- heads of business;
- technical;
- investor relations (IR); and
- security.

Guidance for the CMT on initial steps

The CMT is a high-level body which provides the overall strategic direction of the crisis management response. It should be considering long-term commercial, financial and reputation matters and the global licence to operate of the company.

The initial duties of the CMT are to:

- Assess the situation and its impact:
  - discuss and log what is known about the issue/incident;
  - establish fact-finding requirements and delegate this activity;
  - assess the situation and how serious it is, or could become; and
  - avoid dwelling on knowledge gaps or attempting to solve the problem.
- Agree team membership:
  - keep the CMT tight to aid effective decision-making; and
  - each CMT member to name an alternate.
- Confirm crisis footing:
  - if a crisis is confirmed, discuss which support teams should be activated.
- Recall key personnel from business as usual, as required:
  - agree how other business needs will be fulfilled during the crisis; and
  - ensure facilities and resources are available.
- Set objectives for the CMT:
  - write clear objectives on the whiteboard;
  - ensure the role of the CMT, as against operational teams, is fully understood;
  - determine how the CMT will operate; and
  - establish clear communications channels with any other teams.
- Assess options and set strategy:
  - summarize the situation and known facts;
  - keep strategy discussions at high level at this stage;
  - write outline strategy on the whiteboard;
  - agree an outline of a communications strategy for the communications team to develop further; and
  - agree workstreams that arise from the strategy.
- Agree early deliverables and actions:
  - write an action plan on the whiteboard, with owners and due time.

Overview role of the CMT leader

The CMT leader has executive responsibility to manage the crisis and be the ultimate decision-maker on the team. The CMT leader chairs all CMT meetings and fosters an environment for strategic decision-making, creates time to think and ensures that all potential scenarios (including best and worst cases) are considered. The CMT leader should ensure that there is regular liaison with the ExCo and board.

Key responsibilities include:

- determining which additional CMT members are required, taking into account the details of the crisis and the specific skill sets and knowledge;
- chairing the CMT with the support of the coordinator; and
- identifying the CMT's objectives and determines the strategic direction of the response.

Overview role of the communications lead

The CMT communications representative is responsible for the overall communications strategy and response to a crisis, including media and stakeholder handling.

Key responsibilities include:

- providing an assessment of the reputation risk;
- managing the development of the communications strategy;
- approving all internal and external communication (with legal); and
- updating the CMT on media and stakeholder reaction and feedback.

The crisis coordinator role

The coordinator is a key role on a CMT and, whilst it is a supporting rather than a decision-making role, it is one of the most demanding. Also known as a 'facilitator' or 'chief of staff', the coordinator runs the crisis management room, is the most senior support to the CMT leader and acts as guardian of the process.

The tasks assigned to the coordinator role in a crisis management manual usually include:

- helping the CMT leader put together the right CMT, advising on roles that are required and the availability of those who can perform them;
- mobilizing the team (with administrative support);

- establishing connection with other teams that may be involved in the crisis response;

- overseeing the information management capability in the CMT, working with an information management team and ensuring legal endorsement of how information is being captured and shared;

- organizing and helping to run meetings, checking actions are taken and completed, keeping a rolling agenda, ensuring attendance etc; and

- ensuring the crisis manual is 'in the room', that structures are adhered to and helpful templates/checklists used as appropriate.

The coordinator also sometimes has a peacetime role, coordinating preparedness in their geography, function or business. This might involve overseeing regular updates of the crisis manual, ensuring key staff members are given appropriate crisis training, checking crisis facilities and keeping contact lists updated. This is not the right positioning. The crisis coordinator should be, and be seen to be, senior, not secretarial.

Crucially, the crisis coordinator should be a member of the senior management team, because the role needs to have a good understanding of the business, its strategy and its key personnel. The role is sometimes performed by communications professionals, but this is not always the most appropriate solution. Indeed, the skills required of this role – project management, an eye for detail, time management – are not always those associated with the communications function!

Some organizations allow CMT leaders to select their own coordinators, as the relationship between the two roles needs to be a strong one. This seems sensible, provided the coordinators are trained and that they can balance the needs of two masters: the CMT leader and the crisis manual.

As the above practical guide shows, manuals should be simple and user friendly. If they are weighty tomes, people will simply not refer to them in a crisis. They should also not be filled with templates, phone lists, facilities checklists etc. These are important but should not confuse a simple manual. Instead they should be covered in a separate handbook.

Given that in some organizations crises can be called at different levels, some prefer to have a manual for each level. However, my preference is for one 'universal' manual, relevant at all levels and against which everyone can be trained. Functional manuals can be a good idea. Communications, for example, can have a manual that provides further details on the roles and responsibilities of the function and its specific challenges.

Procedures are still crucial, which is why the fact that they are changing is a good sign. They are getting shorter, more user friendly and less comprehensive. Most companies have now binned the A4 bound manuals in favour of a thin A5 folder, a credit card sized version and/or an electronic version. And enlightened companies are realizing that manuals will never provide the answers to the many questions that a crisis poses. They are therefore designing them as enablers, not straitjackets; guidance, not instructions.

After the London bombings of 7 July 2005, a Review Committee was set up to see what lessons could be learned from the crisis response. One of its observations was that 'procedures tend to focus too much on incidents, rather than on individuals, and on processes rather than people'. One of its recommendations was therefore 'a change in mindset... from incidents to individuals, and from processes to people'.[6]

The lessons of this crisis, and of all crises, are clear: people must come first. Competent, trained people will find their way through convoluted process; incompetent, untrained people will make a mess of the best processes in the world. But – best of all – good process can enable competent people to make better decisions.

5. Preparing people

Principle: crisis management requires trained, skilled professionals to fulfil specific responsibilities.

PAS 200, the crisis management guidance document from the British Standards Institute and the Cabinet Office, is a little light on preparing people. This is surprising when almost all the 'possible barriers to success' in crisis management mentioned in *PAS 200* are people and cultural barriers. They include 'rigid and inflexible core beliefs, values and assumptions' which make it difficult to challenge norms, failure to identify and learn from lessons from previous crises, a culture where 'admitting mistakes, uncovering latent failures or critically analysing systems or management action is equated with disloyalty or disruptive behaviour', and a lack of training and resources.[7]

There are plenty of training sessions – crisis best-practice workshops, crisis spokesperson training, crisis communications training, media response, relative response etc – which companies habitually run to prepare their people. First and foremost, people must understand their roles as detailed in the crisis manual or supporting guidance (eg functional manuals like the crisis communications manual). But competence development should also look at 'soft' skills and behaviours: team-working, persuading, speaking up.

Perhaps the most important people intervention is the crisis exercise, which can take place over a few hours or even a few days and which tests aspects of an organization's crisis preparedness. Working through a realistic scenario under pressure is an invaluable way to assess the strengths and weaknesses within the crisis response, the abilities of the individuals on the CMT and other teams, and dynamics within and between these teams. Of course, the 'real thing' will pan out differently to the crisis exercise, but that does not matter: leadership, structure, processes and competencies can and should be tested.

Exercises do not need to be surprises. In fact, they require so much preparation, and senior diaries are so difficult to juggle, that it is almost impossible to run a meaningful surprise exercise. Some people think the surprise element is part of the challenge: you do not know when a real crisis is going to happen, so you shouldn't know when the exercise will happen. But knowing the exercise is going to happen puts a helpful focus on crisis preparedness in the organization. Nobody wants to put in a poor performance in front of their peers and superiors, so participants may well spend time ensuring they have access to refresher training and have read the manual. If they prepare themselves to 'get it right' in an impending exercise, they are more likely to get it right if a real crisis were to occur. Getting it right is not cheating; getting it right is good.

Running a crisis management exercise

The key steps in preparing a crisis exercise are: planning, developing, rehearsing, delivering and debriefing/learning.

1 Planning
The planning phase ensures clarity, from the outset, of objectives and scope: it clarifies what kind of exercise it is, who it will involve, where and when it will take place, what (basic) scenario will be used, and how it will run. Key steps include:

- Setting clear objectives. What is being tested? Process? Escalation? Facilities? Communications? HR? Leadership? Decision-making? The country CMT team? The group CMT? The answer cannot be 'all of the above'. It is far better to pick a few aspects of crisis preparedness to exercise. Further, clear objectives will both determine the design of the exercise and will help measure success afterwards.

- Deciding which type of exercise is most appropriate to meet the objectives. There are two basic types of exercise. 'Full simulations' are realistic, high-pressure 'stress tests'. They can be run across multiple teams, sites and geographies to test information flows under pressure. 'Desktops' are more measured, coaching exercises, usually designed to familiarize team members with crisis procedures and roles and responsibilities, but also to test critical decision-making. They are less stressful, facilitated conversations, but should still involve elements of time pressure. Organizations that have not run a crisis exercise before should start with a desktop.

- Choosing participants. Crisis exercises take out large chunks of executive time, so the list of participants needs to be drafted early on. The participants will depend on the scenario and the elements of preparedness that need to be tested.
- Choosing a scenario. The scenario will serve as the platform to test the response and meet the objectives set out above. It should be hypothetical but realistic, with potential to threaten the organization's business and reputation. It should not be based on a recent issue or incident unless it is heavily disguised: the danger of ruffling feathers is too great. At this stage, it is important to get agreement on a very basic scenario outline. This can be built up during the course of preparation. There is no need to develop a Michael Creighton thriller. The scenario is a tool to test preparedness, not proof of creative writing ability.
- Planning the exercise format. The format of the exercise will drive content creation, so needs to be agreed at this early stage. How long will the exercise run for and how will it be structured? How will it be facilitated? Will role-players be used? Whilst role-players tend not to be necessary for desktops, they help ensure realism in simulations by replicating internal and external stakeholder pressure. Involving internal subject matter experts on the day can also help to input technical information needed to move the scenario on and answer key questions, helping ensure credibility is maintained.
- Booking the date, time and venue. The exercise date needs to be secured as early as possible. The best venue is the venue most likely to be used in a real crisis. Rooms need to be of appropriate size and have access to landlines, good mobile service, Wi-Fi and printers.
- Setting a timeline. A crisis exercise is a major undertaking. It is like preparing for a theatre performance, but for one night only and in which the cast does not know the plot! Creating a project plan with clear milestones will ensure all tasks are completed in a timely fashion before the date of the exercise.

2 Developing

The development phase is the most complex – from designing and stress testing the details of the scenario to developing the exercise materials and framework that will enable its delivery. Key steps include:

- Developing the scenario outline and Main Events List (MEL). The MEL outlines the key events and the critical decision points. These can later be supplemented with background 'atmosphere' and 'noise' to add pressure. Subject matter experts should be used to ensure the details are accurate, and that there is full understanding of the events' impact and implications. Taking the time to interrogate and question everything at this stage will mitigate the risk of participants picking holes in the scenario on the day.

- Developing the scenario chronology. This is the sequence of events that will unfold throughout the exercise, mapping out which information (input) is going to whom, when and how. The key to a good chronology is to check and check again that all participants will be tested and all inputs have a defined purpose and clear expected outputs.

- Developing the exercise materials. These can be in the form of situation updates, e-mails, technical data sheets, media inputs or scripts for role-played calls. Even in a desktop, the scenario is brought to life through mocked-up video clips and media coverage.

3 Rehearsing

For full simulations, preparing and testing logistics, as well as rehearsing the 'order of play', are key to ensuring smooth execution on the day. Steps include:

- Compiling the exercise directory. This document lists all those who can be contacted as part of the exercise (including mobile phones and e-mail addresses, exercise room landlines, teleconference details, control room numbers etc). It must be made clear that participants are not to contact anyone who is not listed on the directory.

- Sending joining instructions to participants. Joining instructions provide a summary of the exercise objectives, explain how it will work, outline any specific requirements and provide any pre-reading.

- Setting up and testing the logistics. Logistical issues can put the delivery of an exercise at risk. Facilitators should have access to the rooms well in advance so the logistics – including IT connectivity, mobile phone coverage, landline/teleconference numbers, systems – can be tested.

4 Delivering

And so to the day itself...

- Briefing and managing participants. The most senior person in the room (usually the CMT leader) should be given the opportunity to provide a welcome address and set the tone for the day. The exercise facilitator should then introduce the exercise objectives, format and rules of engagement.

- Reading the room. During the exercise, experienced facilitators will 'read the room', ensuring everyone is involved. They may need to intervene to ratchet up the pressure, delay inputs whilst important conversations are ongoing, or 'kill' certain inputs that might be obsolete given the direction of the exercise. The facilitator is the stage manager, there to make sure the exercise goes well.

- Exercise coordination (for simulations only). There should be a direct link between the exercise control room (where exercise coordinators and role-players are based) and the crisis response rooms, so facilitators can keep track of timings and manage input coordination as well as monitor the teams' progress to control the tempo of the exercise. Flexibility is a must.

5 Debrief and learning

Once the exercise ends, there needs to be an immediate debrief. This should be structured to ensure the feedback is captured against the objectives. It is also good practice to send out a post-exercise report in the weeks following the exercise, summarizing key lessons and providing an action plan for improvement. Additional feedback can be gathered through online surveys and separate telephone calls with team leaders, observers, facilitators and other participants.

There is no merit in deconstructing all the mistakes and leaving the participants feeling that the whole exercise exposed their personal weaknesses. A good exercise will leave participants feeling that they learned something and can identify areas for improvement. It should reinforce the culture of crisis-readiness and lead to behavioural changes if necessary. Indeed, after an exercise, the lessons must be taken on board. Practice should not engender complacency; it should lead to continuous improvement.

In crisis management, people matter. And the best way to prepare people is to give them plenty of opportunities to practise. Practice does not make perfect, but practice makes better.

6. Preparing culture and relationships

Principle: crisis management requires a culture that values reputation and the importance of external goodwill and relationships.

This book has already looked at the importance of culture and emotional interventions in reputation management. I will not repeat the analysis and advice here, except to stress that a positive internal culture where reputation is genuinely understood and valued as a strategic asset provides a good context for successful crisis management. It makes people want to exhibit the right behaviours, do their best, do the right thing and work hard for a company under pressure and scrutiny.

Culture is the internal context; goodwill and relationships provide the external context.

For all large organizations, managing a future crisis starts today. All the crisis policy, structure, process and competence will come to nothing if you do not have goodwill and good relationships to call upon when things are not going well. One of the most important things a company can do to prepare for a crisis is to ensure during peacetime that it has a good reputation and a good network of support.

This is what BP found when it experienced the Deepwater Horizon oil spill in the Gulf of Mexico in 2010. News International also learned the same lesson after the phone hacking scandal. The company was tolerated (and even feared), but certainly not loved, by most stakeholders. It found that, when it was down on its luck, there was a queue of politicians and others ready to make matters worse rather than lend it their support. And banks are experiencing the same problem now. Now is not a good time for a bank to have a crisis. There is currently limited goodwill for banks amongst stakeholders and the general public. Any issue or incident is likely to escalate into a crisis given the strength of bad feeling.

The importance of relationships and goodwill is especially salient for the communications department, usually tasked with driving stakeholder engagement and measuring the organization's reputation. But it is something that an entire organization should be aware of. Third-party advocates give their support based on trust. Trust is in short supply in the middle of a crisis, but can be established in advance.

BP Deepwater Horizon – a crisis of preparedness

A case study about the 2010 BP Deepwater Horizon explosion and oil spill could fit almost anywhere in this book. It has become one of the most memorable, and most financially and reputationally destructive, corporate crises in history, with lessons in crisis management that will be studied, remembered – and hopefully learned – for decades. Discussing the incident within a chapter on crisis preparedness seems most appropriate, as the key question is: Was BP, an international oil company that had been through incident-driven crises before in the United States, in a sufficiently advanced state of crisis preparedness when the disaster struck?

The crisis itself was a typical internal incident. On 20 April 2010, an explosion and fire destroyed the Deepwater Horizon oil rig in the Gulf of Mexico. Eleven rig workers lost their lives and the subsequent oil spill became the largest marine spill in the history of the petroleum industry. The leak took nearly three months to fully seal, with the operational and reputational crisis playing out under the glare of the world's media. A Pew Research Centre study found that the oil spill dominated the mainstream news media for 100 days after the explosion.[8]

The crisis has had far-reaching repercussions for BP. The company lost $25 billion in market value in the week after the explosion. BP was fined $4.5 billion for the oil spill by US authorities in 'the largest criminal settlement in US history'.[9] The total cost of the disaster including clean-up costs and fines – put aside and paid out – currently stands at $42 billion,[10] including a $20 billion fund for victims of the oil spill. The crisis has resulted in asset sales to raise cash, lost contracts and a share price that remains significantly below the pre-incident high.[11] It cost Chief Executive Tony Hayward his job (he was replaced by Bob Dudley on 27 July 2010). BP's reputation was severely knocked and the brand fell out of Interbrand's Best Global Brands ranking.[12] Legal liabilities could increase further (The *Financial Times* estimates a total bill of $90 billion[13]) as the company awaits the results of a trial determining the apportionment of blame between BP, Halliburton and Transocean. This initial phase of the trial will also determine any fine imposed under the Clean Water Act, which could reach $21 billion.

The crisis was the stuff that simulation exercises are made of – deaths, destruction, spills and potential impacts so huge that the future of the company is under threat. And yet, in various aspects, BP fell short of crisis management expectations.

Preparedness of leadership

BP's Chief Executive, Tony Hayward, flew out to the United States on the morning of the disaster. This was the right thing to do. The incident was catastrophic and it was appropriate for there to be immediate senior attention. Hayward's actions echoed those of his predecessor, Lord Browne, who had received praise for his initial response to the Texas City Refinery disaster of 2005.

But the visible leadership strategy soon ran into problems: Tony Hayward's on-camera performances started to hinder, rather than help, the crisis response. His 'gaffes' are now infamous, and included: 'What the hell did we do to deserve this?';[14] 'The Gulf of Mexico is a very big ocean. The amount of volume of oil and dispersant we are putting into it is tiny in relation to the total water volume';[15] 'The environmental impact of this disaster is likely to be very, very modest';[16] and 'There's no one who wants this over more than I do. I would like my life back.'[17] Most people who remember anything about the Deepwater Horizon spill remember one or more of these slip-ups. It is a cruel fact of crisis management that a good operational response can be overshadowed by a few ill-chosen words.

Hayward conducted dozens of media interviews during the course of the crisis. To be fair to him, anyone under such enormous strain, whilst also trying to be on top of the operational response and the wider organization's needs, would have made some errors. But he should not have been put in a position where he could make such media mistakes: he was used too often.

BP's Swedish Chairman, Carl-Henric Svanberg, fared little better. His absence from the media was noted, especially in the United States where Chairmen are more visible than they tend to be in Europe. When he eventually did emerge, he said in an interview that BP cares 'about the small people'.[18] The unfortunate phrase resulted in yet more negative publicity for the communications effort and Svanberg was later forced to issue an apology.[19]

BP did not appear to have a spokesperson strategy. There were few senior American executives visible (and therefore few American accents audible) during the crisis. The overexposure of Tony Hayward emphasized the 'Britishness' of BP and allowed politicians and the media to continue to blame a non-American entity. US Congressman Anthony Weiner, himself no stranger to crisis and controversy, summed up the suspicion when he said in an interview: 'Here's a viewer's guide to BP media briefings. Whenever you hear someone with a British accent talking about this on behalf of British Petroleum they are not telling you the truth. That's the bottom line.'[20]

After a while, Tony Hayward got stuck in the spokesperson role. The opportunity to withdraw him passed and he became a lightning rod for criticism and anger. After it became apparent that the crisis would almost certainly end his tenure as BP Chief Executive, it was perhaps right to keep him as the spokesperson to allow a new Chief Executive to enter at an appropriate time and provide a fresh start. But his overexposure was an early – and avoidable – error. Chief Executives should be seen and heard in a crisis for short periods only.

Preparedness of structure, process and the value chain

Another famous Tony Hayward gaffe was his assertion: 'This was not our drilling rig and not our equipment. It was not our people, our systems or our processes. [It was] their systems, their people, their equipment.'[21] Hayward was referring to Transocean, the Swiss-based drilling contractor which owned and operated Deepwater Horizon. He was right. But Deepwater Horizon proved a crisis fact: big companies cannot outsource a crisis to their contractors.

BP's strategy seemed from the start to be to emphasize the legal and contractual situation. The first press release that BP issued on the day of the explosion was entitled: 'BP confirms that Transocean Ltd issued the following press release today'[22] and the only text was Transocean's own copy. This was a major error. It portrays a company that is ducking the crisis or shifting blame to others, worrying more about the court case tomorrow rather than the human and environmental tragedy today. It also jarred with Tony Hayward's decision to fly to the United States immediately: the Chief Executive was showing ownership but the company as a whole was avoiding it.

Perceptions of buck-passing were to hang over BP for the rest of the crisis. It put the company on the back foot and gave further opportunity for criticism. BP, Transocean and Halliburton (the cement contractor for the rig) appeared before a congressional hearing on 11 and 12 May where the blame game continued. US President Barack Obama criticized the buck-passing as a 'ridiculous spectacle' where the three companies were 'falling over each other to point the finger of blame at somebody else'.[23]

Multinationals have complex value chains. Crisis management and pre-paredness need to take this into consideration. BP did not seem to recognize that, whilst crisis preparedness and crisis management can and should be shared and rehearsed through a value chain, in terms of responsibility the buck stops with the big global corporate at the top of the pile.

Preparedness of relationships

BP was also unprepared in terms of relationships and goodwill. At the time of the incident, BP was emerging from a difficult few years in the United States. The 2005 Texas City refinery explosion had left a stain on its record and reputation, as too had an oil spill in Prudhoe Bay, Alaska, in 2006. This left the company with little credit in the reputation bank and with some strained relationships that needed attention. But BP had in fact made cuts in its communications and government relations functions in the United States shortly before the Deepwater Horizon disaster. Its links with federal stakeholders (particularly the White House) were not sufficiently strong.

The result was a situation of perpetual stakeholder conflict. Arguably there was no way of avoiding this conflict as, given the nature of the crisis, the President and others would have had to have portrayed BP as the villain of the piece. But the strength of the tone from the White House was surpris-ing. Obama was quoted as saying he wanted to know 'whose ass to kick'[24] whilst the White House vowed to keep its 'boot on the throat of BP' to ensure the company took due responsibility.[25]

BP's Deepwater Horizon crisis will be remembered for many things: the Chief Executive's gaffes; the sheer volume of the spill and the time it took to stem it; the performances at the Congressional hearing; the social media response; the sudden and politically expedient re-emergence of 'British

Petroleum' (rather than BP) as a brand; the size of the fines. This crisis lessons list goes on and on and will overshadow the extraordinary feats of engineering that eventually saw the operational problem solved.

Future crisis management students will have much to discuss and debate, but the incident was perhaps not a crisis management 'game-changer'. The response fell down on some basic aspects of crisis management that have been part of discourse in the discipline for many years: picking the right spokesperson, taking ownership, preparing relationships. The primary accusation against BP is that it was simply not as 'crisis ready' as it should have been.

This chapter has focused on general crisis preparedness, but there are times when an organization – or a number of organizations – need to prepare for a specific event. Major event preparedness takes crisis preparedness to a different level, as the following case study explains.

BT and the London 2012 Olympic and Paralympic Games

In July 2012, London was set to host the Olympic and Paralympic Games. With such high scrutiny and global exposure, the London Organising Committee for the Olympic and Paralympic Games (LOCOG) undertook a programme of crisis preparedness that engaged a wide range of stakeholders and encouraged partners, suppliers and the public to execute extraordinary measures to help make the Games a success.

One of those partners was BT, one of the world's largest communication services providers, confirmed in 2008 as the official communication services partner of London 2012. BT was responsible for fulfilling a wide range of communication needs for the Olympics, from connecting all 94 venues, providing the Wi-Fi and hosting the London 2012 website, to managing connectivity for the media and participating athletes. BT was the sole organization to be granted the communication services contract. This was a first: past hosts had chosen to spread the risk across multiple providers.

Described as 'the most connected Games ever', and with billions of television viewers worldwide, it is fair to say that the stakes were high for BT. Like LOCOG, BT recognized that preparedness was the key to success, and began planning accordingly.

In 2011, with a year to go until the opening ceremony, crisis preparations were fully under way. BT identified two primary crisis impacts that would present the most acute reputation threat: disruption of the Games due to technology failure; and disruption of media coverage of the Games due to technology failure.

These outcomes could come from various causes, which I have mapped in Figure 12.3 using the categorization model from the first section of this book.

FIGURE 12.3 Crisis impact model

INTERNAL	• Failure of/disruption to Games Network supporting critical Games applications • Failure of/disruption to Local Area Network (internet, phones, cable TV) for LOCOG • Failure of/disruption to london2012.com website	• Corporate ethics failings (perceived/real) • Sponsor ticket allocation
EXTERNAL	• Games security breach • Cybercrime attack • Sabotage • Terrorism attack • Severe weather	• High-profile negative perception/scrutiny of corporate sponsors
	INCIDENT-LED	**ISSUES-LED**

Although recognizing the potential for issues-led crises during the Games, the matrix demonstrates that the nature of the event and BT's role meant that the primary risks were incident-led.

The responsibility for planning and responding to external incidents would be shared between multiple partners, but led by LOCOG. The responsibility for internally driven incidents would potentially fall squarely with BT, as one of the key technology partners supporting the Games, and present a higher degree of reputational risk for the company.

With the Games approaching, the BT communications team's primary remit was to prepare BT for 'Games time'. This included media awareness training across the delivery programme, encompassing a combination of workshops and online training for 1,000 staff members, and intensive training for spokespeople who might be needed in the event of a crisis.

The BT communications team developed a range of tools, including a London 2012 crisis communications handbook, to support preparations. This complemented LOCOG's own crisis communications handbook that identified a range of threats to the Games which LOCOG and its partners might have to manage, and mapped out how each response should be implemented. Over the course of preparations, BT's London 2012 delivery programme grew from 12 people to 1,000 trained and competent staff members who would support the provision of communications services during the event, and were prepared for disruptions.

The International Olympic Committee (IOC) ran general exercises, but expected LOCOG and its technology partners to run 'technical rehearsals'.

BT participated in two technical rehearsals, both lasting a week each: TR1 was run three months prior to the Games; TR2 was run six weeks before.

Technology personnel were based in the Technology Operations Centre (TOC) at Canary Wharf in London. The TOC was the 'nerve centre' of the Games and was where all 12 technology partners, LOCOG, and other key stakeholders were located during the event. The TOC was based off site from the Olympic Park for business continuity purposes and was responsible for the evaluation and initial response to any technology threats once the Games began.

By conducting the scenario and rehearsal exercises at the TOC, the teams could replicate the set-up they would experience during 'Games time' and test multi-agency operations and communication. This provided an invaluable opportunity to practise communication between BT and the LOCOG press team, and agree key principles for managing the media together. One of the biggest challenges of London 2012 was bringing the extensive planning that had been undertaken to life. This is why the opportunity to practise in the real setting was one of the most important aspects of the planning process, lessening the risk of the unknown for when the Games began.

BT's crisis management structure follows a three-tier model of Gold, Silver and Bronze. When it came to 'Games time', the magnitude of the event led BT to rank London 2012 at a Gold level even before any issue or incident had occurred. This enabled the organization to bring together teams and individuals within the crisis management structure, and was referred to internally as 'Gold made flesh'. When the Games began, BT established the 'Games Time Operating Board' (GTOB) as the primary management team for the event. The GTOB consisted of 25 people from different functions who attended a meeting twice a day to stay abreast of news from across BT and information that was being fed in from the TOC. BT also joined the daily LOCOG and the IOC press conferences where live issues were discussed, and LOCOG partner calls to discuss the issues of the day. Multi-agency collaboration was further enhanced by a private intranet site set up for sponsors to help manage communication and ensure the mechanisms for a swift crisis communications response were in place.

Unlike some other partners, BT did not experience a crisis during the Games. However, some issues did arise that drew external attention. One was the perception of empty seats at events, with the initial focus on corporate sponsors. Careful management by LOCOG and the partners stopped this issue from escalating.

One technical incident arose during the men's cycling road race. The bikes relayed positional information back to the Commentary Information System (CIS), but the timing network became overloaded due to use of the public Wi-Fi and mobile network, and the remote countryside location of the race. The timing network was not BT's responsibility but, as the communications provider for London 2012, BT considered this to have the potential to implicate its brand, and as a result recommended and initiated further action to safeguard the following day's women's road race.

Chapter summary

Crisis preparedness is about being ready for the worst at a strategic level. This means preparing leaders and others to perform at their best in the toughest of circumstances. They need policy, structure and process to help them, and they perform best in a culture that values reputation and the importance of goodwill and relationships. But above all they need the competence and confidence that come from awareness raising, training and testing.

The key lessons from this chapter are:

- Most crisis management work in organizations is actually crisis preparedness: preparing the organization to face the worst and providing assurance to senior management, shareholders and stakeholders.

- The decision on where to house crisis preparedness within an organization should be pragmatic. But, all other factors being equal, it should sit in corporate affairs as this is where a crisis is felt. And crisis management is about the strategic management of impacts rather than operational problem solving.

- All organizations should have a crisis policy that provides a clear definition of what a crisis is and who has the power to declare one. The policy should explain how crisis management fits with operational responses to incidents/issues within a wider resilience framework.

- Leadership is a major differentiator in a crisis. There is no one right style of leadership, but leaders across the organization should be aware of their strengths and weaknesses and be given the opportunity to rehearse.

- A crisis structure delineates the roles and responsibilities of different teams or 'tiers' of crisis management. Many organizations are reducing complexity in their structures.

- Crisis procedures (also known as the crisis manual) should be a simple set of rules within a framework that is designed to help trained people make good decisions. Procedures should not be complex documents such as those seen in business continuity and incident response.

- People, not procedures, manage crises. Training and exercising give people the opportunity to practise how they would respond in a crisis.

- Goodwill and relationships are vital assets in a crisis. Organizations should invest time to build these, just as they invest time in other aspects of crisis preparedness.

- Crisis preparedness does not stop at the corporate borders. Coordination is needed through the value chain, although big companies should be aware that a crisis can never be outsourced to a contractor.

Organizations hope that all the crisis preparedness work they undertake will never need to be used in anger. But most organizations now see the value in being 'ready for anything'.

Notes

1 British Standards Institution, *PAS 200:2011 Crisis Management Guidance and Good Practice*, BSI, London

2 British Standards Institution, *PAS 200:2011 Crisis Management Guidance and Good Practice*, BSI, London

3 Mitroff, Ian (2005) *Why Some Companies Emerge Stronger And Better From a Crisis: Seven Essential Lessons For Surviving Disaster*, AMACOM, New York

4 British Standards Institution, *PAS 200:2011 Crisis Management Guidance and Good Practice*, BSI, London

5 Kotter, John P (1996) *Leading Change*, Harvard Business School Press, Boston

6 London Assembly [accessed 28 February 2013] *Report of the 7 July Review Committee Volume 3: Views and information from individuals*, paragraphs 1.15 to 1.17, London: Greater London Authority [pdf] www.london.gov.uk/sites/default/files/archives/assembly-reports-7july-vol3-individuals.pdf

7 British Standards Institution, *PAS 200:2011 Crisis Management Guidance and Good Practice*, BSI, London

8 Pew Research Centre's journalism project staff [accessed 2 March 2013] '100 Days of Gushing Oil – Media Analysis and Quiz', journalism.org [online] www.journalism.org/analysis_report/100_days_gushing_oil

9 Godsen, Emily [2 March 2013] 'BP agrees record $4.5bn settlement over Gulf spill', *The Telegraph* [online] www.telegraph.co.uk/finance/newsbysector/epic/bpdot/9680668/BP-agrees-record-4.5bn-settlement-over-Gulf-spill.html

10 Macalister, Terry [2 March 2013] 'BP hopes $4.5bn fine will draw line under Deepwater Horizon disaster', *The Guardian* [online] www.theguardian.com/business/2012/nov/15/bp-fine-draw-line-deepwater

11 Asset sales: Chazan, Guy and Crooks, Ed [accessed 2 March 2013] 'Claims may push BP's spill bill to $90bn', *Financial Times* [online] www.ft.com/cms/s/0/097ca8f4-6f6b-11e2-b906-00144feab49a.html#axzz2eldYM682 Lost contracts: Linton, Eric [accessed 2 March 2013] 'BP Loses US Contracts; Execs Plead Not Guilty', *International Business Times* [online] www.ibtimes.com/bp-loses-us-contracts-execs-plead-not-guilty-907328 Share price: Chazan, Guy [accessed 2 March 2013] 'BP eyes Russia cash for buyback', *Financial Times* [online] www.ft.com/cms/s/0/6273ccf2-3196-11e2-b68b-00144feabdc0.html

12 Interbrand [accessed 3 March 2013] 'Best Global Brands: 2010 ranking of the top 100 brands' [online] www.interbrand.com/en/best-global-brands/previous-years/Best-Global-Brands-2010/best-global-brands-2010-report.aspx Interbrand [accessed 3 March 2013] 'Best Global Brands: 2009 Ranking of the Top 100 Brands' [online] www.interbrand.com/en/best-global-brands/previous-years/best-global-brands-2009.aspx

13 Chazan, G and Crooks, E [accessed 2 March 2013] 'Claims may push BP's spill bill to $90bn', *Financial Times* [online] www.ft.com/cms/s/0/097ca8f4-6f6b-11e2-b906-00144feab49a.html#axzz2eldYM682

14 Krauss, Clifford [accessed 18 July 2013] 'Oil Spill's Blow to BP's Image May Eclipse Costs', *The New York Times* [online] www.nytimes.com/2010/04/30/business/30bp.html?pagewanted=all&_r=0

15 Webb, Tim [accessed 18 July 2013] 'BP boss admits job on the line over Gulf oil spill', *The Guardian* [online] www.theguardian.com/business/2010/may/13/bp-boss-admits-mistakes-gulf-oil-spill

16 Milam, Greg [accessed 19 July 2013] 'BP Chief: Oil Spill Impact "Very Modest"', *Sky News* [online] http://news.sky.com/story/780332/bp-chief-oil-spill-impact-very-modest

17 Staff reporter [accessed 18 July 2013] 'BP CEO Tony Hayward (VIDEO): "I'd Like My Life Back"', *The Huffington Post* [online video clip] www.huffingtonpost.com/2010/06/01/bp-ceo-tony-hayward-video_n_595906.html

18 Svanberg, Carl-Henric [accessed 19 July 2013] 'BP Chief: "We Care About the Small People"', Associated Press, YouTube [online video clip] www.youtube.com/watch?v=th3LtLx0IEM

19 Leach, Ben [accessed 19 July 2013]'Oil spill: BP chairman apologises for referring to Americans as "small people"', *The Telegraph* [online] www.telegraph.co.uk/finance/newsbysector/energy/oilandgas/7834577/Oil-spill-BP-chairman-apologises-for-referring-to-Americans-as-small-people.html

20 Johnston, Douglas [accessed 19 July 2013] 'Weiner says anyone from BP with a British accent is lying', *YouTube* [online video clip] www.youtube.com/watch?v=FBIdZYOUNS8

21 Crooks, Ed and Edgecliffe-Johnson, Andrew [accessed 19 July 2013] 'BP counts high cost of clean-up and blow to brand', *Financial Times*, www.ft.com/cms/s/0/776c0f46-57a7-11df-855b-00144feab49a.html#axzz2eldYM682

22 BP [accessed 18 July 2013] 'BP confirms that Transocean Ltd issued the following statement today' [press release] www.bp.com/en/global/corporate/press/press-releases/bp-confirms-that-transocean-ltd-issued-the-following-statement-today.html

23 Bohan, Caren and Gorman, Steve [accessed 19 July 2013] 'Obama slams oil companies for spill blame game', *Reuters* [online] http://uk.reuters.com/article/2010/05/14/us-oil-rig-leak-idUSTRE6430AR20100514

24 Driver, Anna and Allen, JoAnne [accessed 19 July 2013] 'Obama says ready to "'kick ass" over Gulf oil spill', *Reuters* [online] http://uk.reuters.com/article/2010/06/08/us-oil-spill-idUSTRE65204220100608

25 Crooks, Ed [accessed 19 July 2013] 'Washington to keep 'boot on the throat' of BP over oil spill', *Financial Times* [online] www.ft.com/cms/s/0/fee351b6-5714-11df-aaff-00144feab49a.html#axzz2ebD7TJNI

13
Resolving risks to reputation

With the organization now prepared for the worst, we come to resolution. The *resolve* phase in the six-stage life cycle is the strategic issues management phase, where organizations seek to manage identified issues down a benign curve to limit reputational damage and to avoid the possibility that they could escalate into full-blown crises. This phase is different from the *prevent* phase: it is not about having the capability in place to stop something from becoming a risk; it is about resolving something that is already 'live' either within the organization or, more likely, amongst external stakeholders.

This chapter covers the management of both external issues and internal issues. As we saw in Chapters 4 and 5 these are very different and often managed by different parts of an organization. External issues have a more political slant to them, whereas internal issues could arise from any aspect of the company's performance or behaviour. But good communication is central to addressing – and resolving – both.

This chapter provides:

- an overview of issues management;
- advice and practical guidance on issues management process;
- advice on developing issue management strategies;
- a (short) note on communicating risk; and
- some commentary on 'change' as an issues management strategy.

Issues management/issues resolution

Some issues are not fully resolvable, so need management over time. Climate change, for example, is an externally driven issue that many global companies perceive to be a risk to reputation, but it is not one that they can resolve. They can mitigate their risk exposure to it through change and innovation, but it is unlikely they can completely eliminate it as an issue. But most issues can be resolved, and the objective of issues management must surely be resolution wherever possible. For this reason, the risk life cycle diagram from Chapter 9 has an 'end of the line' for resolved issues. Other life cycles show a benign curve continuing through the risk life cycle, suggesting an issue is being successfully managed but is still present. I prefer issues resolution and the direction it provides, but as the more familiar terminology is 'issues management', I will use this term for the purposes of this chapter.

Issues management is the management over time of non-acute risks to an organization's strategic, commercial and reputational interests which, if left unmanaged or ignited by a 'trigger' event, could escalate into crises. Issues management has the same reputational goal as crisis management, but it implies more space and time: there may be periods of pressure and scrutiny, but it takes place within a 'business as usual' context.

Some organizations and commentators refer to issues being the gap between performance and expectation, and that issues management is about closing that gap, either through improving or realigning performance (change) or changing expectation (reshaping the debate/agenda). As case studies throughout this book have shown, many crises have arisen from a failure of issues management. The News International crisis, which hit the headlines in 2011, actually started as an issue for the company many years before it came to a head.

News International – an unresolved issue becomes a crisis

In July 2011, media company News International found itself at the centre of a scandal which has led to major change in the British print media industry. News International's best-read title, *News of the World*, was accused of illegal phone hacking (accessing of private voicemails) in its pursuit of tabloid stories. The scandal resulted in the arrest of high-profile individuals, criminal inquiries and the closure of the *News of the World*. One far-reaching consequence of the scandal was the establishment of the Leveson Inquiry, an investigation into journalistic practices that put the British print media industry on trial and made recommendations for tough new regulation.

Allegations about phone hacking had been circulating for some time, but the trigger event was a report in rival newspaper the *Guardian* on 4 July 2011 that claimed the *News of the World* had hacked the phone of Milly Dowler, a teenager who was missing at the time of the alleged hacking and who was later found dead.[1] Rebekah Brooks, Chief Executive of News International, who was editor of the *News of the World* at the time the alleged hacking took place, denied knowledge of the practice. Another former editor, Andy Coulson, resigned from his role as UK Prime Minister David Cameron's media advisor and was arrested on 8 July. The crisis played out over many months, with criminal investigations and the Leveson Inquiry keeping it at the top of the news agenda.

Gestures and decisions

Crises are a time for creative decision-making and one of the notable aspects of the News International crisis was the string of gestures and decisions that the company made in an attempt to manage the consequences of the crisis. On 8 July, the first, and perhaps most extraordinary, major decision that the company took was to axe the *News of the World* brand altogether. At the time, the newspaper was achieving a circulation of 2.6 million sales a week, making it the most widely read English-language newspaper.[2] If News International was hoping that sacrificing the title would be enough to show change and remorse, it was wrong. Many stakeholders wanted more, and particularly wanted heads to roll. Leader of the Labour Party, Ed Miliband, said: 'It's a big act but I don't think it solves the real issues... One of the people who is remaining in her job is the Chief Executive of News International who was the editor at the time of the hacking of Milly Dowler's phone.'[3]

The second big decision was made by News International's parent company, News Corporation, and its Chairman and Chief Executive, Rupert Murdoch. Just prior to the Milly Dowler revelation, News Corporation was bidding to take over media company BSkyB. It was believed that Jeremy Hunt, who as Culture Secretary had the final say on the bid, was sympathetic to the takeover. However, when Rupert Murdoch flew to London to deal with the crisis, he bowed to pressure and withdrew his takeover bid on 13 July.

On 15 July, Rupert Murdoch met with and apologized to the parents of Milly Dowler, saying he was 'appalled' by what had happened. This was followed by a formal apology published in national papers on 16 July 2011. The apology read: 'We are sorry. The *News of the World* was in the business of holding others to account. It failed when it came to itself.'[4] Murdoch later paid the Dowlers £2 million in compensation and donated a further £1 million to charities of the Dowlers' choice.[5]

But these further decisions and gestures were still not enough. It was well known that Murdoch wanted to 'save' Rebekah Brooks (he had said on his return to London that she was his 'first priority',[6] a message that played badly with stakeholders and the media) but this was the scalp that opponents wanted. On 15 July, Brooks resigned from her role as Chief Executive of News International. She was arrested on 17 July.

Long-term consequences for the company and industry

Crises, especially those that are not handled well, often result in tougher regulation. The need (and opportunity) for governments and regulators to be seen to 'do something' is too great to resist. Regulation affects entire industries, not just individual companies.

The outcome of Part I of the Leveson Inquiry was published on 29 November 2012. The report recommended a self-regulatory body to replace the Press

Complaints Commission (PCC) with a statutory framework which enforces newspapers to sign up. However, the main UK political parties did not agree on the extent to which Leveson should be adopted: Labour and the Liberal Democrats wanted the recommendations to be implemented in full, whilst the Conservatives (the majority party in government) opposed the idea of statutory legislation. Before a Parliamentary vote on three different proposals took place, a deal was struck to establish an independent regulator by royal charter, which could only be changed if amendments achieved a two-thirds majority in both Houses of Parliament. Most of the press industry has rejected the royal charter put forward by the three parties, claiming that state regulation undermines one of the fundamental pillars of a liberal democracy: press freedom. The debate continues, but the likelihood remains high of significant new regulation of the printed press.

The scandal has had a tremendous impact on News Corporation. One of the major structural changes is the separation of News International into two entities: a publishing arm by the name of News Corporation and an entertainment arm, Fox Corporation.[7] News International in the United Kingdom has become News UK. Commenting on the change, the company said in a statement that the rebranding follows 'fundamental changes of governance and personnel that have taken place to address the problems of the recent past'.[8]

Poor media management from a media company

The phone hacking scandal was also notable for the crisis media management performance of News International. The company did not put up Rupert Murdoch, James Murdoch or Rebekah Brooks as media spokespeople at any stage of the crisis. Instead, relatively junior executives were nominated to talk to media that were hungry for scandal and emboldened by the public's heightened sense of moral outrage. Whilst there may have been good reasons to shield the senior executives at the beginning of the crisis – to hold them in reserve should it escalate further – it became clear that News International had no intention of using them at all. For a company that had such high-profile and well-connected personalities at its helm, their lack of visibility seemed bizarre and became part of the story.

This media strategy ensured that the first public appearance of the Murdochs would be one of intense scrutiny. Rupert and James Murdoch appeared before the House of Commons Culture, Media and Sport Select Committee on 19 July. This became a media circus and set-piece political lambasting, complete with a protestor hurling a custard pie at Rupert Murdoch. Rupert Murdoch was not a good performer (perhaps proving why he was not used as media spokesperson), with one newspaper reporting: 'Like the company's share price, he was stuttering, unsure, confused and at times bewildered in which direction he should go.'[9]

Under the circumstances, the committee appearance was always going to be an uncomfortable and humiliating piece of political theatre. The committee concluded in its report that Murdoch was 'not fit' to lead his media empire.[10] The lack of a convincing media communications strategy served only to heap significance on this committee and its conclusions.

An issue unresolved

There are many other interesting lessons to be drawn from the phone hacking crisis. The need to forge good stakeholder relationships and build goodwill as part of crisis preparedness is one. The senior leaders at News International could not have been better connected, but it appears these relationships were shallow. Perhaps the company's leaders were more tolerated than supported; feared rather than loved. But once the senior leaders were embroiled in crisis, there was no shortage of people lining up to level criticism and scorn at them and the company.

But most relevant to this chapter is the fact that the phone hacking crisis was as much a failure of issue management as it was a failure of crisis management.

Allegations against News International had emerged as early as 2005, when the Royal Editor of the News of the World, Clive Goodman, was suspected of phone hacking. Goodman and private investigator Glenn Mulcaire were charged with phone hacking in 2006. Editor Andy Coulson resigned as a result. Ex-*News of the World* journalists admitted that phone hacking was prevalent and, indeed, encouraged. The industry's trade publication, the *Press Gazette*, alleged at the time that the practice was 'widespread throughout Fleet Street'.[11] News International settled claims during this time, paying compensation of approximately £1 million.[12]

In 2007, a report by the PCC found no evidence of wrongdoing at *News of the World*.[13] But there was clearly an issue that needed addressing. The risk was a typical internal issue relating to the performance of the company, its products and people, its culture and practice. The issue still went unresolved when it resurfaced in the run-up to the crisis. Phone hacking allegations were made, but the targets for hacking were celebrities and politicians. Whilst this was still a story, the public did not respond with outrage and anger at this, believing celebrities have a reduced right to personal privacy.

The Milly Dowler allegation was the trigger from issue to crisis. It gave the scandal a victim, and in so doing turned News International and the *News of the World* into villains. Could this have been predicted? Quite possibly. There are enough enquiring minds at News International to imagine how an issue that had been rumbling for years could develop given a suitable trigger event. Could it have been resolved? Of course. Resolution might not have been easy or pretty, but it would have surely been preferable to the crisis that ensued and its consequences.

As News International's experience demonstrates, mismanaging, ignoring or otherwise failing to resolve issues can lead to crises. The escalation from 'something we have been managing for months' to 'the Chief Executive has called a Group crisis and the media are camped outside' can be extremely sudden, and occasionally based on a trigger event that seems in itself innocuous. Such a trigger can be the proverbial straw that breaks the camel's back.

An issue does not, however, have to escalate into a crisis for it to be reputationally damaging. Many issues have dogged many companies for many years without ever becoming crises by the definitions used in this book. The point about issues resolution is that, if you wait until a crisis is declared before taking a stronger interest, you may have waited too long to save your reputation.

Issues management process

The principles of good issues management are essentially the same as those for crisis management as set out in the previous chapter on preparedness: leadership, structure, process and competence within a culture that understands and values reputation. For internal issues that have emerged and need more urgent management, the structures and processes of crisis management might be necessary to get on top of the situation. Just because a situation has not (yet) been declared a crisis does not mean that it would not benefit from the discipline and clarity that crisis process brings. But for longer-term (primarily externally driven) issues management, the two key elements here are process and competence.

A good issues management process must encourage ownership, empower decision-making and provide helpful guidance and tools. To that end, organizations should focus on ensuring the lines of responsibility are clear and fair, that individuals tasked with managing a particular issue are trained and confident, that they know their powers, limitations and reporting requirements, and that they have access to a toolkit.

Ownership is the first step. The danger with a non-acute reputation risk which affords the luxury of time is that ownership can be unclear: many people might be involved in managing the issue across many parts of the organization. It is vital that strategic issues that have been identified as potentially high-risk are given a clear owner.

Whilst the owners need to have clout and the right technical or business knowledge to take on the task, the last thing you want to do when confronted by an issue is to turn it into a crisis yourself, by taking the organization's most senior people away from their day jobs and getting them to focus on something which should be handled at another level. By virtue of their involvement, the issue is already on a path of escalation, from which it may be difficult to pull back. Further, this is not really a communications responsibility. The communications function is often responsible for facilitating and supporting the issues management process, but responsibility for actually managing issues rests with an issue 'owner' who normally has a business, rather than a functional, role.

Moving from ownership to management, the best issue management teams are cross-functional. Major issues – whether internally or externally driven – are potential crises. It makes sense for them to be staffed in a similar way, bringing in the expertise of, for example, communications, legal, operational/technical, product, marketing etc. One of these may be appointed the issue 'focal point' or 'coordinator', reporting to the issue owner.

The process for issues management should be simple. Convoluted systems encourage procrastination, not resolution. The more time people spend managing an issues management system, the less time they spend actually managing the issues.

A practical guide to issues management

This seven-step guide (which is 'inspired' by a client's own process) to managing issues covers the 'predict' as well as 'resolve' phases of the reputation risk life cycle.

1 Horizon scanning

- Analyse the business environment for potential or current issues (eg forthcoming legislation changes, new technologies/products).
- Define what impact the issue might have on the business or geography.
- Scan and monitor what is being said, written and done by key stakeholders.

2 Identification

- Identify potential or current issues (long list).
- Identify the issues that will most impact on the company and are gaining widespread interest.
- Look for new patterns/trends.
- Assess the potential for becoming a poster child for specific issues.
- Define issues as precisely as possible and assess their position in the life cycle (eg emerging, current, mature).

3 Prioritization

- Identify whether a robust strategy for managing and resolving the issue already exists.
- Identify the triggers that might escalate the issue, and how likely they are to occur.
- Plot whether the issue has a low, medium or high likelihood of emerging/escalating and whether it has a low, medium or high potential impact.

4 Analysis

- For the issues in the higher-risk areas of the matrix, identify and prioritize stakeholders (internal and external).
- Conduct full reputation risk assessments on the 'red box' (high likelihood, high-impact) issues; conduct a scenario planning exercise to look at triggers, escalators and impacts for 'red box' issues.

5 Strategy

- Develop an issue management (or resolution) strategy for each priority issue.
- Test the strategy against different scenarios and expected stakeholder reaction.
- Where appropriate, refine the strategy after stakeholder engagement (internal and external).
- Develop an issue brief to articulate the issue, challenges, key messages, Q&A, actions and owner.

6 Implementation

- Deliver the strategy through tactical actions.
- Ensure a communications protocol is in place.
- Review and adjust the implementation plan as the issue develops – this may include issue escalation/de-escalation.
- Keep monitoring the issue.

7 Evaluation

- Assess the strategy and plan at regular intervals.
- Identify learnings from the issues management process.
- Identify the specific parts of the plan that succeeded in influencing stakeholders – this will help inform future strategies.
- Feed learnings into the process; share learnings with colleagues.
- Write up case studies in the spirit of continuous improvement.

Managing issues, just like managing crises, usually involves a great deal of stakeholder outreach and engagement. For serious issues, specific stakeholder maps should be created. Some organizations claim to create stakeholder maps, but many turn out to be lists. Of those that are presented diagrammatically, most are matrices that map stakeholders against two variables: influence and interest in the issue. This is better than nothing, but a true stakeholder map will also show the interconnectivity between the different key stakeholders. In order for companies and organizations to truly understand how opinions are being formed – and ultimately identify what they can do to help shape these views – they need to have a more sophisticated understanding of who their stakeholders are and how they relate to and influence one another. Taking the time to create a detailed yet clear stakeholder map can be the difference between having a 'stakeholder engagement plan' that ticks a box and one that can potentially change opinions. A short workshop followed by the plotting/drawing of a map will help identify trends, gaps and opportunities to engage.

The stakeholder map can also be used to assess whether a communications strategy is working. By periodically bringing together the same group of people (or different people from the same parts of the business) and running a new workshop to develop an updated stakeholder map, you will be able to see how your issues management is delivering over time.

Issues management competence

As ever, these process interventions need to be backed up with competence. Whilst most organizations offer crisis management training of some sort to their key staff, few offer issues management training. This is perhaps understandable considering the vast number of people that have important roles in issues management teams at any given time. There are some key competencies in issues management, however, that can be assessed and improved even without a full training programme.

The communications function in particular should consider issues management training, as the competencies needed to contribute to a cross-functional issues management team are not always those required on a day-to-day basis, especially for more junior communications professionals:

- **Flexibility** – being part of a multidisciplinary issues management team requires flexibility and an ability (and willingness) to understand the needs of the business as well as other functions.

- **Outside-in thinking** – as many issues are externally driven, it is often for the communications function to help bring in external knowledge and analysis. Communicators must be able to think like stakeholders.

- **Solution focus** – the objective of an issues team must be to want to disband, with the issue resolved. All team members must understand what resolution looks like and devise strategy and tactics to achieve it.

- **Objectivity** – teams must approach the issue in as objective a way as possible, seeing it not as a battle between right and wrong but as a problem that needs solving.

- **Empathy** – the problem, however, might not be solved with science and logic. The communications representative on the team will need to bring emotional intelligence into the room.

- **Influencing** – communicators are not in issue management teams to take notes and draft messages. They are there to advise based on their professional experience and expertise. They must be reassured that they have a positive contribution to make.

Issue strategy development

The ultimate objective of an issues management process, such as the one described above, is to find and execute the right strategy that will move an identified issue from a state of reputation risk to a managed state or to resolution. For any given issue, there are usually many strategic response options. An issue management team (IMT) should spend time identifying and assessing those options and actively deciding which ones to discount and which to take forward.

The key options will usually fall into two main categories: change what the organization does, or change the debate. Of course, there may be many options within each of those categories. 'Change' might be anything from tweaking one particular aspect of the business to taking a fundamental strategic decision about the future direction of the company. 'Change the debate' might mean suggesting to the industry association that they might quietly improve their government relations work on a certain issue affecting the sector or it might mean hosting a global conference and allowing the Chairman to make a keynote speech on a major societal and political issue.

In fact, most issue management strategies for external issues tend to involve some 'real' performance or strategic change together with an associated communications or public affairs campaign. The goal of this is to mitigate risk through change, whilst at the same time guiding the debate to better (safer) territory where possible. Some refer to this as 'table stakes' – in order to earn your right to participate in (and try to shift) the debate, you need to show that your own house is in order and that you are prepared to put your money, and reputation, where your mouth is.

The need to devise a strategy for any given issue may seem obvious, but many teams either overlook this step or struggle with it. The reason for this is usually that the team is either under intense pressure to 'do something' and/or is composed of problem solvers. Either way, the temptation is to jump to tactics. One of the most valuable services an expert can provide is to take a team or its leaders out of their tactical mindset for a day and give them some structure in the form of clear objectives and strategy, then to recast the actions and delivery plan around that new framework.

The following 10-step guidance combines the strategic with the tactical and works well for both internally driven and externally driven issues. It serves as an agenda for a workshop and also as a written strategy document that the team, and senior management, can endorse.

An issue management strategy template

In this template, where there is *'for example'* text in italics, I have used the issue of alleged corporate tax avoidance (see Chapter 4 for a case study). This will show the template in action, giving an overview of how each section might

look were an international company with complex tax planning arrangements to undertake this exercise.

1 Issue description

- Describe the issue succinctly so that it is clear what the business
  and reputation risk and/or opportunity is.

- *For example, high scrutiny of corporate taxation arrangements of
  global companies.*

2 Issue management ownership, reporting and team

- Be clear about who owns this issue, who is the nominated
  'focal point' or issues manager, who needs sign-off of strategic
  decisions and communications, who is on the team and what
  resource/time commitment is expected. Detail any communications
  protocols.

3 Current situation

- This is similar to a situation report – or 'SitRep' – in crisis
  management: it sets out where the issue is at this moment in time,
  thereby providing readers with a context for the strategic
  assessment and decisions. It may include a simple summary of
  the situation plus some very specific recent developments.

- *For example, with the global economy remaining fragile, the issue
  of perceived corporate tax 'avoidance' has escalated amongst key
  stakeholder groups. Companies including Apple, Amazon, Google
  and Starbucks have already suffered reputational damage; some
  have taken action. Politicians at a national level have been reacting
  to, and further escalating, public outrage. A recent meeting of the
  G8 had this issue high on the agenda and leaders promised
  concerted action. Media coverage is high and critical of
  international businesses.* [This might then go on to give a selection
  of quotes, actions and other developments to give the issue
  'colour'.]

4 Key risks for [company]

- This section sets out the exposures as understood by the IMT and,
  if the IMT is cross-functional as well as representing affected
  businesses, could cover many aspects.

- *For example, as a global, listed company with many consumer
  brands in our portfolio and a heavy footprint in many markets
  where this issue is highly contentious, our risk is high. Further, we
  are tax-domiciled and have other tax arrangements which are
  designed for efficiency. Whilst we abide by all national and
  international tax law, this issue is about outrage not compliance
  and our exposure is ranked as high.*

5 Current business position and communications strategy

- This articulates the current position – ie up to the point of the IMT being set up. It should be a factual statement rather than opinion.

- *For example, the current business position is that it is acting in full compliance with all relevant tax and other laws. A holding line has been agreed for reactive use which states: '[Company] complies with all relevant tax laws in all markets. Tax law is a matter for governments.'*

6 Stakeholder assessment

- The assessment of stakeholder positioning is essential. This section should help the reader understand the views and actions of others (both current and predicted) which will help with strategy development in that it will provide the context for whether the organization is a leader or a follower.

- *For example, in summary, the stakeholder landscape can be characterized as:*
  - *Public: highly interested and outraged at perceived tax avoidance of wealthy companies.*
  - *Politicians: sensitive to this outrage and need to be seen to be responding, but also realistic in expectations of what international tax law change can achieve.*
  - *NGOs: some interest, but NGOs in this space are far fewer and less organized than in the environmental and other spaces.*
  - *[Please see attached stakeholder map/matrix for further information.]*

7 Scenario planning

- Building on section 4, this starts to assess the risk going forward. At this stage, it is best to leave this as an assessment of triggers, scenarios and impacts, rather than to suggest mitigation measures (that comes after objective setting, below). This section may explain what a crisis might look like were this matter to be unresolved or if a particular trigger caused a certain acute risk. However, it is not this team's primary responsibility to go into crisis preparedness mode; at least not yet. This document is about mitigation and resolution and should stay positively focused.

- *For example, worst-case scenario: a trigger event, such as disclosure about our total tax payment for the year just ended, happens in [market] which raises our profile on the issue. This could get global media attention, put our senior management in an extremely difficult position and potentially lead to consumer action such as a product boycott, as has happened to other companies. The impacts of this could be extremely serious, both reputationally and commercially. We recommend that this group looks at crisis triggers and crisis preparedness in due course.*

8 Objectives of the issue management strategy

- This is a vitally important, if short, statement of intent. Everyone must understand and buy in to the objective, from which the strategy, delivery and communications plan will flow. Some objectives might be opportunity-focused; others might be pure risk avoidance. Clarity about this is essential.

- *For example, the objective is to protect our reputation and our licence to operate in all markets whilst protecting the financial interests of the company and its shareholders from unreasonable or unworkable new tax law.*

9 Strategic options

- There are always many options to consider and a good IMT will identify a comprehensive list, before whittling it down to a few for careful consideration. This does not need to be an exhaustive process, describing the ins and outs of every strategic option. It needs to explain succinctly the main approaches that the business could take to the identified issue. It is helpful to give each option a snappy title to encapsulate the essence of it and assist discussions about options.

- *For example, strategic options include:*
  - *Option 1: No proactive engagement on tax law matters with governments or any other stakeholder; reactive communications only in line with existing holding statement. [The 'non-engage' option.]*
  - *Option 2: Proactive but non-public engagement on the matter with key stakeholders including governments, encouraging a 'no change' policy. [The 'quietly engage for no change' option.]*
  - *Option 3: Proactive but non-public engagement on the matter with key stakeholders including governments, offering support in making changes that will meet political and public needs and which are acceptable to us and other companies. [The 'quietly open to change' option.]*
  - *Option 4: Proactive and public engagement, encouraging a 'no change' policy and utilizing third parties and the media to lobby. [The 'public conflict' option.]*
  - *Option 5: Proactive and public engagement on the matter, offering support and ideas in public as well as private. [The 'public solution-providers' option.]*

10 Strategy recommendation

- The IMT may not be the final decision-maker, but it should have the courage of its convictions and make a firm recommendation on strategy. This recommendation should come with a strong rationale for why this is the best of the identified options.

- *For example, our preferred route is Option 3. This positions us as 'open for solutions' amongst political audiences struggling for answers. It will help any future legislative change be sensible rather than knee-jerk and it will build goodwill amongst stakeholders, which we might need should a trigger event occur. Keeping this engagement low profile minimizes the risk of public scrutiny and is more in keeping with our corporate style.*

A (short) note on communicating risk

Chapter 2 looked at the dynamics of real and perceived risk as part of the challenging climate in which reputations are managed. Chapter 4 explained that issues requiring the communication of risk have somewhat different dynamics and require a special set of strategic management skills. These risks to reputation arise when communities, politicians, interest groups or society at large is 'outraged' by a perceived new risk that they believe is being imposed upon them by an organization or sector.

Risk communication is a specific communications discipline. A quick internet search will find many books and articles written about it, various organizations set up to discuss it and many academics devoted to researching it. There is a mass of best practice advice and guidance on risk communication for those who are interested. I cannot hope to do it justice here, but no book on reputation and issues management should fail to mention it.

The basic premise of risk communication is that perceived risk is as important as real risk and that perceptions of risk are emotional rather than rational. Greek philosopher Epictetus said 'perceptions are truths because people believe them'.[14] If somebody believes something – even if it is something that facts and science show to be irrational – it is a truth to them. Risk communication, as part of a wider communications strategy, seeks to address concerns and respond to emotion, thereby restoring some rationality to controversial debates. Below are some observations from experience in many risk communication projects.

- Individuals are primarily concerned about risk to themselves. The 'greater good' is no response to that, so arguments that focus on wider societal benefits rarely work without very specific risk/benefit communication aimed at individuals and communities. The alternative is to marginalize opponents who believe (whether genuinely or expediently) they are suffering risk, and appeal over their heads to a silent majority. This almost never works as the risk-suffering minority is louder, more determined and more focused than the silent majority, and they know how to share and disseminate information to stakeholders and the media to further their cause. However 'wrong' they are, their concerns must be actively addressed, never ignored.

- Risk communication is much easier when there is a direct and tangible advantage for those bearing the risk. If people do not believe that they will get any direct benefit from a risk, they are far more likely to oppose it. Indirect benefits, such as the wider economic good, do not work on those who believe themselves to be suffering a risk. For example, opposition to mobile telephone and Wi-Fi infrastructure lessened over time, partly because of good work by issues managers in the industry, but partly because the convenience of mobile phone ownership turned sceptics into enthusiasts.

- Part of communicating risk might be to advocate for greater regulation. Part of the fear of the unknown is the feeling that those who are policing it, or making sure it is safe, are ill-equipped or are being sidelined by organizations with an interest in pushing forward with the risk. People must be confident in the regulatory regime around a real or perceived risk. There have been instances where industries have not only developed their own safety standards or codes of conduct around a perceived risk, but have also encouraged lawmakers or regulators to turn this 'soft law' into 'hard law' to give communities and others the comforts they need that the risk is being well managed.

- Consultation on risks must be genuine. Risk communication best practice encourages openness, listening, active communication and feedback above anything else. Companies should provide multiple channels for feedback, including innovative ones such as focus groups or 'citizens' juries' which test perceptions and get better information into a debate which might otherwise be characterized by distortion, assumption and rumour.

- Successful risk communication strategies almost always involve working with third parties. This is a characteristic of most issue management strategies where the objective is to change the debate or agenda rather than change strategy. But with risk communication it is an absolute necessity. Communities and others who fear a risk are unlikely to believe the organization behind the risk, however powerful its facts and arguments. Bringing genuinely independent third parties into the mix, and ensuring they are seen to have no financial or other personal interest in the outcome, changes the dynamic. Understanding the stakeholder influencer map and identifying those whose support will matter is one of the most valuable parts of a risk communication strategy.

- Finally, learn from others. There are always relevant comparisons from the past and people willing to share their issues management and risk communication experiences.

Mobile phones and health – resolution through engagement

Mobile telephones are now part of everyday life, with most people's concerns about the technology centring on whether they have enough coverage and data to go about their everyday lives. But this was not always the case. In the 1990s, alarmist headlines began to emerge in key markets such as the United States, Australia and the United Kingdom, linking the use of mobile phones to health impacts, including cancer. The focus of these concerns soon spread from mobile phones to the infrastructure required for mobile phone networks, such as masts and base stations.

The industry quickly found itself entangled in court battles, its reputation and commercial future threatened amidst comparisons with the tobacco industry. But in most countries this issue has now largely been resolved. How?

Issue history

A lack of public knowledge about mobile technology, coupled with rapid growth in the mobile phone market, created an environment of mistrust, misunderstanding and increasing scrutiny of the technology in the early 1990s. This translated into negative media coverage, the mobilization of public opinion against mobile infrastructure, growing frustration with the industry and ongoing attempts to demonstrate causation between the radio frequencies (RF) emitted by mobile technology and health impacts.

In the late 1990s, the mobile operators' main point of differentiation was the level of coverage they could offer their customers. This, coupled with the fact that governments designed the network auction process to be as competitive as possible to drive consumer value, resulted in a period of intense activity. Networks were being rolled out at a fast pace, with operators flooding planning authorities with hundreds of applications that they did not have the time, resources or expertise to deal with. This resulted in a growing perception that mobile operators were conducting themselves with a lack of public consultation and transparency.

In the United Kingdom, public opposition to mobile phones was focused on masts and base stations. This was largely prompted by impact on visual amenity – few people wanted masts in their neighbourhoods – and the lack of influence that people felt they were able to exert on mobile phone operators over the siting of network infrastructure equipment. Protests in the United Kingdom were initially small scale and localized, with resident groups opposing the siting of base stations. But as the issue started to gather momentum, an increasingly vocal, coordinated and influential 'anti' movement started to emerge at a national scale.

Radio technology had long been established through radio and television, but it was the new application of an old technology that resulted in mobile network operators encountering a low-trust, sceptical public. In the mid to late 1990s, scientists started to carry out research into the potential impact of RF emissions on health. A few high-profile research studies claimed to have established causality between RF emissions and adverse health effects; this risked validating claims that mobile technology represented a public health risk and dramatically raised the stakes for the industry.

In 1999, the BBC broadcast an investigation into the potential health risks associated with mobile technology. This, combined with ongoing opposition to infrastructure developments, resulted in a sharp escalation in scrutiny. The government commissioned the Stewart Report – an investigation into the health risks associated with mobile technology – to be conducted by the Independent Expert Group on Mobile Phones. The precautionary approach recommended by the report forced operators onto the defensive, compelling an industry-wide response to the issue.

Resolving the issue in the United Kingdom

This external issue was clearly gathering momentum. Abandoning their case-by-case approach, industry players recognized there was a non-competitive issue that posed a threat to business and found a way to coordinate an industry-wide response. In 1999, the operators set up the Mobile Telecoms Advisory – renamed the Mobile Operators' Association (MOA) in 2003 – as a means of coordinating the industry response to the issue. By sharing knowledge and information on best practice relating to network roll-out, the MOA developed its 'Ten Commitments to Best Siting Practice'.[15] These principles formed the basis of a code of best practice against which the industry would hold itself to account, and included guidelines on consulting key stakeholders as part of the planning process.

The MOA helped steer the issue and shape the agenda by driving the development of a range of objective information relating to the issue, which was then channelled to stakeholders via operator websites and leaflets, third-party endorsement and a proactive media campaign.

The industry undertook raised awareness on the issue amongst key stakeholders, targeting the national government, local government, as well as the public and media. These audiences were engaged on the responsible action that the industry was taking to manage public concerns, including devising a code of best practice, bringing greater transparency to the network roll-out process, and building masts and base stations in compliance with independent health guidelines. Numerous meetings were held with local planning authorities and government associations to provide them with information on network technology and the latest scientific research on the RF health issue. This information was then cascaded onto local authorities and councillors.

Just when you thought it was safe...

The RF health debate re-emerged in 2006/07, sparked by the installation of wireless technology in classrooms as part of the government's interactive learning initiative and another BBC 'exposé' on the health risks of Wi-Fi technology. It became linked to a debate about 'electro sensitivity' when a teacher at a British school claimed to have developed adverse health symptoms after Wi-Fi technology was installed in his classroom.[16]

This issue re-emergence was, again, based on a new application of a tried-and-tested technology, but with added emotional charge in the context of potential health risk to children. Sir William Stewart (the lead author of the Stewart Report), the Health Protection Agency (HPA) and the Professional Association of Teachers (PAT) called for research to be carried out into the safety of Wi-Fi.

This time, an organization called the Wi-Fi Alliance (WFA) took the lead on behalf of industry. The emphasis of their work was on engaging government agencies and, in 2009, the HPA released a report stating that RF emissions measured in classrooms fell well within ICNIRP guidelines.[17] The HPA thus became a credible third-party advocate in media coverage. Much of the groundwork had already been laid by the MOA: the industry had the benefit of relying on networks, relationships and research established during the initial mobile phone issue.

Where is the issue now?

Scientific consensus has helped to calm public concerns, but engagement of key stakeholders remains ongoing, as does the drive to raise awareness via the development of objective scientific research. The industry remains committed to managing the issue to ensure it remains on a benign trajectory. This includes ongoing monitoring for signs of escalation through regular consumer polling as a means of gauging opinion and attitudes to the industry.

The issue of perceived health risk from mobile phones and associated infrastructure is a good example of how an issue crept up on an industry, requiring coordinated industry action across markets to protect the industry's licence to operate. Whilst the issue continues to generate some attention internationally (it has emerged as an issue in India, for example), it has largely been resolved in many countries.

Change as an issue management strategy

The case study on mobile phone technology is primarily a story of issue management (and near resolution) through changing the debate. The industry did not fundamentally change its products or services or plans; it essentially won the argument. But sometimes companies are on the wrong side of the argument and change is the only strategy. An example would be the 'sweatshops' issue that peaked in the 1990s, causing reputation and commercial damage to many famous clothing brands, including Nike. This was a classic example of an issue where societal outrage, driven by well-organized external stakeholders, focuses on organizational behaviour and performance.

Nike and 'sweatshops' – resolution through change

In the early 1990s, Nike (amongst other companies) faced a media, political and societal backlash because it was perceived to be using Asian 'sweatshops' to produce garments cheaply that were then sold on to Western consumers at high prices. The conditions and pay of factory workers became a significant externally driven reputation risk but one that was based on internal matters: corporate standards and behaviours.

As criticism of Nike (and its Indonesian subcontractors) started to appear in reputable journals, the company's initial response was seemingly to distance itself from the issue, claiming it could not be held responsible for the practices of suppliers. But in June 1996, *Life* magazine published pictures of a child in Pakistan assembling Nike soccer balls.[18] According to one commentator, this became a seminal moment for Nike, and the company started to see the matter differently.[19] But some damage was already done. The issue had become a consumer issue, and Nike's stock price fell in value by 50 per cent going from $38 per share in 1996, to $19 in mid-1997.[20]

In 1997, a Nike audit of a Vietnamese factory was obtained and leaked by the Transnational Resource and Action Center (now known as CorpWatch).[21] This was the trigger for a change of issue management strategy. The 'debate', if there ever was one, was over. It was time for change. Nike's Chairman and Chief Executive, Phil Knight, issued a *mea culpa*: 'The Nike product has become synonymous with slave wages, forced overtime, and arbitrary abuse,'[22] he said at a 1998 press conference at the National Press Club. It was at this conference that Nike announced that it would introduce a more rigorous auditing regime and, in a crucial declaration of change, insist that overseas contractors were bound by the same rules and processes as would be expected from US contractors.

Knight did not stop there. He sought to turn an issue that had damaged Nike's reputation into an opportunity to be seen as a leader. 'We believe that these are practices which the conscientious, good companies will follow in the 21st century,' he said. 'These moves do more than just set industry standards. They reflect who we are as a company.'[23] The company brought in reforms designed to improve how workers were treated, and opened operations to inspection. It wrote a code of conduct for contractors, requiring them to provide workplaces free of harassment, banning the employment of underage workers, mandating the payment of at least the minimum wage and requiring employees to have paid leave.

In parallel to this change programme, Nike engaged its critics. 'The most significant shift for Nike was when we began to sit down with the very people who had been critical of us and started to engage not in a denial conversation but in a conversation on how to solve the problems,'[24] stated Nike's Vice-President of Sustainable Business and Innovation. The issue did not immediately die. Nike had made enemies and had created a perception amongst stakeholders – and most seriously, its consumers – that it was not a good corporate citizen. This perception took time to shift, but Nike continued to engage and continued to change.

Today, the issue of 'Asian sweatshops' still spikes occasionally when there is a trigger event, such as the Bangladeshi factory collapse in April 2013 which left 1,129 dead and once again brought to the world's attention the conditions in which some developing world workers produce goods for developed world consumers. But the issue is far less high profile. In terms of major reputation risk and issues management, it may appear 'resolved', but after such reputation and commercial damage, Nike is unlikely to be complacent. The company has successfully repositioned itself as a corporate citizenship leader, and the issue of manufacturing features prominently in the responsibility section of the Nike Inc website. It states: 'We're looking end-to-end, from the first phase of our product creation process to the impacts of our decisions on the lives of workers in the factories that bring our products to life.'[25] So, not an issue fully resolved perhaps, but an issue seemingly under control.

Chapter summary

It sounds like a corporate cliché, but in every issue there really is some sort of opportunity. As Chapter 4 explained, opportunity comes from change – accepting that an issue needs to be addressed, working with stakeholders to resolve it and potentially stealing a march on competitors. Opportunity can also come from tackling an issue head-on and, like the mobile phone industry, protecting and enhancing your product and business.

The key lessons from this chapter are:

- Issues management should focus on resolution to encourage the organization to find ways of closing out the issue as a reputation risk. An issue that has rumbled on for years is perhaps institutionalized.

- Many major corporate crises of recent years have started as issues which could, and perhaps should, have been resolved.

- Trigger events can turn unresolved issues into crises. But an issue does not need a trigger and does not need to become a crisis in order for reputation to be damaged: unmanaged issues can be chronic risks that eat away at reputation over time.

- High-priority issues must be given a clear owner – preferably in the business rather than in communications – and a cross-functional team should be established to devise and execute an issues resolution strategy.

- Issue management strategies – for externally driven issues – usually fall into two types: changing the debate or changing performance/strategy.

- Risk communication is a specific discipline, which has as its premise the contention that perceived risk is as important as real risk and that perceptions are emotional rather than rational. Risk communication seeks to address concerns, respond to emotional dynamics and restore some rationality into controversial debates/issues.

Whether it is through changing your policies and practices or changing the debate – or both – resolution is the key. If issues management fails to resolve reputation risk, organizations may find themselves in crisis response mode. This is the subject of the next chapter.

Notes

1 Davies, Nick and Hill, Amanda [accessed 9 April 2013] 'Missing Milly Dowler's voicemail was hacked by News of the World', *The Guardian* [online] www.theguardian.com/uk/2011/jul/04/milly-dowler-voicemail-hacked-news-of-world

2 Murdoch, James [accessed 9 April 2013] 'Statement from News International regarding the Metropolitan Police Service's new investigation into police payments', News UK [press release] http://news.co.uk/2011/07/06/statement-from-news-international-regarding-the-metropolitan-police-services-new-investigation-into-police-payments-2/

3 Gabbatt, Adam and Batty, David [accessed 10 April 2013] 'News of the World closure announced – Thursday 7 July 2011', *The Guardian* [online] www.theguardian.com/media/blog/2011/jul/07/news-of-the-world-closes-live-coverage

4 Murdoch, Rupert [accessed 9 April 2013] 'We are sorry', News International [pdf] www.ft.com/cms/86624338-aef1-11e0-9310-00144feabdc0.pdf

5 Deans, Jason [accessed 10 April 2013] 'Phone hacking: NI confirms £2m for Dowlers and £1m charity donation', *The Guardian* [online] www.theguardian.com/media/2011/oct/21/phone-hacking-dowlers

6 Staff reporter [accessed 10 April 2013] 'Murdoch says chief Rebekah Brooks is his first priority', BBC News [online] www.bbc.co.uk/news/uk-14100053

7 Staff reporter [accessed 9 April 2013] 'Have I got news for you', *The Economist* [online] www.economist.com/node/21563721

8 Darcey, Mike [accessed 9 April 2013] 'News International renamed News UK', News UK [press release] http://news.co.uk/2013/06/26/news-international-renamed-news-uk-3/

9 Reece, Damian [accessed 10 April 2013] 'Phone hacking: "Bewildered" Rupert Murdoch suffers a close shave at select committee', *The Telegraph* [online] www.telegraph.co.uk/finance/comment/damianreece/8648665/Phone-hacking-Bewildered-Rupert-Murdoch-suffers-a-close-shave-at-select-committee.html

10 Sabbagh, Dan and Halliday, Josh [accessed 10 April 2013] 'Rupert Murdoch deemed 'not a fit person' to run international company', *The Guardian* [online] www.theguardian.com/media/2012/may/01/rupert-murdoch-not-fit-phone-hacking

11 Greenslade, Roy [accessed 10 April 2013] 'Yes, hacking was a disgrace – so why did most newspapers ignore it?', *The Guardian* [online] www.theguardian.com/media/greenslade/2013/mar/25/press-freedom-sundaytimes

12 Davies, Nick [accessed 9 April 2013] 'Murdoch papers paid £1m to gag phone-hacking victims', *The Guardian* [online] www.theguardian.com/media/2009/jul/08/murdoch-papers-phone-hacking

13 Davies, Nick [accessed 9 April 2013] 'Timeline: how the News of the World phone-hacking scandal developed', *The Guardian* [online] www.theguardian.com/media/2010/dec/15/timeline-news-of-the-world-phone-hacking

14 Epictetus, 1st Century AD

15 Mobile Operators Association [accessed 21 March 2013] 'Developing Mobile Networks: Ten Commitments to best siting practice' [pdf] www.swindon.gov.uk/ep/ep-planning/forwardplaning/ep-planning-localdev/Documents/Mobile%20Operators%20Association%E2%80%99s%20(MOA)%20Ten%20Commitments%20(2006).pdf

16 Claire Heald [accessed 21 March 2013] 'Wi-fi worry', BBC News [online] http://news.bbc.co.uk/1/hi/6172257.stm

17 Peyman, Azadeh and Mann, Simon [accessed 21 March 2013] 'Wi-Fi in schools', Health Protection Agency [pdf] www.hpa.org.uk/webc/HPAwebFile/HPAweb_C/1254510618866

18 Epstein-Reevees, James [accessed 23 March 2013] 'The Parents Of CSR: Nike And Kathie Lee Gifford', *Forbes* [online] www.forbes.com/sites/csr/2010/06/08/the-parents-of-csr-nike-and-kathie-lee-gifford/

19 Epstein-Reevees, James [accessed 23 March 2013] 'The Parents Of CSR: Nike And Kathie Lee Gifford', *Forbes* [online] www.forbes.com/sites/csr/2010/06/08/the-parents-of-csr-nike-and-kathie-lee-gifford/

20 Palmquist, Rod [accessed 3 April 2013] 'Student Campaign Takes on Nike Like Never Before', *The Huffington Post* [online] www.huffingtonpost.com/rod-palmquist/student-campaign-takes-on_b_643375.html

21 Epstein-Reevees, James [accessed 23 March 2013] 'The Parents Of CSR: Nike And Kathie Lee Gifford', *Forbes* [online] www.forbes.com/sites/csr/2010/06/08/the-parents-of-csr-nike-and-kathie-lee-gifford/

22 Cushman Jr, John [accessed 3 April 2013] 'Nike Pledges to End Child Labor And Apply U.S. Rules Abroad', *The New York Times* [online] www.nytimes.com/1998/05/13/business/international-business-nike-pledges-to-end-child-labor-and-apply-us-rules-abroad.html

23 Cushman Jr, John [accessed 3 April 2013] 'Nike Pledges to End Child Labor And Apply U.S. Rules Abroad', *The New York Times* [online] www.nytimes.com/1998/05/13/business/international-business-nike-pledges-to-end-child-labor-and-apply-us-rules-abroad.html

24 Jones, Terril [accessed 3 April 2013] 'What Apple Can Learn From How
    Nike Dealt With It's Chinese Labor Scandal', *Business Insider* [online]
    www.businessinsider.com/what-apple-can-learn-from-how-nike-dealt-with-its-
    chinese-labor-scandal-2012-3

25 Nike.com [accessed 3 April 2013] 'Manufacturing' [online]
    http://nikeinc.com/pages/manufacturing

14
Responding to immediate reputation risk

This is the crisis management phase of the risk life cycle. Whether an incident has occurred, or an unresolved issue has suddenly escalated, a crisis has been called. Scrutiny and pressure are high, many teams may have been mobilized and much work is being done.

There is a heavy communications focus to this chapter, because communication is so central to crisis management in so many ways. Good crisis management demonstrates to stakeholders directly, and to the wider public via the media, that the organization is in control, acting responsibly and committed to resolving the situation. This, together with the need to keep internal audiences informed and involved, requires a lot of good communication.

But whilst this chapter has tactical advice for the communications function, one of the core arguments of this book is that crisis management is strategic. The first part of this chapter therefore looks at the strategic decision-making required of the crisis management team (CMT), and the role of communications on that team. The chapter covers:

- strategic crisis decision-making;
- the communications response;
- crisis media management, including content generation, the role of the spokesperson and managing traditional and social media; and
- the role of other functions in a crisis response, and how communications interacts with and supports them.

Strategic crisis decision-making

Chapter 12 argued that crisis preparedness is about getting to a point where an organization's leaders can make, implement and communicate good decisions in a crisis to protect reputational, financial and commercial interests. Once a crisis is called, the CMT must free itself to perform this strategic function, avoiding the temptation to solve tactical problems. When a fire is burning, either literally or metaphorically, this is not easy.

Once assembled, the CMT has two primary roles. First, it must oversee the response to an incident or issue that is sufficiently serious for a crisis to have been called. Some sort of response is likely to be under way already: a rescue effort, incident management on site, media management, product recall etc. The CMT's role is not to duplicate this response or manage it in detail; others are better equipped and have been trained to do that. The CMT should rather oversee it, endorse it and guide it... and then move beyond it. The CMT must not descend into the detail of the response; it must remain high level and strategic. Its focus should be on the big picture, long-term impacts and recovery.

Take, for example, a classic 'internal incident' crisis of the sort described in Chapter 7: a major explosion and fire at a company's manufacturing facility. Some people have lost their lives, some are unaccounted for and others are seriously injured. The fire is still burning and there is a chemical leak into a local waterway. This is certainly an incident. But what makes it a *crisis* is not the detail of what has happened, but the potential impacts on the company.

The CMT assembles at corporate headquarters, recognizing that the company needs to protect its people and the environment and that what it is seen to do and heard to say now could impact its long-term interests and even determine whether the company survives. In this case, the CMT must make sure that the operational response is proceeding as expected. First and foremost, it must stress that the safety of people is the overriding priority and that the company will do whatever it can to protect people and the environment. It should demand that the operational response reports regularly into the CMT; it should closely oversee the communications and HR response.

But beyond this, there is little the CMT could or should actually *do* in terms of the operational response. The CMT does not itself put fires out. Therefore, it should soon start to focus on the second aspect of the CMT role: thinking about perceptions, impacts, recovery and survival. In fact, I would argue that before it does *anything*, a CMT should remind itself of what it is there to do. The clue is in the name: a crisis management team is there to manage the crisis, not the incident or issue that has triggered it. After assuring itself that everything is being done in terms of incident management, it should start to ask other questions. What are the potential consequences of this? What could this mean for us? What could be the commercial impact, the share price impact, the impact on morale and the impact on our reputation? What can and must we do to minimize negative impacts? The answers to these questions may bring the team regularly back to the operational response – especially in an incident-driven crisis where doing the right thing, and being seen to do so, is the fundamental objective – but it will also involve high-level stakeholder management, customer and contract considerations and financial decisions.

Put simply, the job of the CMT is, through high-level decision-making, to protect those things recognized to be of utmost value: the trust of stakeholders and the reputation that they collectively assign to the organization.

A CMT therefore has to get to the heart of the matter as quickly as possible. It has to think beyond the incident or issue that is being managed and understand why the company is in crisis mode, rather than just incident or issue management mode. Applying the definition used throughout this book, it must assess what this 'abnormal, unstable and complex' situation really is and understand why it represents 'a threat to the strategic objectives, reputation or existence' of the organization. BP's crisis in the Gulf of Mexico in 2010 was not, harsh as it may seem, a crisis about the deaths of 11 people working on the Deepwater Horizon rig. It was a crisis about BP's competence, performance, safety record and trustworthiness.

Toyota recall

The story of Toyota's product recalls in 2009 and 2010 provides another example.

Between September 2009 and early 2010, Toyota initiated the biggest vehicle recall in its history. A series of accidents had led to safety concerns being raised about trapped accelerator pedals. Two recalls during this period involved nearly seven million vehicles globally.

Toyota was slow to respond. After the second recall announcement in January 2010, a week elapsed without any communication from the company. Toyota's Chairman and Chief Executive, Akio Toyoda, did not appear in public until 5 February. This indicated that the company had not grasped the nature of the crisis it was facing. The problem Toyota needed to address at the crisis management level was not 'some of our cars are faulty' but 'the reputation we have built for safety and reliability is under serious threat'. The CMT should not be worrying about the exact nature of the mechanical fault, but about the consequences that a multi-million vehicle recall could have on a company that has a brand promise based on quality. As one automotive industry analyst observed, 'People don't buy [Toyotas] for their good looks. They buy them because they have a lot of confidence in the quality and safety of the vehicle.'[1]

This was therefore a perceptions of safety and quality crisis for a company that built its leading market share based on those key customer propositions. Moreover, the reasons given for why the problems may have arisen in the first place compounded the issue. At a congressional hearing, Toyota's Chief Executive apologized and admitted: 'We pursued growth over the speed at which we were able to develop our people and our organization and we should be sincerely mindful of that.'[2] The international media picked up on this, pointing to Toyota's rapid globalization and desire to be the world's largest automotive manufacturer as an explanation for why safety and quality had been compromised. One UK broadsheet newspaper said the recall crisis 'is about a company too fixated on becoming the world's number one to avert tragedy'.[3]

By refocusing on quality and reliability Toyota has recovered well from the recall crisis. But the faltering crisis response and lack of appropriate communication suggested that the CMT (assuming one or more was formed) had not initially spotted the fundamental problem and was not operating at a strategic and future-focused level.

Once a CMT has understood the problem it is facing and the reason that the organization is 'in crisis' rather than just managing an issue or an incident, it needs to start thinking outside the box. Again, using the definitions from earlier chapters, crises require creative thought and decision-making, as opposed to the implementation of prepared solutions.

No manual, for example, tells you to ditch your biggest brand to try to fend off wider commercial and reputational damage, but that is what News International did when it decided its *News of the World* title was too reputationally toxic to continue. No manual tells you to allow your Chief Executive to travel in an aircraft through a layer of supposedly dangerous high volumes of volcanic ash, yet that is what Willie Walsh of British Airways did in an attempt to put an end to the ash cloud crisis of 2010.

Big things happen in crises: senior people resign, independent investigations are launched, business models are changed, products are jettisoned, and huge sums are promised before liability is established. This is the strategic crisis decision-making that CMTs are there to perform.

A final but important point to raise here is that the CMT should, to an extent, be 'protected' from the operational response so that it can think strategically and make the big decisions. If constituted and operating properly, it should not look or feel like a 'war room'. People should not be rushing in and out, waving papers, tuning in to broadcast news and generally causing chaos. The CMT should be a tight decision-making body. Equally, however, it should not it sit in glorious isolation from the response or the unique context in which the crisis will be managed.

Every crisis has a context. An example of how the context and the stakeholder mix affects a crisis is the situation in which security provider G4S found itself only months before the London Olympics.

An unwinnable Olympic crisis for G4S

G4S is the largest security company in the world, providing security services to a diverse range of industries, including government. In 2010, the company was awarded the contract to provide security services at the 2012 London Olympics. The contract involved recruiting 2,000 security staff for the venues and managing 8,000 additional personnel. The contract, thought to be worth £284 million, began in March 2011, with G4S reporting to the London Organising Committee of the Olympic and Paralympic Games (LOCOG).

In December 2011, seven months prior to the commencement of the Games, the UK's Department of Culture, Media and Sport released an Olympics progress report. The report revealed that the number of security personnel was to be increased to 23,700 (10,400 to be supplied by G4S). The report identified this as a 'significant recruitment challenge'.[4]

In March 2012, the Public Accounts Committee (PAC) – the UK's parliamentary spending watchdog – raised concerns about LOCOG's requests for more personnel. The PAC stated that G4S faced a 'significant challenge to recruit, train and coordinate all the security guards in time for the Games'.[5] Following up concerns about the quality of management information from G4S and its communication with job applicants, LOCOG ordered a report in May 2012 from Deloitte. The Deloitte audit recommended a number of actions, including an overhaul of the project's governance structure; G4S later stated that these recommendations were implemented within a week of publication.

At a meeting of the Olympic Security Board on 27 June, with exactly one month until the opening ceremony, G4S revealed it was experiencing 'scheduling problems' as staff were unavailable until the opening ceremony on 27 July. On 11 July, G4S indicated to LOCOG that it would not be able to deliver on the contract. Contingency plans were consequently scaled up, with support from the armed forces increasing from 725 to 3,500 personnel and police forces from around the United Kingdom contributing forces to make up the shortfall.

G4S Chief Executive, Nick Buckles, appeared before the House of Commons Home Affairs Select Committee on 17 July. He apologized and accepted that G4S was '100 per cent responsible' for the failure in fulfilling the security contract and, when asked by a committee member whether he agreed the incident was a humiliating shambles, he replied 'I cannot disagree with you.' But despite agreeing that G4S's reputation was now in 'tatters', Buckles remained adamant that its £57 million management fee should still be honoured.[6]

The body that came out of this debacle unscathed was LOCOG. Lord Sebastian Coe, LOCOG's Chairman, was asked by journalists whether G4S was solely to blame. He replied: 'It is difficult to look beyond their inability to deliver when we were consistently being assured they would deliver.'[7] Paul Deighton, Chief Executive of LOCOG, pointed out that the organizing committee itself had successfully recruited and was ready to deploy 70,000 volunteers to work during the games without mishap.

The report of the Home Affairs Select Committee, published after the Games in September 2012, towed the LOCOG line. It stated that: 'The blame for G4S's failure to deliver on its contract rests firmly and solely with the company. There is no suggestion that LOCOG, the Home Office or anybody else involved in the process contributed to the problem in any way.'[8] Indeed, the Committee said that it was only thanks to the far-sighted planning of officials at the Home Office, LOCOG and other Olympic security partners that a catastrophe was averted.

This was not, however, the view of Her Majesty's Inspectorate of Constabulary, which had been commissioned to look into security arrangements back in 2011. Its September 2011 report found that LOCOG was 18 months behind in the production of policies and standard operating procedures, causing delays to its delivery of venue security plans and, in turn, delays to accessing the number of staff required. Further, when problems regarding G4S's ability to deliver new targets were identified in four reports, LOCOG failed to share these reports with Olympic Security Board Members.

The truth, as ever, is unlikely to be black and white. G4S was a contractor to LOCOG. Both had responsibilities on security and both had stakeholders to assure. But G4S is a private contractor with a reputation already challenged (during a previous incarnation as Group 4, it had come under heavy fire for its record on prisoner management). LOCOG, on the other hand, was an organization put together under the stewardship of a former British Olympic hero, charged with delivering a major sporting event that the public was being urged to rally behind. In Chapter 12, the case study on BP asserted that a crisis 'cannot be outsourced'. This is true for global companies who must take ultimate responsibility for problems in their supply chains; but government agencies can, and do, outsource crises to their private sector contractors.

In a crisis, political, societal and stakeholder context is key. The communications function can help a CMT understand this, bringing the outside in. This is just one of many roles that the Head of Communications must play.

In the CMT, the Head of Communications (which should always be a core role, rather than an optional role) has one of the hardest jobs. He/she has oversight of one of the most complex aspects of the response, likely to involve a large number of people performing many different roles. He/she brings the outside in to the CMT and takes the inside out to the public via the media. And, as so many aspects of a crisis response involve communications, they are likely to be in regular contact with heads of other functions such as legal, operations, IR, government relations and HR.

The Head of Communications is also a key contributor to CMT strategy. Thankfully, the days of 'We'll make the decisions, you write the release' have long gone and, in most organizations, the senior communications person is a valued strategic adviser. In a situation where there are no right answers and where decisions and solutions need to be creative, the Head of Communications can apply a reputation lens to the situation and help make the substantive decisions. How will these decisions and actions be perceived by stakeholders? Do they reflect the public mood? Sometimes, reputational considerations override technical or operational logic.

Crisis management is about substance, not spin. The communications lead should help get the response right as well as help communicate it.

The wider crisis communications response

This dual role is a difficult one to pull off for any communications leader: contributing to the (hopefully) calm decision-making in the CMT, whilst maintaining oversight of and responsibility for the Crisis Communications Team (CCT) where the mood is likely to be more frantic and the needs more immediate. For this reason, the Head of Communications should not seek to 'double hat' as the CCT Lead as well as being the CMT representative, but should delegate the CCT role to a trusted deputy. The relationship between the CMT Communications Lead and the Head of the CCT is like that of a Chief Executive and Chief Operating Officer: ultimately the Chief Executive takes the decisions and maintains oversight, whilst the Chief Operating Officer advises, supports and makes it happen.

The CCT will be performing a number of different roles: monitoring the media, drafting content, coaching the spokesperson, checking facts before they are signed off for communications use, manning the phones, overseeing stakeholder engagement, liaising with other functions, ensuring internal communications are not overlooked, engaging with social media and much more. The following case study paints a picture of a communications function in a crisis.

Gas leak in the North Sea

On Sunday 25 March 2012, a gas leak was detected on the Elgin field in the UK North Sea, about 150 miles (240 km) east of Aberdeen. Production was stopped and 238 personnel were safely evacuated onshore. The leak was stemmed eight weeks later, on 15 May 2012.

The response of the operator, French energy giant Total, has been commended as an example of good incident and crisis management.[9] Total was seen to do everything possible to stem the leak operationally, and heard to communicate transparently all the actions being taken. The company I run was involved in the response, so we had a first-hand view of the crisis. But this is a case study 'from within': it is based on interviews with many of the key senior Total executives and managers involved.

In many ways this was a classic crisis: an energy company, an incident, an ongoing gas leak, an evacuation, political interest, media interest etc. It should be stressed, however, that the impacts on people and the environment were limited: no deaths, no injuries, and no lasting environmental damage. This is in part thanks to the effectiveness of the evacuation and operational response. As one senior executive put it, 'to take care of reputation, you have to take care of people and the environment first'. And, of course, gas is invisible... unlike oil. So there was no visual imagery for the front pages.

The first few hours

As would be expected of a company in its sector, Total has the structures, processes and trained people in place to respond to an incident of this nature. It did not take long for the Aberdeen Duty Manager to realize something serious was happening following the initial incident notification call and to activate local emergency response procedures. A crisis was declared in the United Kingdom, a crisis team mobilized in Aberdeen and Group executives in Paris notified.

The Aberdeen team made three calls to Group that Sunday afternoon. The first was to notify Group of the decision to evacuate all non-essential personnel as a precaution, keeping 19 people on board. This was in line with the initial technical assessment that the leak would not last long. The second, a few hours later, confirmed the evacuation was complete. The third, later that night, relayed the decision to evacuate the remaining 19. This decision was taken after it became apparent that the leak could not be quickly contained. One executive recalled a sense of shock at this realization – Elgin was a showcase for High Pressure High Temperature (HPHT) technology and led the world in this new form of drilling.

By the Sunday night, once news of the full platform evacuation was confirmed, it was clear that, although the epicentre of the crisis would be the United Kingdom, the impacts could be felt more widely. Resource and support would therefore be necessary from Paris. The decision to mobilize a 'crisis cell' in Paris was taken late on the Sunday night. It was mobilized overnight, and held its first meeting at 7 am on the Monday.

Managing the initial external pressure

The communications response was principally managed from Aberdeen, at least in the early days. Trained media responders (from within the company and from a local agency) were mobilized to fill the communications resource gap. Five statements were released that first day, 12 interview requests were received and the first interviews given.

A 'dark site' (an alternative website set up but not visible until activated, designed to inform and update key audiences on a crisis) was activated within an hour of the leak being detected, providing the team with a central platform for the release of information. The local team in Aberdeen had recently received approval for a new social media protocol; this allowed the team to establish its presence on social media channels.

However, the Aberdeen communications function soon acknowledged it was overwhelmed. Media interest in the first 24 hours was high. As one remarked, 'Nothing can quite prepare you for the sheer volume of attention you receive, the number of phone calls and requests you get, especially in the first 24 hours. However much training and preparation you've had, it still takes you by surprise.' The team struggled to keep pace with the ongoing requests, feeling that, however much information was being put out, it still wasn't quite enough to feed increasingly demanding journalists. 'You simply can't please everybody – you just have to prioritise demands and manage as best you can.' Although the media shout the loudest, there are also many other stakeholders to engage in those first hours, each with their own agenda.

By Monday afternoon, and over the following 24 hours, additional specialist support was being deployed by Group, drawing on both external and internal resource. This included communications experts from within other areas of the business being redeployed to Aberdeen. Soon, there were five different communication units handling different aspects of the response. One senior executive recalled: 'We just didn't have enough communicators. We realized we would need to develop a list of those who could help and draft them in.' This global 'skills inventory' was partly created during the crisis but it was recognized that this would be a key 'peacetime' task to be completed once the crisis was over.

Group response

Although the crisis cell in Paris had met on Monday morning, Group was not yet feeling the pressure. External inquiries into Total's headquarters in Paris were limited. It was later that day when the gravity of the situation began to hit home. When the French stock exchange closed on Monday night, it was apparent that the incident had had an effect on the markets. By extension, it was clear for the Total Group in Paris that this incident in the United Kingdom constituted a Group crisis by virtue of the impacts it could have on reputation, commercial and financial interests. Group recognized the need to set up a strategic committee to enable senior management to think through the implications of the crisis, away from the more operational focus of the teams already mobilized. 'I don't recall one single conversation where we talked about the cost of any action,' stated a senior Total executive. With reputation on the line, cost just wasn't a factor. Group communications response was also up and running by the Tuesday.

Digital communication

Digital communication quickly became a key pillar of the response. Through coordination between the Aberdeen and Paris teams, the 'crisis website' dedicated to the incident became the central hub of information and a precious tool to which all stakeholders could be referred. In total, 28 press releases and 55 'visuals', including photos, videos and diagrams, were published on the website, along with the publication of all the results of third-party analyses of, for example, air and water pollution.

The use of graphics was highlighted as a key part of the communications response: it helped to explain complex technical matters to the media. 'We did lose some time on that in the beginning,' recalled one member of the team. 'Engineers wanted technical perfection; communicators wanted something simple and understandable.' Preparing some basic graphics in advance for key assets, together with key facts and figures, was seen as another communications lesson of the Elgin crisis.

Social media also formed a key part of the response, with 127 tweets sent by Total between 25 March and 21 May, 24 comments posted on Facebook, 20 videos uploaded on YouTube and 23 photos hosted on Flickr. A complicated sign-off process caused delays to some messages being released; it was the first time the company had used social media in such circumstances. However, a few weeks into the crisis, an effective process was established.

Although the social media response worked well overall, it didn't come without challenges. The danger of 'creating news' through overzealous social media use was ever present. One of Total's communications leaders later reflected: 'In a crisis, social media [are] good for pushing out new information, but providing a "running commentary" is less helpful, and trying to use it to push out "messages" or opinion is better avoided.'

The 'information desk'

In a situation where 800 media calls were received in the first week, coordination of approved information was always going to be a serious challenge. Although the coordination of information flows between all teams and stakeholders did not come without difficulty, it improved as days went on and a clear reporting structure was established. A central information desk (*guichet unique d'information*) was created in Paris, an internal resource to which communicators could go for the latest approved information, including update statements, detailed Q&As (updated every evening in coordination between Aberdeen and Paris), and 'pick and speak' documents (including key messages and background information). This was not part of the official crisis procedure, but was an invaluable enhancement. It ensured that everything that was said in broadcast media and elsewhere was validated information.

The spokespeople

The development of a spokesperson strategy happened early on in the crisis. In the United Kingdom, the spokesperson (a Paris-based, but native English-speaking, communications professional who relocated to Aberdeen) admitted to being 'slightly rusty at first', having last been trained approximately four years previously. But he soon got into his stride and gave many interviews over the course of the crisis. Over the years, crisis best practice has tended to suggest that professional communicators should not be the spokespeople in a crisis. The reasoning for this is usually that they are likely to be 'too slick', less well informed on the operational aspects of a crisis and perceived to be 'PR people trying to spin their way out of a problem'. But times change and, as the Elgin incident demonstrated, this advice may now be outdated. That said, there were times when technical experts were more suited and times when others would be required to deliver messages to the investor community. It's a case of horses for courses, which is the result of a well thought-through spokesperson strategy.

Importantly, a decision was taken not to use the Chief Executive of Total Group, Christophe de Margerie, as a spokesperson in the early stages: 'We realised that if we used him too early we might never get him back.' This was a lesson that Total had learned from BP's Deepwater Horizon crisis in the Gulf of Mexico, during which BP's Chief Executive, Tony Hayward, became 'stuck' in the spokesperson role. Mr de Margerie was eventually used, but much later on and to deliver some good news: the extinguishing of the flare. The burning flare (a safety mechanism on an oil/gas platform to burn off excess gas) had become a perceived safety concern as the gas leak continued, so the moment it was extinguished was an important one.

The UK spokesperson, too, recalled that this was a 'key moment' but that he was careful not to appear too triumphalist at the good news. 'It was important for me and for Total to remain humble even at times of good news. The fact is we were putting right a bad situation; we had still created a crisis.'

Stakeholder management – internal and external

As one interviewee quite rightly remarked, 'much of crisis management is stakeholder management'. The key stakeholder was the UK government. The government had been burnt by an oil pipeline leak the previous year and was determined this incident would be managed more tightly. Total worked closely with government throughout and the close working relationship with this pivotal stakeholder was a huge part of the successful management of the incident. But this was just one of many stakeholders. In all, 383 stakeholders, across multiple geographies, were contacted. Whilst tremendous focus was put on the external response, managing internal communications was treated as a high priority, with information released via internal platforms where possible (including via dedicated intranet sites, internal briefings and newsletters) before being published externally.

Managing workload

This crisis unfolded over many weeks. It was recognized that long-term manpower planning was a gap. Many worked 17-hour days, for weeks on end, with little rest. 'We needed a manpower planner: that's definitely a lesson,' said one Total executive. The teams were, however, skilled and willing, pulling together to manage the response.

Interestingly, however, many also felt too involved to be able to 'let go'. Despite the general exhaustion, many felt so closely committed that they could not step out. 'The most difficult thing for me was not the standing up but the standing down,' according to the Group Head of Communications. 'It was harder to get out of crisis mode than into it. We were probably operating as a crisis for a couple of weeks too long.'

Total has received praise for how it handled Elgin, both for its dedicated operational response and transparent communications strategy. But, looking back, as one executive explained, an incident did happen, knocking the share price and employee morale: 'Yes, we seemed to manage it well. But we were still managing a problem, not a positive. It makes you humble, and it stays with you.'

Crisis media management

As the Total case study demonstrates, a large part of the communications function's value in a crisis is in managing the media. No CMT should be driven solely by the headlines, but the media are the conduit through which the organization in crisis – and its many stakeholders – communicate with the wider world. The media are not the ultimate audience, but they are still a primary channel to those who determine reputation.

Those who still think that 'Our job is to get the operational response right; if we do that, the media will report it' should talk to BP. Many in the energy industry believe that BP's response to the Gulf of Mexico oil spill was operationally excellent: an extraordinary engineering feat within an enormous response in which thousands of people were involved. But those who are not in the energy industry remember only what they saw in the media: a company struggling to deal with a catastrophic leak of its own making, and a Chief Executive struggling to cope with the pressures of the spokesperson role.

The media strategy is a fundamental component of the wider crisis strategy. This section looks at:

- setting objectives and devising strategy;
- content and message;
- the apology;
- the spokesperson role;
- managing the volume of mainstream media interest; and
- managing online media.

Setting objectives and devising strategy

The objective of crisis communications is to ensure that the decisions and actions taken and implemented by the organization reflect stakeholder expectation and demands and are then communicated back to the right stakeholders in the right way, thereby preserving as much goodwill and reputation as possible given the circumstances. Getting a fair 'share of voice' – and preferably becoming the trusted source of information about the crisis – requires the right approach, tone and content. The approach must be open, engaging and transparent; the tone a mix of humility, empathy and control; the content based on good actions being taken to remedy the situation.

And communications must be fast. Crisis communications experts used to speak of the 'golden hour': a short period during which the organization at the heart of a crisis could assess the problem it faced, compose itself, set strategy, develop messaging and then inform the world via the media. Today, such a period does not exist. News spreads extraordinarily quickly and, whatever the risk that presents itself, it is possible that the organization is on the back foot from the moment it hears of the crisis. This certainly applies for incidents, where citizen journalists may be uploading images of the event to various social media platforms before any response teams are formed. It can also apply to internal issues, where for example the trigger for a crisis could be a leak from an internal source to the media.

The trap that communications professionals, as well as the wider response (including the CMT), must avoid is to wait for information. Communication must start immediately, to establish the organization as one that will be open and willing to engage. In the early stages, information may be sparse. Even crises that stem from an issue that has been rumbling for some time will have new content and dynamics, thanks to the trigger that caused the spike in interest. But this does not mean that there is nothing to communicate: 'We are aware of a situation and are urgently investigating it' says little, but is better than nothing. What is certain is that, if you do not start communicating, others will. A story will not wait until the organization at the centre of the crisis has had a chance to organize itself internally and formulate that all-important first response. The media will find experts, eyewitnesses, industry commentators or other journalists to talk around a subject until information comes in. They will happily fill the gaps, whether or not they are familiar with the facts known or situation. Speculation starts to circulate about what might be happening and what could have caused it. A vacuum of information from the organization at the centre of the storm sends exactly the wrong message. It creates a perception of mistrust and incompetence, potentially pushing inquisitive journalists into hostility: 'Just what are you trying to hide?'

A phrase to be very wary of in crisis response, therefore, is 'Let's wait until we get some new information.' It is understandable to want to communicate new facts, but the problem is they might not come. And when they do, they might not be complete. And even if they are, they will only be part of the story. There is always another piece of information just around the corner, and organizations in crisis that wait for it tend to find themselves sidelined as others take the conversation forward.

The order of priorities in a crisis is not 'do it, then explain it'; it is 'explain it as you are doing it'. This means setting and sticking to a strategy of regular proactive statements, making spokespeople available at the right level and the right time and being seen to be resolving the problem.

Perhaps the most famous example of crisis communication in a vacuum of information came in 1989, when the Chairman of UK-based airline

British Midland entered the crisis management hall of fame with his pro-active and sensitive handling of the media after an aircraft accident. On 8 January 1989, a British Midland Boeing 737 flying from Heathrow to Belfast crashed near the M1 motorway in the United Kingdom, killing 47 people and seriously injuring 10. The aircraft crash-landed short of East Midlands airport after an engine malfunction. Company Chairman, Michael Bishop, offered himself openly and immediately for media enquiries. On his way to the scene of the accident, Bishop gave a live broadcast interview from his car phone when he had no knowledge about the cause of the accident or even whether there had been casualties. He told of his concern and pledged to keep the media constantly updated about the situation. Bishop said of his handling of the crash: 'I suppose it was a bit of a gamble, but I had given the matter of what to do if we had a crash a lot of thought over the years and it seemed to me the best way to tackle the crisis when it actually happened.' He added that he had 'probably set a new style for dealing with such crises'.[10] UK newspaper the *Daily Telegraph* commended the response, stating that 'a weaker man might have hidden behind the need for an official inquiry. Instead, Bishop displayed a masterful understanding of adversity leadership: sympathetic, transparent and helpful.'[11] Reputations can be won – or at least saved – as well as lost in the early stages of crises.

Content and message

The British Midland example shows that messages in the early stages of a crisis can be short on facts, but they do need to be based on proven action. The three Cs[12] are a good guideline for developing crisis messages:

- Care and concern (for those affected).
- Control (of the situation).
- Commitment (to resolving the problem).

Messages along these lines can potentially contain the situation as the organization gets to grips with the specifics.

Those charged with developing content in a crisis can also remember the key things to think about when developing any communication for any reason: audience, message, medium. Any communications professional knows that good messaging starts with identifying the audience first. In a crisis, there will be multiple audiences, both internal and external. First and foremost, you are addressing those affected. All crises involve people. Even dry financial crises involve people. There are almost always victims, whether they have been killed in an incident or impacted by financial impropriety. You are addressing their families and friends. You are addressing your colleagues, whose place of work has suddenly become embroiled in a crisis. You are addressing regulators, shareholders, partners, suppliers and many others on your stakeholder list, which, if the communications department is doing its job, has already been drafted.

All of these stakeholders want to hear basically the same thing: what has happened, what you are doing about it and how you feel about it. As suggested above, you might have to start explaining how you feel about it before you fully appreciate what 'it' is.

As the situation develops, and the organization is hopefully taking and implementing the right decisions, messaging must move on. It is vital that content develops with the crisis, and does not become stuck in the initial promises of action and expressions of empathy. People do not tolerate platitudes for long. Crisis communications is about communicating actions, not just picking the right words. And this, again, is why the communications leader must be a central figure in the strategic crisis response. If the messaging is stuck, it might be because the response is faltering: the answer is not better messages, but better action.

Fairly obviously, messages must be truthful. There is absolutely no room for error here. Content can in no way be speculative (speculation being one of the cardinal sins of crisis communication) or economical with the truth. The truth will always surface eventually – be it during the heat of the crisis or months later in a subsequent inquiry.

Good crisis communication is no substitute for good performance. There have been instances where a company has communicated well in the immediate aftermath of a crisis, generating goodwill, only to be heavily criticized down the line. An example of this was another crisis suffered by energy giant BP.

On 23 March 2005, a cloud of volatile hydrocarbon vapour ignited at BP's Texas City Refinery after it had escaped from an octane unit. Fifteen people were killed and 170 injured. BP's crisis communications response was in line with best practice. The most senior people in the organization were seen to be taking the right actions and heard to be expressing the right sentiments. Lord Browne, then the company's Chief Executive, visited the scene, saying it was the worst tragedy he had known during his 38 years with the company: 'All of us have been profoundly affected. All of us want to know what happened... I came to Texas City to assure people the full resources of BP will be there to help the bereaved and the injured.'[13]

The day after the Texas City Refinery explosion, the media seemed to be giving BP a fair hearing and the coverage was fairly benign. *The Wall Street Journal* gave credit for Lord Browne's actions: 'In a sign of how seriously the company was taking the incident, Lord Browne flew to Texas City yesterday and pledged to "leave nothing undone in our effort to determine the cause of the tragedy".'[14] The *Financial Times* said that BP 'will need more than sympathetic words and free meals for the families hit by the blast to repair its tarnished reputation'. But the newspaper was also complimentary: 'In moving swiftly, Lord Browne has avoided the negative fallout that hit ExxonMobil when its tanker ran aground in Alaska, creating the largest oil spill in the US. Many bristled at the perceived arrogant tone of ExxonMobil, whose Chairman left subordinates to deal with the crisis. In contrast, Lord Browne has been suitably humble.'[15]

The immediate crisis response, including the communications, had worked well. But this was not to last. It soon became apparent that the refinery had a chequered safety record leading up to the explosion. In March 2004, for example, the refinery had been evacuated after an explosion, costing the company $63,000 in fines. In September 2004, two workers had died and one was injured when they were scalded by superheated water that had escaped from a high-pressure pipe.

People will forgive errors, and they will forgive crises if they are handled well, but they will not so easily forgive companies that do not appear to have done everything they could have done to prevent crises happening in the first place. Good crisis communication can buy time, but it cannot alone save reputation.

Sorry

Part of almost any discussion about crisis management messaging is the apology. Saying sorry in an internally driven crisis (whether an incident or an issue), where the organization is, or is perceived to be, at fault from the outset, is almost always the right thing to do. It shows empathy, emotion and compassion and can be done in such a way as to avoid accepting liability.

Still, however, some apologies can seem forced. 'I'm so sorry about what has happened' is far better than 'We regret the situation that has arisen.' Both say the same thing, so why not use the more personal and emotive words?

The apology argument has been largely, but not completely, won: there are now few senior lawyers who would tell a company not to apologize because the legal liability implications are too great. But the apology still presents some difficulties, especially when more than one culture is involved. Finding the right way to say sorry is not always easy for a global company. The Japanese culture, especially when compared to the United States and other Western cultures, provides the most interesting study in corporate apologies.

Take a fictional US consumer product company with a successful subsidiary in Japan. The subsidiary has been accused of lying in promotional materials and an independent investigation into the claim has commenced. The media and stakeholders have taken a keen interest both in Japan and in the United States, where the company's headquarters is based. The Japanese crisis management team is keen to apologize immediately at a specially convened media event, whilst the US crisis team is concerned that this will play badly in the United States as it will undermine the independent investigation. They would prefer a carefully crafted written statement of regret.

This mismatch is cultural. In Japan, a corporate apology is first and foremost an expression of regret that an unseemly situation has arisen. It shows remorse and humility. Delaying it can lead to reputation damage. There is great symbolism and nuance in a Japanese corporate apology, with importance placed on the individuals apologizing, the way in which the apology is delivered and the measures that will be taken to restore trust. It is expected that a company's top executives will issue the apology and face the media and public. If holding a press conference, company representatives will be expected to bow deeply to the audience as a public expression of remorse.

In 2011, Sony Corporation experienced a security breach of PlayStation Network, its online gaming platform, causing the loss of personal data from 77 million accounts worldwide. This was compounded by a prolonged outage of the service. In the days following the incident, the company debated whether they should wait until internal investigations were complete and the PlayStation Network service was restored before making a public apology. During this time, Sony was increasingly criticized in the media. Ten days later, Sony held a press conference in Tokyo chaired by its most senior leaders. As soon as Mr Kazuo Hirai, Sony President and Chief Executive, and the heads of the company's communications and gaming divisions stepped onto the podium, they bowed together in a silent, prolonged apology.

Another unique aspect to apologizing in Japan is the need to demonstrate a company's commitment to change through self-imposed disciplinary or 'corrective actions'. Examples include leadership resignations, temporary pay cuts for the executive leadership team and temporary suspension of company membership and participation in industry bodies. In 2012, Mr Ryuji Yamada, President of NTT DoCoMo, the Japanese telecom company, announced that he would take a 20 per cent pay cut for three months. Five other executives also took a 10 per cent cut over the same period as 'a clear means of taking responsibility for causing the series of network malfunctions and leakage of personal information'.[16] Other major Japanese companies which have taken similar measures include Toyota in 2010, which docked the management team's pay by 10 per cent following product recalls, and Nomura, Japan's biggest brokerage, which cut the pay of its Chief Executive by 50 per cent in 2012 following an internal probe into leaked information and insider trading.

The spokesperson

It is probably not the most coveted role in a response, but a company in crisis needs to have a spokesperson – or spokespeople – able to perform competently in the most high-profile and high-pressured media interviews. As discussed in Chapter 12, preparing leaders for a crisis includes preparing them to face a grilling or two from journalists who are determined to get to the heart of the story.

Journalists love a crisis. Covering the main news event of the day presents a significant opportunity for them to gain profile and respect. They get resources and they get bylines. But they are not necessarily out to 'get' the company at the heart of the crisis. They will want interesting angles and they will want to unearth facts or developments that other journalists in competitor outlets have not found. But an interview with the company spokesperson is certainly a huge opportunity for them to make their mark.

Training a spokesperson for the first time is not something you want to do when a crisis has hit.

All large organizations must therefore invest time in identifying and preparing spokespeople. This book is not the place for a crisis media training session, so suffice it to say that competent spokespeople should be found from various parts of the business, should be told that they have been put on the approved list and should be offered regular opportunities to refresh their skills. A well-prepared organization will have a bank of well-trained spokespeople who between them could perform the role on any number of issues or incidents from all parts of the business. Ideally there will be a mixture of nationalities, ages, styles and seniority.

As the aforementioned contrasting examples from BP's Gulf of Mexico oil spill of 2010 and British Midland's crash near Kegworth in 1989 demonstrate, the spokesperson makes a real difference. People do not remember the details of crises for very long, but they remember how the spokespeople fared for much longer. A spokesperson whose performance in one broadcast interview led directly to his resignation was George Entwistle, Director General of the British Broadcasting Company (BBC).

A crisis of management at the BBC

In 2012, the BBC was accused of sacrificing journalistic standards to protect its own reputation after it shelved an investigation by one of its own flagship news programmes into Sir Jimmy Savile, a prominent (and recently deceased) BBC television presenter who had been accused of decades of sexual abuse. The crisis that ensued – one of the biggest reputation challenges the BBC has ever faced – was compounded some weeks later when journalists of the same news programme, *Newsnight*, reported on Twitter that another public figure was about to be implicated in child sex abuse allegations in an upcoming *Newsnight* episode. The tweets fuelled speculation resulting in the wrongful implication of a senior politician.

These editorial decisions, and the way in which they were handled and communicated, led to the resignation of the Director General of the BBC after just 54 days in the job.

A public service broadcaster funded by a licence fee paid by British households, the BBC is a trusted international brand. It enjoys strong stakeholder and public support, and its news output is world renowned for quality and impartiality. Allegations of interference in journalistic independence, cover-up and incompetence therefore hit hard, especially when associated with a famous personality. DJ and entertainer Sir Jimmy Savile had been a household name in the United Kingdom from the mid-1960s until his death in October 2011. He was particularly associated with programmes aimed at a young audience.

Although allegations of sexual abuse had followed the star for years, the issue came to a head when the BBC became aware that commercial broadcaster ITV was to broadcast a programme entitled *The other side of Jimmy Savile*, featuring interviews with alleged victims of Savile's sexual abuse. On 2 October 2012, the night before this programme was broadcast, *Newsnight* editor Peter Rippon wrote a blog explaining why the BBC news programme had dropped its own investigation into Savile. He explained that the investigation had not established any 'institutional failure' by the police or the CPS (Crown Prosecution Service) and that this 'weakened the story from a *Newsnight* perspective'.[17] The programme, he added, was not associated with celebrity exposés and Savile was no longer alive to defend himself.

After the ITV programme was aired, many more allegations came to light that spanned Savile's entire BBC career. The police were soon following hundreds of lines of inquiry (300 potential victims had been identified by 25 October), it became 'fact' rather than 'allegation' that Savile was a sex offender and the Savile sex abuse scandal was the biggest news story in the United Kingdom.

At a news conference on 12 October, BBC Director General George Entwistle (who had become Director General only a month before) apologized to Savile's victims and announced two inquiries. The first was to look at whether there were any failings by the BBC in how it managed the *Newsnight* investigation, to be led by former head of Sky News, Nick Pollard. The second was to look at the culture of the BBC during Savile's career there, to be led by a former High Court Judge, Dame Janet Smith.

On 22 October, *Panorama*, another BBC news programme, aired a programme entitled *Jimmy Savile – what the BBC knew*. This programme looked at the events surrounding the shelving of the *Newsnight* investigation. On the same day, the BBC issued a correction to Peter Rippon's blog post of 2 October, saying it was 'inaccurate or incomplete in some respects' and announced that the *Newsnight* editor was to 'step aside' for the duration of the Pollard inquiry.[18]

Political interest in the unfolding crisis was high, and the House of Commons Select Committee on Culture, Media and Sport had the opportunity on 23 October to question George Entwistle. His performance was un-rehearsed and uninspiring. His leadership was looking decidedly shaky.

The crisis deepens

On 2 November, the crisis took a different turn. *Newsnight*, the programme that had been accused of shelving a story when strong evidence existed, became embroiled in a new controversy when it was accused of airing another story with insufficient checks and poor journalistic standards. The report featured an interview with a former resident of a children's home who claimed a senior Conservative politician had sexually abused him some decades earlier. Although the story did not name the politician in question, it led to internet speculation that it was Lord McAlpine. A week later, the BBC was forced to apologize when the accuser admitted he had mistakenly identified Lord McAlpine. *Newsnight* carried a full apology at the start of the 9 November programme.

The following morning, George Entwistle appeared on the BBC's morning radio news programme, *Today*. By the evening, he had resigned. The next day the BBC Trust Chairman, Lord Patten, stated that the corporation needed a 'thorough, radical, structural overhaul'.[19] In mid-December, the Pollard Inquiry published its report which found that there was 'chaos and confusion' at the BBC.[20]

Unresolved issue, unmanaged crisis

It is now clear that Savile's behaviour had been on many people's radars for many years, but it only spiked into a crisis for the BBC after his death and in the context of editorial decisions. The Savile scandal was less about the failure by the BBC (and other organizations such as the National Health Service and the police) to prevent abuse or deal with it when suspicions were first aroused; it was about how the BBC is managed and led, its culture and its decision-making. It was less about the fact that its employee had committed the abuse – this was to an extent seen as 'history' – and more that the BBC was perceived to have tried to cover it up.

There were, it should be said, some good aspects to how this crisis was managed. The announcing of independent inquiries, although generally accepted (including by the Director General himself) to be somewhat late, was the right decision. It helped to keep political interest at a manageable level. Throughout the crisis, in fact, the BBC managed to avoid overt government intervention. The Prime Minister and the Culture Secretary both held the line that the BBC was taking the matter seriously and they repeatedly stated that they had confidence in the inquiries that had been set up.

The BBC was perhaps on track to resolve the crisis and begin the process of recovery when the second *Newsnight* scandal hit, exacerbating the concerns about editorial decision-making and a lack of internal scrutiny and control. In a crisis there is no such thing as 'a series of unfortunate events'. This was now a management and performance issue. The BBC and its leadership, rather than Savile, were the focal points of the crisis.

Leadership in the media

Like other leaders of organizations in crisis or under the spotlight in recent years (Bob Diamond at Barclays, David Brennan at AstraZeneca, Tony Hayward at BP), George Entwistle eventually had to resign. He had come to 'personify' the crisis and a large part of the unfolding media story was about what he knew, what he didn't know and whether he had been sufficiently on top of events.

The select committee appearance cast doubts on the new Director General's abilities as a spokesperson for the corporation. His poor performance on the *Today* programme was the final nail in his coffin. The *Today* interview was interesting from a crisis communications perspective.[21] Listening to it – a 15-minute-long grilling from one of the UK's most famous news journalists – it is clear that Entwistle has key messages that he is trying to get across: that the *Newsnight* report which led to the wrongful naming of Lord McAlpine as a sex offender was unacceptable, that something went wrong, that he was taking clear and decisive action, that there were two formal inquiries into the Savile story, and that we should understand what happened before we leap to judgement. He had prepared a good answer to the inevitable questions about resignation: 'The Director General isn't appointed only if things are going to go well. The Director General is appointed to deal with things which go well and things which go badly.'[22]

But these messages fell by the wayside when he admitted that he had not seen the *Newsnight* report on the allegations made by a former children's home resident until the following day. He had, he explained, been 'out' that evening. Indeed, under further questioning, he appeared to be busy doing other things as the crisis unfolded around him. The interview showed a leader who was either not asking the right questions of his organization or not intervening when it was going through a major crisis of trust.

He was not seen to be in control. By that evening, he had gone. Indeed, such was the BBC's hurry to negotiate Entwistle's exit, another issue was created by his severance payment (a year's salary rather than the six months he was entitled to under his contract). Lord Patten had to issue a letter explaining the Trust's decision in this matter.

On the face of it, this crisis was a disaster for the BBC. It lost its leader and it lost trust and reputation in the immediate aftermath.[23] But one silver lining was that the *Newsnight* brand survived. A comparison here with the crisis that engulfed News International is interesting (see Chapter 13). News International jettisoned its highly popular title, *News of the World* (circulation 2.6 million) after the phone hacking scandal, calculating it had become too toxic a brand, whilst the BBC retained *Newsnight* (viewership of a few hundred thousand). It was able to do this because underlying support for the integrity of that brand and the BBC was high. The BBC has earned the trust and reputation that, to an extent, shielded it from further damage.

But this was a crisis of management, a crisis of organizational structure and culture, and a crisis of leadership. The Director General's performance as spokesperson sealed his fate. Should George Entwistle have been shielded better by his communications advisers? Should a less combative interviewer have been chosen? In this case, the answer is no. The severity of the crisis by this stage meant that the Director General had to step up. Choosing a gentler interviewer or nominating a more junior spokesperson would have been seen as weak leadership and would have become part of the developing crisis of management capability at the BBC.

Choosing the spokesperson

But if an organization is more nimble in a crisis, it can give itself options for the spokesperson role. This, again, is a key strategic decision that the Head of Communications should bring to the CMT at an early stage. Although the organization may have created a good bench of possible candidates for the job, the details of the crisis usually narrow the field significantly. It is still a crucial decision: pick someone too senior and you have self-escalated the crisis; pick someone too junior and you may face criticism for shielding the leaders. Pick a technical expert and you may be accused of trying to present an emotional issue as a scientific one; pick a 'suit' and the response may look too corporate.

There is of course no right answer. But wherever possible the company in crisis should leave itself room for manoeuvre. Going in too quickly with the most senior person, unless it is a major catastrophe from the outset, may make it difficult for them to take a back seat as the crisis develops. If the most senior leaders are to be used in the early stages of a crisis, they should be used in a specific situation – such as before or after a visit to the incident site or around a specific part of a developing issue – then retracted. BP's decision to field Tony Hayward early and often looks, with the benefit of hindsight, like a calamitous choice. But at the time the company was expecting a far swifter operational solution. This was perhaps a failure of scenario planning as much as spokesperson choice. By contrast, News International chose to shield the Murdochs and senior executives from media interviews during the phone hacking scandal. This simply did not work. It was one of the biggest news stories of the year; the media and public wanted the senior people to explain themselves.

And what about the communicators themselves? Traditional crisis management best practice has suggested that the Head of Communications should not perform the spokesperson role in case it is seen as the spin doctors trying to paint a negative situation in a positive light. As the case study in this chapter on Total shows, this guidance may now be outdated. Why shouldn't a professional communicator communicate?

Whoever is chosen will need support in fulfilling their role. A member of the CCT should be assigned to be the spokesperson coach, helping the chosen representatives to stay abreast of the developing situation, the decisions taken and the messaging as well as rehearsing them before each major interview. This role is also a 'minder' role, ensuring that the most appropriate media bids are granted and that media interviews do not take up too much precious time.

Managing the volume of mainstream media interest

Communications functions come in many different shapes and sizes. Few, however, have sufficient manpower in one location to deal with the volume of media calls that the organization might receive in a crisis. Further, the communications team does not want to be entirely distracted by incoming media calls: it has many other roles to play. The communications leader will want to separate reactive response to endless journalists' questions from the proactive work that his or her team needs to be doing.

Setting up a Media Response Team (MRT) is the best solution. Big organizations can potentially move people from one part of the company to another to bolster the media response capacity. This can be done physically or virtually. There is no reason why communications professionals in one market or division shouldn't pitch in to support those in another, but they must have basic knowledge of the market/division they are supporting. This is rarely the case, although there will often be some who fit the bill. Another solution is to use local agency support, if any is available. Many PR agencies will have the capacity and capability to provide support to what might be a 24/7 media response operation.

Better still is to use people from the organization itself, but from outside the communications function. Many companies train up staff from administrative functions to form MRTs in the event of a crisis. Such colleagues are usually more than willing to help in a crisis, and often have 'peacetime' roles where they are often on the phone or otherwise dealing with people.

When a crisis is called, the Head of Communications or the Head of the CCT decides whether the nature of the crisis is suitable for the creation of an MRT. This MRT solution can work well for incident-led crises, but is much less suitable for issue-led crises. Using examples from this chapter, it is easy to imagine Total using such a solution during the gas leak in the North Sea (and indeed they did) but it would have been inappropriate for the BBC to have tried to use such a team during the *Newsnight* crisis. Issue-led crises, where the performance of the organization is under immediate scrutiny, are more complex; journalists want to get the story from the beginning, not just the facts.

Once assembled, the MRT – which will usually consist of a dozen or so people – needs a leader. This is a job for an experienced member of the communications function. The leader is in charge of ensuring that facts and lines to take are clearly displayed in the room and are updated regularly. The role of responders is thus to answer calls, take down journalists' contact details, ensure they have the latest press statement (and offer to send it to them if not) and to offer answers to factual background information. Their role is absolutely not to engage in an 'interview': they are not spokespeople for the organization and are not trained to have a complex dialogue with a journalist. But they can be the first line of defence: taking down numbers (using standard log sheets they have been trained against), making a note of questions asked and passing these sheets on to the MRT leader who can then decide whether the journalist in question needs to be called back.

Of course, journalists need to know the number to call. This makes the first proactive statement in a crisis very important. It should get to as many journalists as possible, via wire services and media lists, with the number to call for further information clearly displayed.

Managing online media

The above section on managing calls from journalists may seem a bit passé, but it is not. Even in today's online world, communication with media in a crisis is still primarily about press statements and telephone calls. What the main press and broadcast media report about your organization in crisis is still the main concern for crisis media managers. But there is a new show in town, and the question everyone currently asks about crisis communications is: 'Has the advent of social media changed how you respond to crises?'

Chapter 2 discussed how social media have changed the climate in which reputations are managed. It concluded that social media may have sparked a paradigm shift in how companies think about communications, but the change is tactical rather than strategic. The same is true of crisis communications response. Social media rarely come up as a subject for strategic consideration in a CMT, but they do require tactical management within the CCT.

Whoever is tasked with managing social media should start to do so from a position of knowledge. They should know who the organization's key online stakeholders are, which social media sites they use, how they interact with offline stakeholder groups and what their existing views are of the organization and industry. This, ideally, is information that is already available as part of a good stakeholder database.

There should also be clarity about ownership, powers and limitations. This is vital given the anarchic and immediate nature of social media. Key questions to ask upfront are:

- Who is responsible for doing what on social media? Who is in charge of monitoring, who is liaising with the broader crisis communications team, and who is collating and analysing all the data being received through social media activity?

- How is social media activity being signed off? Are members of the social media or broader communications team trusted to use their judgement to respond to social media activity, or is greater control over messaging being retained centrally?

- What advice is being communicated internally to employees about their use of social media during the crisis? Are employees being deployed as ambassadors for the company, or is all activity being kept to a minimum? Should special guidance about employee behaviour online during the crisis be provided?

Again, ideally, the communications function would know the answers to these questions before the crisis strikes. Social media may not lend themselves to structure; but organizations must remain structured in a crisis.

A crisis is not the best time to try out something new. You do not want your first ever corporate tweet to be the one that announces a major incident or issue to the world. But assuming that the organization has some sort of existing social media footprint, the best way to structure a social media crisis response is to listen, plan, engage and reflect.

Listen

Speed is of the essence in responding to a crisis via social media. But the desire to jump in and start communicating should be resisted until the organization has properly listened. This does not mean shying away from proactively reporting what may have happened, if that is in keeping with the organization's online personality. It means that entering a non-hierarchical conversation is dangerous before understanding how others involved in that conversation are reacting to the news. Questions to ask in this phase are:

- What are social media users saying about the issue/incident and the organizations involved? What are their main concerns? What has prompted them to join the conversation online?

- Who is getting involved in the conversation, both directly and indirectly? Are they customers, members of the public, consumer groups, NGOs, politicians, journalists, or any other important stakeholder group?

- Where is most of the commentary coming from? Twitter, Facebook or elsewhere?

- What are online commentators expecting the organization to do?

An active listening capability should also be set up at this stage. This will enable you to track what is happening, whether sentiment is being moved by your organization's online and offline activities, and whether there are specific issues to which the organization should respond. However, 'listening' to conversations online in the midst of a crisis is not straightforward. It is easy to get overwhelmed by the volume of traffic: thousands of tweets or Facebook posts can appear in minutes.

First, do not think you need to watch and respond to each and every post. An important part of a successful social media response in a crisis is to be discriminating about what content or coverage is isolated for further action. Second, make sure you have the right tools in place to help you be discriminating. Whilst metrics around volume, reach and share of voice are relatively straightforward to source, social media influence is difficult to pinpoint. The size of a social media following is not directly correlated to influence. Likewise, a person who is influential offline is not necessarily as respected by online communities.

Plan

The initial 'listening' phase is not something that takes place over many hours or days. It is more a mindset than a time-bound activity. The need to plan a response will come very quickly. Questions to ask in this phase are:

- What, given the circumstances of the crisis, will your online audiences expect to see from you (online and offline) and how will they expect you to behave?
- What social media platforms will enable you to target your key stakeholders most directly and effectively?
- How is the story likely to develop online? For example, what sites will stakeholders use for immediate information about the issue/ incident? Who might pick up the story and where might they take it?
- At what point (if at all) will it be appropriate for the organization's leaders and employees to be deployed? Will the now ubiquitous 'YouTube apology' be appropriate? If so, from whom and when?
- Is it possible to leverage existing supporters and allies on social media? Who might support us and what will they need from us?

Once you have mapped out your social media plan, it is critical to double-check that you have the governance in place to ensure continuous alignment with your offline communications strategy. Once this is done, it is time to engage.

Engage

Once the planning stage is complete, the engagement strategy will become apparent. At this point, the organization will decide to proceed in one of the following ways:

1 **Do not engage.** Whether engagement is not in keeping with the brand personality or the planning stage has unearthed too many problems, non-engagement is still an option. There will, however, be a consequence of non-engagement. It is the online version of 'no comment' and should only be used when, for whatever reason, it is decided that it would make matters worse.

2 **Engage with facts only.** This is the safest option. The social media strategy is a simple one: when new facts become available, they can be disseminated through appropriate online channels. This is one-way communication, though, and not in keeping with the 'rules' of social media. It will attract some criticism but will prevent the organization from becoming embroiled in uncontrollable and risky conversations.

3 **Engage with dialogue.** Empowering communicators (and others) to engage in genuine conversation presents risks but is most in keeping with the spirit of social media.

I always start with the premise that option 2 is the most appropriate option, then look at the specific circumstances to advise on whether there is a case for changing this to option 1 or 3.

In terms of style at this engagement phase, there are some important questions to consider:

- How will you respond to offensive posts? Removing them from your webpages is an option, but this should only be done if you have already made it clear, or if you can make it clear, that it is a matter of policy at your organization.

- Is humour appropriate? Social media lend themselves to informality. But crises do not. Humour is rarely appropriate, even if this is the peacetime personality of the organization online.

- How is your corporate website supporting traffic to your social media platforms? In a crisis, an organization's website is one of the most obvious sources of information for journalists, stakeholders and customers. Irrespective of whether the incident or issue merits the activation of a dark site, it is critical that your website both echoes the messaging, positioning and content, and acts as an effective conduit of traffic to and from them.

- Are there any social media conversations that could be more effectively handled offline? Not all engagement that originates on social media should be handled through social media. Where customers or stakeholders have significant, or complex, concerns or complaints about your organization, providing an offline outlet to discuss these issues in detail can prove effective.

Reflect

As with any aspect of communications, there is an ongoing evaluation requirement. Typically, this will look at: volume, reach, engagement, influence and share of voice. Questions to ask at this stage are:

- To what extent are we moving opinion amongst our priority online audiences?

- What activity is generating the biggest impact? And what isn't moving the needle?
- Do our stakeholders believe we are listening and responding to their concerns? How are they showing this?
- How effectively is our online strategy complementing our offline one? And vice versa? Have we seen any disconnect between the two and do we need to recalibrate the emphasis on either (or both)?

Communications working with other functions

A crisis is a time for cross-functional working. The CMT is likely to have representatives from different functions, all of which have their own needs and roles to fulfil. This section looks at the roles and some of the challenges faced by three important functions – legal, HR, and IR – in a crisis response, and how communications interacts with them.

Legal

In-house legal counsel can be, should be, and often is a constructive and forward-thinking part of a CMT. There are still too many examples, however, of legal dogmatism taking precedence over the need to find 'creative solutions'. The first press release issued by BP after it learned of the explosion on the Deepwater Horizon rig was entitled 'BP can confirm that Transocean today issued the following press release' and then simply repeated the Transocean copy. This is not something a communications person would have advised. The crisis may have been on a Transocean rig and the contractual situation would have stipulated that Transocean had primacy in managing incidents, but the sentiment was interpreted by just about everyone to mean: 'We are trying to distance ourselves from this problem.'

In-house counsel must, of course, think of the court case that will inevitably result from the crisis. On the CMT, for example, they should have oversight of how the room is run and how communications are managed within and between teams. Actions that are logged but then not completed, for instance, may come back to haunt the organization when the matter reaches court: ('At 10.20 am on Day 1, the company decided it should consider withdrawing the product from the market and yet we know this was not done until two days later. Why is that?')

But it is no good planning to win in the court of law when the court of public opinion has already reached its judgement. BP's initial legalistic response to the Deepwater Horizon crisis helped seal its fate in the court of public (and political) opinion, and it would be hard to argue that it helped the company in the many court cases it went on to face (and will be facing for some time to come).

There is the assumption amongst some non-legal people, including, it seems, some CMT leaders, that the lawyer is always right, because law is fixed. But the law is anything but clear in some areas, and legal advice is only one voice around the table. Of course, the legal function should ensure that the organization is not about to do anything illegal in its crisis response. But this is rarely the case. It is not illegal to take public ownership of a crisis in which your oil is spilling into the water; it is not illegal to say sorry. Indeed, lawyers are routinely pragmatic in their day jobs, helping to find solutions that are only partly driven by the legal right and wrong. A lawyer might advise you to settle an employment dispute before a tribunal, for example, as it will save money and time even if you are convinced you are legally right.

It is wrong to characterize these two functions as at loggerheads, one wanting to say nothing and admit nothing, the other wanting to communicate transparently and with emotion. This can still happen, but in companies that are mature in crisis preparedness and response (especially engineering companies, whose senior people are rational, logical problem-solvers), legal counsel can contribute creatively to major decisions. In this way, legal counsel and the head of communications often work well together.

Human resources (HR)

In an incident, whether internally or externally driven, the HR function is likely to be heavily involved. This department will own the response to staff and to relatives of staff who may have been impacted. They should have access to persons on site lists, next of kin information and trauma counsellors. They should be able to produce the right policies and procedures for managing all employee related matters.

HR works closely with communications in a crisis in various ways, but there are two that are of particular importance: communicating with families of impacted staff, and communicating with the wider organization when it is in shock and/or grief.

Many companies train Relative Response Teams (RRTs) which operate similarly to the MRTs described earlier in this chapter. Again, they are staffed by those who have people-facing roles and who will be able to perform the very different task of taking calls from distraught family members looking for information. Like the MRT, this is a 'call centre' approach: the RRT should take calls, log details, pass on any information available and cleared for use but not engage in deep dialogue. There are many rules and much advice around the subject of relative response, but the reason it is so important for communications is that it is about 'information in' and 'information out'. The information that the RRT, the MRT and the wider CCT use must be the same. If the media and relatives are hearing something different, this is a recipe for confusion and disaster.

Three mining incidents in recent years provide an interesting 'compare and contrast' case study on relative and media response. On 5 April 2010, a coal dust explosion occurred at Massey Energy's Upper Big Branch coal mine in Raleigh County, West Virginia. The subsequent Mine Safety and Health Administration (MSHA) investigation found that Massey Energy had failed to properly maintain ventilation systems in the mine. This created the conditions for an explosion that would claim the lives of 29 mine workers.

Methane explosions at the Pike River coal mine in New Zealand's West Coast region on 19, 26 and 28 November 2010 resulted in the deaths of 29 mine workers. The Royal Commission Report into the tragedy found Pike River Coal, the mine's owner, guilty of multiple safety breaches. Peter Whittall, the company's Chief Executive, currently faces 12 ongoing charges of safety breaches, including failing to manage methane levels and ventilation in the mine.[24]

On 5 August 2010, a tunnel collapse at San Jose copper-gold mine in Copiapó in the Chilean Atacama Desert, left 33 men trapped 700 metres underground. The 'Chilean miners', as they would become known by the world's media, were eventually brought to the surface after 69 days underground following a high-profile rescue attempt.

In their initial stages, both the Pike River and Upper Big Branch responses were characterized by confusion and misinformation regarding how many people had been involved in the incidents. In the case of Pike River, the Royal Commission Report found that 'the emergency response was hampered by a lack of information. The number of men missing underground remained uncertain until 20 November (24 hours after the initial explosion).'[25] The report also found that, faced with a lack of information, Peter Whittall, the Pike River Coal Chief Executive, had a tendency to allow the desire for a positive outcome to influence the information he supplied to anxious relatives: 'Some families consider they were given false hope concerning the prospects of their men's survival... but this was inadvertent.'[26]

Perhaps one of the most tragic tactical missteps occurred when Peter Whittall decided to notify relatives of the trapped miners that there had been a second explosion in the mine at a press conference, rather than informing them in private. This judgement was subsequently critiqued in the report: 'Mr Whittall began by referring to improved gas levels and preparations to go into the mine. This caused great excitement. But as soon as order was restored he referred to the second explosion... The scene turned to one of profound distress. Mr Whittall agreed that his announcement went horribly wrong.'[27]

Similarly, the official investigation into the Upper Big Branch disaster noted 'a great deal of chaos as state, federal and company officials tried to determine who was underground, where they were and what condition they were in'.[28] This confusion had a direct bearing on relative liaison efforts, with responders unable to state definitively whether or not some miners had even been in the mine at the time of the incident.

The confusion also impacted the respective crisis communications responses, with misinformation being circulated to the media in the initial stages of the crises. At Upper Big Branch, initial statements reported that seven people had been killed, with 19 unaccounted for.[29] Twenty-four hours later, Massey Energy released a statement claiming that 24 miners had been killed, with four miners unaccounted for.[30] The report into the incident found that misinformation was caused not only by faults in the personnel systems, but by misinformation in the media being allowed to influence information logging in the crisis centre.

In contrast, initial confusion over the number of miners trapped at the San Jose mine in Chile was clarified within a few hours. A relative site, subsequently named Camp Hope, was soon set up to provide relatives with a permanent base whilst they waited for the rescue effort to run its course. The camp included community bulletin boards, scheduled bus shuttle services to nearby cities, and even an on-site school. The President Piñera-led response at San Jose provides some interesting lessons in crisis communications. With some 1,500 local and international journalists permanently encamped at the scene, the Chilean government enacted one of the most media-centric crisis responses ever seen. President Piñera put a personal contact in charge of the media operation, which employed 45 people and eight cameras. This team supplied constant live feeds and updates for use by foreign and domestic media outlets. As one commentator noted at the time: 'The way the Chilean government managed to transform the rescue of the miners into an emotional televised show will become a classic case study.'[31] This communications outcome could only be achieved because the personnel information was available and the family response was comprehensive.

Managing grief

Communications will also be involved in managing grief. Helping families come to terms with what has happened and giving them all the support they need is something for HR to lead, but get this wrong and reputation will suffer. You can never do enough for the families of those who have died in your care, and the cost of doing so is negligible.

The same principles apply for internal audiences. Communications and HR should work together to determine what the appropriate actions and sentiments are in the aftermath of a crisis in which colleagues have been killed. Actions might include: holding a minute's silence, making trauma counsellors available, flying flags at half mast, making online and hard-copy condolence books available, changing the look of the intranet site as a sign of respect and organizing a memorial service. These may seem like simple and obvious actions, but again, companies still contrive to get them wrong, and when they do, reputation suffers.

Investor relations (IR)

IR manages a (listed) company's communication with its shareholders, potential investors, financial media and analysts, ie the investment community. IR is critical to maintaining the investment community's confidence in a company's ability to manage, respond and recover from a crisis and bringing the shareholder perspective into the boardroom.

Unlike other corporate communications functions, IR is a mixture of regulated and voluntary activity. Corporate governance rules for all listed companies dictate the frequency and manner in which a company must communicate its current and likely financial performance to its investment community. Amongst other things, these rules govern peacetime or 'business as usual' financial communication activities such as quarterly results, the timing of the Annual General Meeting (AGM) and the development and distribution of the Annual Report.

In addition to this financial calendar work, all listed companies must also communicate immediately any 'material' event that may affect its share price, ie something that might cause its shareholders and potential investors to lose or gain confidence in its ability to perform and therefore buy or sell more shares. Events deemed 'material' may include the sale of an asset, the 'spin-off' of part of the business, a merger with, or an acquisition of, another company and significant changes to a management team. A crisis is almost always a 'material' event. Therefore, for listed companies, IR officers and an IR strategy are crucial to protecting share price (and reputation with shareholders and others) during and after a crisis.

The investment community does not like surprises. Management of expectations is therefore crucial to effective IR. Whilst there can be no guarantee that communicating in a timely and transparent manner will prevent an announcement from impacting investor confidence and the share price, it is certainly true that a shock announcement will be far harder to control. As with communications functions, IR is most effective when it engages in a long-term, two-way conversation with its stakeholders. This dialogue must be aligned to all other media engagement activity, as investors will be heavily influenced by all media, as well as the financial press.

For a company to communicate successfully with the investment community, and to maintain its credibility and protect its share price during a crisis, it is essential that IR has invested in strong relationships with shareholders and stakeholders in advance.

Should the company face a crisis that threatens its licence to operate and its share price, the role of the IR adviser is similar to other communications experts. During the initial phases, it is likely that the IR adviser, working with the disclosure committee, will judge whether or not the incident or crisis the company is facing is deemed 'material' and should therefore be communicated immediately to the investment community (via the channels determined by the financial regulator). 'Disclosure and transparency become instrumental during times of crisis, when a firm's financial image and reputation are most vulnerable.'[32] IR's relationships with the investment community, analysts and media will be crucial as they communicate the company's strategic response and demonstrate control of the situation to minimize impact on share price and market sentiment.

Chapter summary

Many books have been written just on the subject of crisis response. This book presents strategic crisis management and crisis communications within the context of the reputation risk life cycle. When an organization responds to a crisis, it will be asked whether it could have predicted it, prevented it or resolved it. And it will certainly become apparent whether it was prepared for it.

The key lessons from this chapter are:

- The CMT's role is to oversee, endorse and guide the operational response and then move beyond it. The CMT must not get lost in the weeds of the response; it must remain high level and strategic, with its focus on the big picture, long-term impacts and recovery.

- The job of the CMT is, through high level decision-making, to protect those things recognized to be of utmost value: the trust of stakeholders and the reputation they assign to the organization.

- In a crisis, political, societal and stakeholder context is key. The communications function can help a CMT understand this, bringing the outside in.

- Crisis management is about substance, not spin. The communications lead should help get the response right as well as help communicate it.

- CMTs should not be driven solely by headlines, but the media are the conduit through which the organization in crisis communicates with the wider world. The media are not the ultimate audience, but they are still the primary channel to those who determine reputation.

- If you do not start communicating, others will. A story will not wait until the organization at the centre of the crisis has had a chance to organize itself internally and formulate its response.

- Stakeholders want to hear what has happened, what you are doing about it and how you feel about it. But they do not tolerate platitudes for long. If the messaging is stuck, it might be because the response is faltering: the answer might be in better actions rather than better words.

- All large organizations must therefore invest time in identifying and preparing spokespeople. Whoever is chosen will need support in fulfilling their role. A member of the CCT should be assigned to be coach.

- The communications leader may separate reactive response to journalists' questions from the proactive work that his or her team needs to be doing. Setting up a MRT is the best solution. Many companies train up staff from administrative functions to form such teams.

The communications function is at the forefront of crisis response, developing and communicating facts, actions and emotions to a wide range of stakeholders at a time when the organization's reputation and licence to operate is under threat. But it is far more than a tactical response. Communications leaders help keep reputation in the CMT, ensuring key decisions and actions are scrutinized with a reputation lens. They bring the outside in, as well as the inside out.

Crisis management is strategic. It is about substance, not spin; action, not words. A company that is facing a crisis of any kind, as described by the categorization model in this book, will ultimately be judged on the decisions it makes and the actions it takes. But these decision and actions need to be communicated in the right way, with the right tone, at the right time to the right people.

Get this right, and your reputation may survive intact. Get it wrong, and you will find yourself in reputation recovery mode, the subject of the next and penultimate chapter.

Notes

1 Isidore, Chris [accessed 8 April 2013] 'Toyota's reputation takes a huge hit', *CNN Money* [online] http://money.cnn.com/2010/01/27/news/companies/toyota_sales_halt/

2 Staff reporter [accessed 8 April 2013] 'Toyota boss Akio Toyoda apologises for faults', BBC News [online] http://news.bbc.co.uk/1/hi/business/8533352.stm

3 Staff reporter [accessed 8 April 2013] 'Toyota: A giant crashes', *The Guardian* [online] www.theguardian.com/commentisfree/2010/feb/25/toyota-giant-crashes-editorial

4 National Audit Office, Department for Culture, Media and Sport [accessed 5 June 2013] *Preparationsfor the London 2012 Olympic and Paralympic Games: Progress Report December 2011*, (HC 1596, Session 2010-2012), London: TSO [report] www.nao.org.uk/wp-content/uploads/2011/12/10121596es.pdf

5 House of Commons, Committee of Public Accounts [accessed 5 June 2012] 'Preparations for the London 2012 Olympic and Paralympic Games' (HC 526, Ninth Report of Session 2012–13) London: TSO [report] www.publications.parliament.uk/pa/cm201213/cmselect/cmpubacc/526/526.pdf

6 House of Commons, Home Affairs Select Committee [accessed 5 June 2013] 'UNCORRECTED TRANSCRIPT OF ORAL EVIDENCE, Oral evidence

taken before the Home Affairs committee: Olympics security, Nick Buckles and Ian Horseman-Sewell, Evidence heard in Public Questions 1–287', (HC 531-i, Session 2012-13), London: TSO [report] www.publications.parliament.uk/pa/cm201213/cmselect/cmhaff/uc531-i/uc53101.htm

7 Travis, Alan and Gibson, Owen [accessed 18 April 2013] 'G4S failed to understand size of Olympic security job, says Lord Coe', *The Guardian* [online] www.theguardian.com/business/2012/sep/11/g4s-failed-olympic-security-lord-coe

8 House of Commons, Home Affairs Committee [accessed 5 June 2013] *Olympics Security*, (HC 531-i, Seventh Report of Session 2012–13), London: TSO [report] www.publications.parliament.uk/pa/cm201213/cmselect/cmhaff/531/531.pdf

9 Institute of Mechanical Engineers [accessed 14 June 2013] 'Gas leak on Elgin platform could take six months to fix' [online] www.imeche.org/news/engineering/gas-leak-on-elgin-platform-could-take-six-months-to-fix

10 *PRWeek* [accessed 12 August 2013] 'PR helps Bishop fly – British Midland', retrieved from Factiva database

11 Randall, Jeff [accessed 28 March 2013] 'Why it is better to lose money than your reputation', *The Telegraph* [online] www.telegraph.co.uk/finance/comment/jeffrandall/2804285/Why-it-is-better-to-lose-money-than-your-reputation.html

12 Regester, Michael and Larkin, Judy (2005) *Risk Issues and Crisis Management*, Kogan Page, London

13 Griffiths, Katherine [accessed 26 April 2013] 'Refinery blast fireball kills 15 and fuels fears of global oil price hike', Independent.ie [online] www.independent.ie/world-news/americas/refinery-blast-fireball-kills-15-and-fuels-fears-of-global-oil-price-hike-25996514.html

14 Cummins, C and Gold, R [accessed 26 April 2013] 'BP's Safety Practices Face Closer Scrutiny After Refinery Blast', *The Wall Street Journal* [online] http://online.wsj.com/article/0,,SB111167497732288757,00.html

15 McNulty, S [accessed 8 March 2013] 'BP must repair its tarnished reputation', *Financial Times*,www.ft.com/cms/s/0/ed132a08-9d72-11d9-a227-00000e2511c8.html#axzz2eldYM682

16 Staff reporter [accessed 16 April 2013] 'Japan telecom bosses take pay cuts for system woes', *The Star* [online] www.thestar.com.my/story.aspx?file=%2f2012%2f1%2f28%2fbusiness%2f10554806&sec=business

17 Rippon, Peter [accessed 26 February 2013] 'Newsnight and Jimmy Savile', BBC News: The Editors Blog [online] www.bbc.co.uk/blogs/theeditors/2012/10/newsnight_and_jimmy_savile.html

18 Herrmann, Steve [accessed 26 February 2013] 'Jimmy Savile and Newsnight: A correction', BBC News [online] www.bbc.co.uk/blogs/theeditors/2012/10/jimmy_savile_and_newsnight_a_c.html

19 Staff reporter [accessed 26 February 2013] 'BBC needs 'radical overhaul', says Lord Patten', BBC News [online] www.bbc.co.uk/news/uk-20286198

20 Pollard, Nick [accessed 25 February 2013] *Pollard Review: Report*, London: BBC [pdf] http://downloads.bbc.co.uk/bbctrust/assets/files/pdf/our_work/pollard_review/pollard_review.pdf

21 Staff reporter [accessed 25 February 2013] 'Crisis at the BBC: Timeline of events', BBC News [online] www.bbc.co.uk/news/uk-20286848

22 Staff reporter [accessed 25 February 2013] 'Crisis at the BBC: Timeline of events', BBC News [online] www.bbc.co.uk/news/uk-20286848

23 Furness, Hannah [accessed 26 February 2013] 'BBC will suffer 'lasting damage' over Savile scandal, poll finds', *The Telegraph* [online] www.telegraph.co.uk/news/uknews/crime/jimmy-savile/9642143/BBC-will-suffer-lasting-damage-over-Savile-scandal-poll-finds.html
YouGov [accessed 26 February 2013] '7 in 10 Brits think BBC covered up Savile allegations' [pdf] http://cdn.yougov.com/cumulus_uploads/document/if5y99fw2x/Savile%20release.pdf
McKay, Peter [accessed 26 February 2013] 'Has Dave the guts to take on Patten?', *Mail Online* [online] www.dailymail.co.uk/debate/article-2224530/Jimmy-Savile-scandal-Has-Davis-Cameron-guts-BBC-boss-Lord-Patten.html

24 Staff reporter [accessed 15 May 2013] 'New Zealand Pike River mine boss pleads not guilty', BBC News [online] www.bbc.co.uk/news/world-asia-20077766

25 Royal Commission [accessed 15 May 2013] *Royal Commission on the Pike River Coal Mine Tragedy: Commission's Report - Volume 1*, New Zealand: Royal Commission [report] http://pikeriver.royalcommission.govt.nz/vwluResources/Final-Report-Volume-One/$file/ReportVol1-whole.pdf

26 Royal Commission [accessed 15 May 2013] *Royal Commission on the Pike River Coal Mine Tragedy: Commission's Report - Volume 1*, New Zealand: Royal Commission [report] http://pikeriver.royalcommission.govt.nz/vwluResources/Final-Report-Volume-One/$file/ReportVol1-whole.pdf

27 Royal Commission [accessed 15 May 2013] *Royal Commission on the Pike River Coal Mine Tragedy: Commission's Report - Volume 1*, New Zealand: Royal Commission [report] http://pikeriver.royalcommission.govt.nz/vwluResources/Final-Report-Volume-One/$file/ReportVol1-whole.pdf

28 National Technology Transfer Center [accessed 16 May 2013] 'Upper Big Branch Report: Chapter 4 Confusion in the Command Center' [pdf] www.npr.org/documents/2011/may/giip-massey-report.pdf

29 National Technology Transfer Center [accessed 16 May 2013] 'Upper Big Branch Report: Chapter 4 Confusion in the Command Center' [pdf] www.npr.org/documents/2011/may/giip-massey-report.pdf

30 National Technology Transfer Center [accessed 16 May 2013] 'Upper Big Branch Report: Chapter 4 Confusion in the Command Center' [pdf] www.npr.org/documents/2011/may/giip-massey-report.pdf

31 Staff reporter [date accessed 25 February 2013] 'Canny media operation sends mine rescue around world', BBC News [online] www.bbc.co.uk/news/world-latin-america-11539682

32 Heldenbergh, A, Scoubeau, C, Arnone, L and Croquet, M (2006) The financial communication during a period of transition: The Case of banks and insurance companies in Belgium, *Corporate Communications: An International Journal*, 11(2), pp 174–88

15
Recovering from reputation damage

A crisis always has some sort of reputational impact. In some cases, an organization may have managed a crisis so well that it achieves a reputation 'bounce'. A good crisis response reaffirms belief in the company, its leaders, its values and its products. Johnson & Johnson achieved this rare feat with its management of the product sabotage crisis in 1982, as described in Chapter 6. Far from leading to consumer doubt about the product, the crisis response cemented its leading market position. Even today, the brand owners emblazon 'from the makers of Tylenol' across other products in their portfolio.

Such a positive reputation outcome is most likely to come from a crisis driven by an external incident, such as response to a weather event, a terror attack or (as with Tylenol), sabotage. The organization has been attacked and, whilst it should never attempt to portray itself as a helpless 'victim', a strong response can show its stakeholders what it is made of. Indeed, it is an opportunity to introduce itself to a wider audience in a positive light, even though it would never choose this situation as the context for extending brand awareness.

Such an outcome is much harder to achieve for internally driven crises, where there has been a major safety or (real or perceived) performance failure. Here, the more likely reputational impact is negative. Even those internal crises that have been well managed are more likely than not to have some sort of negative effect on the way the organization is perceived, due to the fact that the crisis happened in the first place. Managing a crisis of your own creation is, realistically, more about minimizing a negative than achieving a positive. So the final phase in the reputation risk life cycle – recovery – is an important one. It will see an organization rebound, possibly stronger than before, or struggle to recover its reputation.

Every crisis has an end. The purpose of entering into a crisis modus operandi is that it is for special and unusual occasions only. As the previous chapter shows, a crisis response saps resources, time and energy. Whilst it is never a black and white distinction – one day frantic crisis response under pressure and scrutiny, the next a calm return to normality – it is important for crisis leaders to know when the moment has arrived for the organization to stand down the crisis response and return to a business as usual footing.

At this moment, when the crisis is seen to be over, there can be the temptation for those involved to heave a sigh of relief and try to remember what it was they were in the middle of doing when they were so rudely interrupted a few days or weeks previously. The inbox will be full of other matters requiring attention. For some, returning to the day job will be the right thing to do. But crisis leaders should see the aftermath of a crisis as an opportunity to learn and improve. Indeed, a crisis can present a window of genuine opportunity for an organization's leadership to effect important and lasting change.

With this in mind, this chapter looks at:

- conducting a post-crisis review of crisis management performance, and improving preparedness;
- rebuilding trust and reputation – internally and externally; and
- changing the organization.

The communications function is a key player in this phase, just as it is in all the other phases of the reputation risk life cycle.

Reviewing performance and improving preparedness

The opportunity to identify lessons from how the organization handled the crisis is short-lived. Unless those involved in the response are interrogated within a few days – a week or two maximum – of being stood down, their memories will start to fade. They will also start to 'polarize' their experience: 'I think we did well because...' or 'I think we managed it badly because...', focusing only on those aspects of the response that suit their overall view.

The crisis leader should therefore kick off the process of identifying lessons and instigating improvements in crisis preparedness sooner rather than later. The best solution is to commission a 'post-crisis review', which looks at crisis management performance against various measures.

First, it should assess performance against the principles listed in Chapter 12. These are:

- Policy – did the crisis experience support or challenge the way we think about crisis management, how we define it and how it relates to other parts of organizational resilience?
- Leadership – how did our leaders perform under pressure and scrutiny?

- Structure – did the structure hold up under pressure? Were the powers and limitations of different parts of the response clear? Did escalation and communication between teams work?
- Procedures – did the manual help or hinder the response? Did people follow the manual or create their own ways of working?
- People – how did our people perform under pressure and scrutiny?
- Culture and relationships – did our organizational culture and our stakeholder relationships help us or hinder us in the crisis response?

Second, the post-crisis review should look at more specific aspects of the crisis response. For example, for the crisis management team (CMT) this might include:

- Set-up – how quickly and effectively was the CMT assembled? Who managed this and what obstacles were there?
- Composition – were the right people in the room?
- Objective setting – did the CMT discuss its purpose and set specific objectives?
- Strategy – was a clear strategy set? Did the CMT return periodically to the strategy to check it still held and to assess progress?
- Decision-making – did the CMT make good decisions? How were key decision points approached and decisions taken?
- Team-working – how did the different functions and business on the team work together?
- Inter-team communications – how did the CMT communicate with other teams in the response?
- Room organization – did the coordinator run the room well?
- Resources – were resources made available from other parts of the organization? Did people have 'alternates' so they could take breaks? Were there sufficient resources available in an extended crisis?
- Information – were 'information in' and 'information out' managed tightly?
- Facilities – did the facilities support good organization and decision-making?

This process can be repeated for as many different parts of the crisis response as the organization wants to assess, including the crisis communications response.

Finally, the post-crisis review should look at external outcomes. This will include:

- Media coverage – did the organization get a good share of voice? Did it mobilize third parties successfully? Did key messages come across at key moments of the crisis?

- Social media sentiment – what was the nature of the conversation online? What were customers/others saying about the organization's management of the problem?

- Stakeholder survey – what did key stakeholders think about how the crisis was handled?

This structured approach focuses on identifying lessons from the crisis response. It does not look at 'why this happened in the first place'. This second piece of work is referred to later in the chapter, but a note of caution: legal and regulatory proceedings may already be under way and will be carefully controlled. It is advisable to keep the legal function involved in all post-crisis review projects as, after the crisis response is stood down, the court of law becomes more pressing than the court of public opinion.

A post-crisis review is conducted through desk work, structured interviews with a cross-section of responders and workshops, culminating in a final report with recommendations for improvement. The crisis leader should then sign off the report and commit to making some or all of the improvements, or at least to escalating them to those who can authorize the improvements. This is where the process can fall down. Organizations are good at identifying lessons; they are less good at learning them.

Whoever owns crisis preparedness in the organization must be involved at this stage (even if they were not involved in the actual crisis response). It is for them to help the organization learn the lessons: change the manual, tweak the structure, focus on leadership training etc. The key here is to be as specific and realistic as possible, and to get the buy-in of senior internal audiences whilst the crisis is still fresh in their minds.

One company that used a post-crisis review process to overhaul its attitude to preparedness is Heathrow Airport.

Rethinking preparedness – Heathrow learns from the snowstorm

On the morning of 18 December 2010, a week before Christmas Day, London's Heathrow Airport was hit by heavy snowfall. By 2 pm, the airport was under nine centimetres of snow, bringing normal operations to a complete halt. Disruption to flights lasted until 24 December. It was not to be a happy Christmas for Heathrow and many passengers.

Heathrow attracted criticism for many aspects of its response, but there were two key areas: its inability to 'solve' the problem (managing the operational response) and its perceived lack of passenger communication and support (managing impacts). Both contributed to what was a crisis of competence and care that was likely to dent the airport's reputation.

Operationally, there was preparedness for, and experience of, serious weather events. The airport – one of the world's busiest – had seen major disruption due to weather events and acts of nature before. The Icelandic ash cloud of April 2010 had forced a full closure, and severe fog in December 2006 caused major travel disruption. The perception of snow disruption is, as Heathrow discovered, different: fog and volcanic ash cannot be dispersed, but snow can be moved. And, as many on social media and in the mainstream media pointed out, Canadian and Norwegian airports can and do move greater quantities of snow on a regular basis to keep operations going. Whilst Heathrow could do nothing about the cause of the disruption, it was perceived to be in control of the solution.

Snow does tend to come in winter, which is when Christmas also falls, so the airport could not say that Christmas snow disruption was entirely unpredictable. But the volume of snow was unusual (the biggest snowfall at the airport for 30 years), and the timing – exactly one week before Christmas – caused immediate chaos and then false hope that the situation would be resolved. Heathrow operates routinely at 98 per cent capacity and rescheduling flights is an operational challenge at the best of times. The prospect of getting passengers to their destinations before Christmas, when nobody's journey is discretionary, were slim. And, of course, the media were in attendance, adding to the crowds and reporting on the countless human-interest stories: the couple waiting to fly to the Caribbean to get married, the American students unable to return home to their families for Christmas, the parents desperate to get home with gifts for their children. The media portrayed Heathrow as the airport that cancelled Christmas.

Heathrow could have put the disruption down to bad luck and, returning to normal operations, made a reasonable prediction that the next snow of such magnitude could be decades away. But the airport recognized that the crisis was about its ability to manage operations and support passengers: its core purpose. Heathrow realized it needed to think differently.

Heathrow immediately commissioned a full review into the events of December 2010. The Heathrow Winter Resilience Enquiry,[1] led by Professor David Begg, was launched before the year was out. Heathrow's key stakeholders – including airline partners, National Air Traffic Control Services (NATS) and the Department for Transport (DfT) – were invited to participate in the review. This inclusive approach was essential, especially as during the disruption the media had sought to create conflict between stakeholders (particularly between Heathrow and the biggest airline at the airport, British Airways).

One of the key findings of the Begg enquiry, published in March 2011, was the need for Heathrow to overhaul its crisis management capability. The report found that strategic crisis management – sitting as it should above the operational response to disruption – was inadequate.

Alongside the Begg Enquiry, Heathrow launched an internal review of the crisis preparedness of its communications function. This review identified a tendency for reactive problem-solving rather than proactive and strategic crisis communication. It also found that the understanding of reputation management in a crisis was mainly limited to the communications function.

Heathrow concluded that its overall approach to crisis management was operational and process-driven. The approach had been driven by the cause, not the consequence. The cause was snow; the consequence was passenger and stakeholder anger and reputation damage at a time when Heathrow needed to build reputation. The London 2012 Olympics were drawing near and the airport was building a case for expansion. As such, it needed to re-build reputational capital, and ensure it didn't expend any more.

In light of the two reviews, Heathrow launched a programme of change to implement lessons and improve crisis preparedness. This was not an improvement project that could be implemented gradually over time. As spring sprung in England, a clear strategic priority for Heathrow was to get to a better state of crisis preparedness for the following winter. Just in case.

Operationally, Heathrow's investment in its 'snow base' – a fleet of bright yellow snow ploughs, tractors and de-icers – was heavily publicized. Over £36 million was spent on improving operational snow response after December 2010.[2]

A key strategic change was the creation in April 2011 of an organization called the Heathrow Airport Demand and Capacity Balancing Group (HADACAB). The purpose of the group, comprising Heathrow Airport, airlines, air traffic control and Airport Coordination Limited, is to help manage anticipated delays in a more strategic and proactive way. By cancelling flights in advance of anticipated weather events, HADACAB's role is to prevent unnecessary passenger journeys to the airport and therefore reduce the possibility of passengers sleeping on the terminal floor: something that nobody, except perhaps the media, wants to see. It also allows passengers on cancelled flights to be rebooked onto spare seats on flights that are operating – maximizing the number of people who can fly when capacity is constrained.

The crisis media strategy was also rethought. Snow disruption is a great broadcast news story. Heathrow has now built three broadcast platforms on the roof of one of its buildings, which allows television crews to see the operational activity on the airfield and gives the airport greater control. This places greater pressure on the operational response: the airport will not want the television crews watching a failing operational response, especially after heavy investment. But the reality is that the communications and operational response cannot be separated, so a media strategy of transparency and control is the right one.

Crucially, Heathrow recognized that the new mindset for crises had to revolve around helping passengers make good choices, and helping passengers in need. Passengers are not only the customer, but also the primary deciders of the airport's reputation. Fundamentally, if passengers are given an explanation as to why their flights have been disrupted, if they know what to do next and who is taking ownership of their problem, their response will be more sympathetic. If this does not happen, they tend to be less so.

The new mindset was about care and control rather than cause and blame. For example, rather than trying to determine who was responsible for a passenger sleeping on the terminal floor, Heathrow understood that any passenger sleeping on the floor was unacceptable. The airport decided it must take greater responsibility for its passengers in such circumstances, providing for them even if the airline (the legally responsible party) did not. Whatever the short-term expediency of finger pointing within a value chain, it does not improve passenger experience.

Heathrow has developed and rolled out a new suite of operational and strategic crisis management plans since 2010. These are continually reviewed, rehearsed and tested to ensure that they continue to be fit for purpose. As well as being familiar with their own crisis procedures, Heathrow employees are actively encouraged to engage with their counterparts from key stakeholder organizations. Airport community calls and webinars encourage a continuous dialogue between Heathrow and its partners, to ensure the airport acts as one. Joint crisis exercises have also been helpful in building trust and mutual understanding with Heathrow's airlines.

Managing tomorrow's crisis starts today, and Heathrow has recognized the need to adopt a more proactive communications stance on the challenges presented by weather disruptions. Its strategy is to educate the media and the public on the enormity of the operation that a heavy snowfall requires and to show the efforts that airport workers need to go to to help passengers on their way. In proactive communications and stakeholder outreach there is an opportunity. Heathrow is currently advocating expansion to accommodate growing demand at an already overstretched airport. The snow event of 2010, and the disruption it caused, could conceivably have been put forward as 'proof' that more capacity is needed. But when the public perceives operational ineptitude and a lack of customer care, this argument would have fallen on deaf ears. You cannot build a good case on a negative experience. Heathrow knew it had to improve, and be seen to improve, its operational response, crisis media management and passenger care in order to have a stronger hand in wider conversations about airport capacity.

Rebuilding trust and reputation

Recovery should be on the agenda of a far-sighted CMT from an early stage. Understanding the probable extent of the commercial, financial and reputational damage, and devising a plan to recover from it, is the sort of high-level, strategic thinking on which the most senior CMT should be focusing. Having clear objectives for reputation recovery may in fact help inform actions whilst the crisis is still being managed.

The crisis may have affected what external stakeholders do, as well as what they think. Regulators, politicians, customers and others may be changing their behaviour, not just re-evaluating their opinions. This has clear commercial implications.

There is an internal element to recovery too. Internal trust might have taken a severe hit; morale might be low. All the good work that has been done over the years to turn employees into ambassadors might have been undone in a matter of days. An internal communication campaign of some sort will be needed.

The recovery period will take many months or even years. Rebuilding trust takes time. PR and 'spin' will not be enough; nor will empty gestures or promises under the banner of CSR. Indeed, trying to 'buy back' trust with a binge of CSR initiatives is likely to be counterproductive. People are very sensitive to companies throwing money at problems. Just as with crisis communications themselves, communications in recovery mode need to be based on substance, not spin. Yes, people want to hear the organization acknowledge failings, express its contrition and make promises of improvement, but actions speak louder than words.

The most important part of reputation recovery will be in proving that performance is once again meeting expectations. Remember, reputation is in the delivery, not the promise, so this will be about showing rather than telling: how can we show that our products are high quality despite the setback that led to the recall; how can we show that senior management is steering the organization in the right direction despite the public failings of some executives (or their predecessors); how can we show our safety commitment is real and substantive despite the terrible accident? If, like Toyota, you have built a reputation on quality and reliability which is then damaged by product faults, the only solution is to show people that you are once again able to produce the goods. No amount of communication will work until this promise has been restored.

But this does not mean there is no room for communications in a recovery based on substance and action. Just as with crisis management, the trick is in *showing* and *telling* whilst you are *doing*. This will mean getting the right messages with the right proof points into many communications with many stakeholders – internal and external.

Shell rebuilds from within

On 9 January 2004, Shell announced that it had been overstating its proven oil and gas reserves by about 20 per cent, or 4 billion barrels.[3] Reserves are a crucial asset for upstream oil and gas companies, indicating the level of future production and revenues. News of the reduction was accompanied by a one-page press release and a conference call in which neither Chairman Sir Philip Watts nor Chief Financial Officer Judy Boynton took part.[4]

The markets and the media were not impressed, and Shell soon found itself managing a crisis of performance and trust. It emerged that senior Shell executives had known about the issue of overstated reserves for some time. This was a classic internal issue-driven crisis: something had gone wrong in the organization, had been known about for some time and had been left unresolved.

Soon after the news broke, the Shell executive board's audit committee commissioned a report by external law firm Davis, Polk & Wardwell.[5] On 5 February, Watts, in his first outing since the crisis began, carried out a results presentation for shareholders in which he insisted he would not resign.[6] But the interim report from Davis, Polk & Wardwell added pressure and shareholder anger grew. On 3 March, Sir Philip Watts resigned, together with Judy Boynton and the head of the company's exploration and production (EP) division, Walter van de Vijver.

The 19 April report by Davis, Polk & Wardwell painted a portrait of Shell as a dysfunctional company where the top two executives, Philip Watts and Walter van de Vijver, were on increasingly hostile terms.[7] Shell needed a fundamental rethink, and committed to conducting a review of its complex dual board structure. At this time, Shell's assets were owned by its two parent companies, listed on different stock markets. Royal Dutch Petroleum, with its headquarters in The Hague, owned 60 per cent of the assets, whilst London-based Shell Transport controlled the remainder.[8] The boards of the two companies would hold separate parallel meetings in two adjoining rooms, then open up the folding divide and have a 'conference' meeting. Shareholders thought this antiquated, and many believed it was precisely this twin-headed structure that led to a lack of oversight and transparency and allowed the reserves scandal to go unmanaged. On 28 October 2004, Shell announced unification of the two separate companies into Royal Dutch Shell to improve management efficiency and accountability. The company would have a single board, a single Chairman (Lord Oxburgh) and a single Chief Executive, Jeroen van der Veer.

As well as the structural change, the new Chief Executive recognized that a major cultural and attitudinal shift was required. Many Shell employees had been hit hard by the scandal, and their pride in working for the company was dented. Jeroen van der Veer wanted to create unity where there had been division and devised the internal change programme and campaign, 'Enterprise First'. The premise of the programme was a simple call to action for Shell employees: whatever you are doing, wherever you are, think of the Shell brand first. This was quite a shift in a company that had many siloes and which had felt more like a family of businesses rather than one united enterprise.

Enterprise First had an official internal communications programme attached to it. It was pushed hard, to the extent that Shell meetings would start with a reminder from the chair that the meeting must think 'Enterprise First'. There was little resistance to the programme. In adversity, employees united around the ideals the programme espoused. The Chief Executive had recognized that he had a window to enforce change and rebuild a positive culture. The programme met its objectives; indeed, so successful was it that it ran for some time, and was only gently 'retired' a number of years after the original crisis that led to its creation.

Changing the organization

The most convincing action in the aftermath of a serious crisis in which reputation is damaged is real and lasting change, such as Shell's restructuring. 'We are changing' is a convincing recovery message, if it is true. The purpose of change is not to rebuild trust alone. A crisis provides a window of opportunity for an organization's leaders to fundamentally change and improve direction, purpose, values and strategy.

'The essence of recovery is not necessarily a return to previous normality,' the authors of *PAS 200* state. 'It may mean moving forward towards a model of business and organizational structures that represent a new normality.' This new normality can of course be a better place: 'Recovery may present opportunities to regenerate the organization and bring forward long-term development plans.'[9]

Seeing a crisis as an opportunity is very difficult when the heat is on and the pressure high. But it is undoubtedly the case that, whilst no leader would wish a crisis on their own organization, far-sighted leaders can make the most of the change opportunity that the otherwise unwelcome crisis presents.

After the LIBOR-fixing scandal that engulfed Barclays in 2012, there was major change in the organization's leadership. Recognizing he had a window of opportunity to make a difference and to recover the bank's badly dented reputation, new Chief Executive Antony Jenkins launched a programme to transform the bank.

Barclays 'transforms' after LIBOR-fixing scandal

In June 2012, against a backdrop of increasing public distrust of the banking industry after the role it played in the global economic crisis, the LIBOR-fixing scandal hit. It was revealed that some banks had engaged in manipulation of the London Interbank Offered Rate (LIBOR) between 2005 and 2009. As the story unfolded, employees at numerous banks including HSBC, RBS, UBS and JP Morgan Chase were found to be involved. But Barclays was hit first and hit hardest, becoming the poster child of the scandal in its home market, the United Kingdom. On 3 July, after a chaotic few weeks of crisis management, Chief Executive Bob Diamond, seen by many as the personification of what was wrong with Barclays and the banking industry, resigned.

The culture of the bank was held up as the primary problem that needed to be addressed. The Salz Review, an independent review commissioned by Bob Diamond shortly before he resigned, examined the bank's values, principles and standards of operation. When the Review was published on 3 April 2013, it criticized a culture that 'tended to favour transaction over relationships, the short-term over sustainability, and financial over other business purposes'.[10]

But by the time the Salz Review was published, change had already taken place. In August 2012, Antony Jenkins was appointed Chief Executive, pledging to make Barclays the 'go-to bank' with a return to its core values and principles. Jenkins recognized that, with the organization in a state of shock and flux, he had the opportunity to change the bank for the better. He instigated a programme called 'Transform', which stood for 'Turnaround, Return Acceptable Numbers and maintain Forward Momentum'. The programme had a number of workstreams, covering amongst other things structure, values, controls, compliance and reputation.

The 'Transform' programme was launched in February 2013 but, to trail it and show both internal and external audiences what he was intending, Jenkins essentially challenged all Barclays employees to make a very public pledge. The pledge was to live the five core values of Barclays: respect, integrity, service, excellence and stewardship. Jenkins stated: 'There might be some of you who don't feel they can fully buy in to an approach which so squarely links performance to the upholding of our values... My message to those people is simple: Barclays is not the place for you. The rules have changed.'[11] This was interpreted as Jenkins laying down the law to those the media and politicians had come to label 'casino bankers' – those investment bankers perceived to be making huge bonuses by taking risky gambles with ordinary people's money.

In an article written by Jenkins in the *Daily Telegraph* on 9 February 2013, the Chief Executive trailed the bank's forthcoming announcement of its strategic review. In the article, he restated the need to change: 'Unless we provide first-class service and correct mistakes immediately, our customers will take their business elsewhere. Those banks which fail to recognize and adapt to these changes will become failing banks.' He outlined the fundamental nature of the change that lay ahead: 'Instead of denial and defeatism, I want the Barclays approach to combine a real change in values and behaviours with an ambitious and focused business strategy aimed at improving long-term returns.'[12]

He then explained the process the bank had been through to get to a point where change would happen: 'Over the past few months, we have looked at every aspect of our business against the challenges of this new environment. In each area we have considered what we want to achieve and how we intend to do it. We have broken the bank down into 75 business units and examined both their potential to generate sustainable profit and their ability to inflict reputational damage. It has been the most fundamental and complete review of any bank's operations. It will set out what we will and will not do in the future.'[13]

Three days later, the strategic review and change programme were officially launched. One of the headline announcements was the closure of the tax planning unit of the bank's structured capital markets division. This was the unit that had been criticized for helping clients avoid tax, whilst generating big profits for the bank. This was a move inspired by reputation and values. Jenkins stated: 'Although this was legal, going forward such activity is incompatible with our purpose. We will not engage in it again.'[14]

The strategic review was commended for its robustness and its efforts to implement far-reaching change. It was notable for its commitment to long-term value over short-term profit. Speaking on the *Today* programme on BBC Radio 4, Jenkins said: 'There is a fundamental difference between short-term profits and shareholder value, and when I talk to our shareholders what they want to know is that they can count on Barclays to deliver sustainable returns over time. The plan we are announcing today is designed to do just that.'[15] One analyst noted that 'Barclays delivered exactly what the trading floor wanted – a solid set of numbers, aggressive cost cutting plans and a reiteration of the strategic overhaul.'[16] After the announcement of major change, the closure of a profitable business and the declaration that long-term value is more important than short-term profit, Barclays share price jumped by 8 per cent.[17]

The purpose of the Barclays 'Transform' programme was to make changes to the bank's culture, structure, process and products to help ensure the decisions and behaviours that led to the LIBOR-fixing scandal never happen again.

This takes us back to the beginning of the life cycle. The recovery phase must involve an honest assessment of whether the organization is well-equipped to predict, prevent and resolve reputation risks. Being better prepared for the next crisis is a good thing, but stopping risks before they become crises is better.

Chapter summary

The key lessons from this chapter are:

- Recovery should be on a CMT's agenda from an early stage. A CMT's role is to consider long-term impacts and to devise strategies to address them.

- Every crisis has an end, but a return to business as usual should not mean that the crisis is forgotten. There is an opportunity to assess, learn, rebuild and change.

- A post-crisis review should be conducted to identify lessons in crisis management. Identified lessons should be learned, not lost.

- The most important part of reputation recovery is showing that performance is once again meeting expectation. Recovery is about substance, not words alone and certainly not CSR initiatives.

- No leader wants a crisis. But good leaders will recognize that, if a crisis does occur, it presents a change opportunity that is potentially transformational.

Notes

1 Begg, Professor David [accessed 12 June 2013] *Report of the Heathrow Winter Resilience Enquiry* [report] www.ft.com/cms/89937494-55ed-11e0-8de9-00144feab49a.pdf

2 Staff reporter [accessed 12 June 2013] 'Heathrow cancels flights and transport is delayed by snow', BBC News [online] www.bbc.co.uk/news/uk-england-london-21063571

3 Staff reporter [accessed 14 June 2013] 'Shellshocked', *The Economist* [online] www.economist.com/node/2494807

4 Morgan, Oliver [accessed 14 June 2013] 'Shareholders want to know where Shell's reserves went', *The Guardian* [online] www.theguardian.com/business/2004/jan/18/oilandpetrol.news1

5 Staff reporter [accessed 14 June 2013] 'Another head rolls in the boardroom', *The Economist* [online] www.economist.com/node/2608070/

6 Staff reporter [accessed 14 June 2013] 'Shell Chairman Resigns Over Reserves Shock', *The New York Times* [online] www.nytimes.com/2004/03/03/business/worldbusiness/03WIRE-SHELL.html

7 Reed, Stanley [accessed 14 June 2013] 'Commentary: Can Shell Put Out This Oil Fire?', *Bloomberg Businessweek* [online] www.businessweek.com/stories/2004-05-02/commentary-can-shell-put-out-this-oil-fire

8 Jay, Adam [accessed 14 June 2013] 'Shell to scrap twin board structure', *The Guardian* [online] www.theguardian.com/business/2004/oct/28/oilandpetrol.money

9 British Standards Institution, *PAS 200:2011 Crisis Management Guidance and Good Practice*, BSI, London

10 Salz, Anthony [accessed 2 April 2013] *Salz Review: An Independent Review of Barclays' Business Practices*, London: Barclays http://group.barclays.com/Satell ite?blobcol=urldatablobheader=application%2Fpdfblobheadername1=Content-Dispositionblobheadername2=MDT-Typeblobheadervalue1=inline%3B+filename %3DRead-the-Salz-Review-report-PDF-3MB.pdfblobheadervalue2=abinary% 3B+charset%3DUTF-8blobkey=idblobtable=MungoBlobsblobwhere=1330697 040891ssbinary=true

11 Staff reporter [accessed 2 April 2013] 'Barclays boss tells staff "sign up to ethics or leave"', BBC News [online] www.bbc.co.uk/news/business-21064590

12 Jenkins, Anthony [accessed 2 April 2013] 'A road map for success and our commitment to real change', *The Telegraph* [online] www.telegraph.co.uk/finance/comment/9859710/A-road-map-for-success-and-our-commitment-to-real-change.html

13 Jenkins, Anthony [accessed 2 April 2013] 'A road map for success and our commitment to real change', *The Telegraph* [online] www.telegraph.co.uk/finance/comment/9859710/A-road-map-for-success-and-our-commitment-to-real-change.html

14 Barclays PLC [accessed 2 April 2013] *Barclays PLC Strategic Review*, London: Barclays [online] http://group.barclays.com/about-barclays/transform/strategicreview

15 Jenkins, Antony [accessed 12 February 2013] *Today Programme*, BBC Radio 4

16 Sharp, Tim (12 February 2013) 'Barclays to axe 3700 jobs in turnaround bid', *Herald Scotland* [online] www.heraldscotland.com/business/company-news/barclays-to-axe-3700-jobs-in-turnaround-bid.20199574

17 Staff reporter [accessed 2 April 2013] 'Barclays shares jump on cuts', Yahoo Finance [online] http://finance.yahoo.com/news/barclays-shares-jump-cuts-234700098.html

16
Where next for crisis, issues and reputation management?

This book has looked at the concept and importance of reputation, the increasingly challenging climate in which it is managed and the different categories of risks to reputation that organizations face. It has provided guidance on how these risks can be managed through the life cycle.

Throughout the book, case studies have illustrated the key points. Some of these case studies may now seem like ancient history (the earliest, the Tylenol case study, dates from 1982) whilst some are still unresolved as this book goes to press (the corporation tax controversy is still ongoing in the United Kingdom). What is noticeable is that the risks that organizations face have not radically changed; nor have the ways in which the risks can and should be managed. Certainly, there is much greater understanding today of the value of reputation than there was 30 years ago. This is in part because more reputations have been so visibly destroyed, with major consequences for the organizations involved. The context has also changed – declining trust, intrusive media, burgeoning social media and the other factors discussed in Chapter 2 – and this has in turn changed issues and crisis tactics to an extent. But the fundamental principles have not changed.

And 30 years from now, it is unlikely that these fundamental principles will have radically changed. The categorization model described in Chapter 3 works for reputation risks past, present and future:

- **External issues** will still emerge, driven by campaign groups, politicians and individuals who will have even more opportunity through technological advances to further their causes. Companies will still find themselves the poster children for some of these issues, needing to respond quickly to avoid long-term reputation damage.

- **Internal issues** will still emerge, because organizations will remain fallible, staffed by people that make human errors, using systems and processes that sometimes fail. Launches will go wrong, bad decisions will be made, bad behaviours will be uncovered. These will continue to provide the biggest risks to reputation, calling into question the values, purpose and performance of the organization.

- **External incidents** will still strike. Whilst cyberattacks provide a new frontier of the externally driven incident, more conventional terror attacks and political unrest will continue. Catastrophic weather events, if climate scientists are to be believed, will become more frequent, more devastating and more widely watched in the interconnected word.

- **Internal incidents** will continue to provide the most acute of reputation risks to organizations, with the spotlight shining on them after a sudden safety or system failure. Safety performance will continue to improve, but accidents will always happen.

In the years ahead, more and more organizations will recognize that they could face reputation risk and crises from any of these categories. The journey from seeing crisis management as an extension of operational emergency response to seeing it as a separate strategic capability will continue.

The reputation risk life cycle as described in the second half of the book is also, I hope, future proof. Organizations will still need to predict risks to reputation, prevent them wherever possible, prepare for the worst, resolve issues before they escalate and respond to those crises that do occur. And they will need to recover from any reputation setbacks.

In years ahead, however, I believe that the centre of gravity of this reputation risk life cycle will shift towards prevention and resolution. But this should not come at the expense of good crisis management response capabilities. What I hope happens is that:

- Crisis management becomes more widely recognized as a high-level, strategic capability for which leaders across businesses, geographies and functions need to be carefully *prepared* in order for them to be able to *respond* successfully.

- Issues management becomes more focused on *predicting* and *resolving* reputation risks, whether the risks emerge from internal performance failures or external agendas.

- Reputation becomes an asset that is understood and valued in more organizations in all sectors, helping them to make decisions that *prevent* risks from arising. This will involve a greater focus on culture.

- Those organizations that still experience crises will have the skills and leaders to *recover*, rebuilding reputation and taking advantage of the change opportunity that a crisis presents.

Will there be more, or less, crisis management? It certainly seems that news stories about bad practice, incidents, controversies and performance failures are more numerous than ever before. Many of the case studies in this book have taken place over the last 24 months or so.

Or is it the case that issues and crises are just more visible than they used to be? It is doubtless the case that issues and incidents that might previously have escaped the media glare can now play out very publicly and in a climate of mistrust. Yes, the world has changed and crises are more visible and acutely threatening than ever before. But if the world in which reputations are managed seems faster, more volatile, more fickle and more judgemental, the harder companies should try to master it.

There is the danger that organizations start to feel a sense of 'crisis fatigue'. They have seen their peers experience crises and suffer reputational damage; they know that one day it will be their turn; they are not convinced that they will get a fair hearing in the court of public opinion. They also see how crises can play themselves out very quickly in the public domain: media, political and public interest moves on and the beleaguered company starts the process of bouncing back. Social media forums start talking about other things and the company is still (usually) there making its products and selling its services.

This, to me, is the modern equivalent of saying 'Today's newspapers are tomorrow's chip paper.' Companies, and their communications function, should not be complacent. Recent crisis case studies involving BP, the BBC, News International, Costa Cruises and many others in this book show how failures in crisis preparedness and/or management lead to enormous reputation, commercial and financial impacts.

But nor should companies be dispirited. Case studies such as those involving Total and Tesco show that good crisis management – actions and words working together as part of a strategic response – can bring results. And the story of Barclays' post-crisis recovery and change programme shows the opportunity to turn the negative energy of a crisis into a potentially positive outcome.

Indeed, this recovery phase of the reputation risk life cycle is often the ideal opportunity to rethink the wider reputation strategy. Chapter 1 advised a mindset change away from seeing reputation as something that needs tactical management and towards something that needs strategic long-term thinking. It argued that 'managing' something does not imply that a comprehensive strategy has been put in place to maintain, enhance, protect and deploy it for the achievement of goals and the creation of value. This change from reputation management to reputation strategy is the step that organizations need to take in order to show themselves and their stakeholders that they not only value reputation but are actively addressing it with positive strategies.

This sort of reputation mindset change often comes to an organization's leaders after the shock of a crisis that has seen reputation damaged and commercial and financial interest hit. But it is much, much better to devise and deliver a reputation strategy *before* a crisis hits. I hope this book will encourage more organizations to do so.

INDEX

CPSIA information can be obtained
at www.ICGtesting.com
Printed in the USA
LVOW13s0353130917

548519LV00026B/1011/P